IMAGES
of America

WARTIME DECATUR 1832–1945

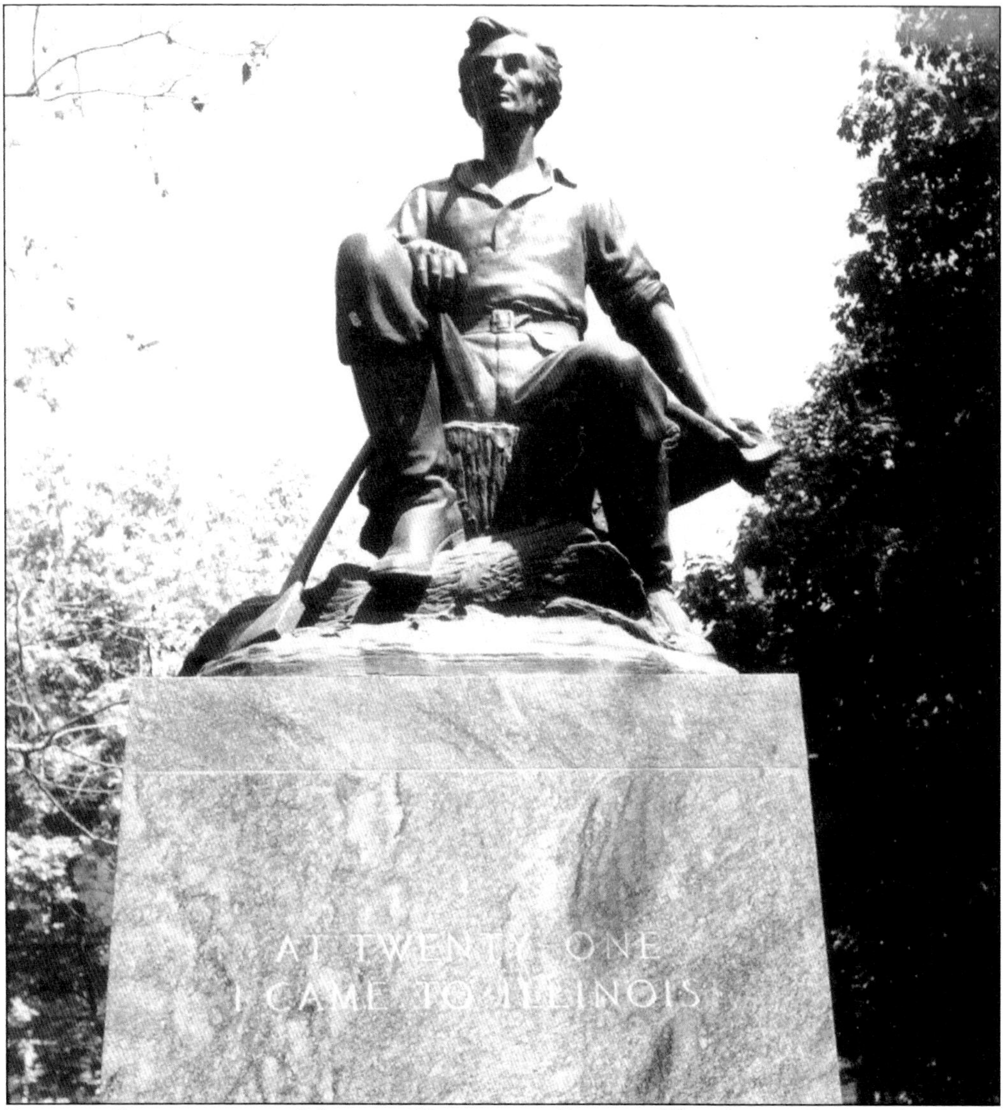

LINCOLN STATUE ON THE MILLIKIN UNIVERSITY CAMPUS. This famous Decatur landmark depicts young Abraham Lincoln on a heroic scale, clutching an axe, and wearing homespun clothing, as he did when he first arrived in Decatur in March of 1830. Two years later, Captain Lincoln commanded a company of New Salem volunteers in the Black Hawk War. (Courtesy Macon County Historical Society Museum.)

IMAGES
of America

WARTIME DECATUR 1832–1945

Dan Guillory

ARCADIA
PUBLISHING

ISBN 978-0-7385-3997-3

Published by Arcadia Publishing
Charleston, South Carolina

Printed in the United States of America

Library of Congress Catalog Card Number: 2005933696

For all general information contact Arcadia Publishing at:
Telephone 843-853-2070
Fax 843-853-0044
E-mail sales@arcadiapublishing.com
For customer service and orders:
Toll-Free 1-888-313-2665

Visit us on the Internet at www.arcadiapublishing.com

*This book is dedicated to my wife Leslie
and daughter Gayle, my most appreciative
and discerning readers.*

On the cover: **DOUGHBOYS AT THE DECATUR CANTEEN.** This busy scene at the train station, with Red Cross volunteers and World War I "doughboys" en route to the front, perfectly symbolizes the intersection of the military and civilian cultures that made victory a reality. This photograph was taken in the fall of 1917. (Courtesy Decatur Public Library.)

Contents

Acknowledgments

Without the generous help and encouragement of the following people, this book would not have been possible: Ann Marie Lonsdale (Acquisitions Editor, Arcadia Publishing); Kim Bauer (Abraham Lincoln Presidential Library); Bob Sampson (University of Illinois); Curtis Mann, Linda Garvert, and Keith Housewright (Sangamon Valley Collection, Lincoln Library); Brent Wielt and Lee Slider (Macon County Conservation District); Pat McDaniel (Macon County Historical Society); Cheri Hunter, Mike Delahunty, and Jolene McCoy (Decatur Genealogical Society); Lee Ann Fisher, Sandi Pointon, Bev Hackney, and Junie Longbons (Decatur Public Library); Peggy Bergen, Doug Imboden, Gary Reynolds, Lew Robbins, David Rush, and Rosie Smith (Shilling Local History Room); John McClarey (for images of Lincoln statuary); and Pat Riley (for vintage postcards). Very special thanks to Dayle Cochran Irwin for permission to use photographs of her great-grandfather and uncle, and for a group of Decatur "home front" images she had originally developed from archival negatives for use in the book *Decatur Serving Others*. Finally, thanks to Jim Parker (Commander, Castle Williams American Legion Post 105).

INTRODUCTION

To the casual motorist, approaching the city of Decatur from the south on U.S. 51, there are few visual cues relating to Decatur's rich and varied wartime connections. A keen driver might spot the small green sign over the Lake Decatur bridge honoring the Korean War veterans, or the red granite marker at the northeast corner of Central Park, paying homage to all of Decatur's prisoners of war and soldiers missing in action. Further exploration would reveal a stately bronze statue of three Civil War soldiers erected in 1904 at the northwest corner of Central Park, a bronze tablet of Civil War dead erected by the Grand Army of the Republic in Fairview Park, and the Korean War veterans memorial in Graceland Cemetery. That inventory generally sums up the signage and statuary that hearken back to wartime experiences. Plans are underway to erect a World War II memorial, fueled in part by the success of the new World War II memorial in Washington, D.C. and the famous Vietnam Memorial. Why, however, should we remember the men, women, and children who are linked to these special moments in the past of Decatur? Is Decatur special in this regard? Does its history deserve recognition, as in the form of this book? Can we better understand our own world by revisiting these experiences of long ago? The answer to all these questions is a dramatic yes.

In spite of its stature as a medium-sized city, Decatur has had a heroic share of American wartime culture and history, including participation in the following military campaigns: the Black Hawk War (1832), the Mexican-American War (1846–1848), the Civil War (1861–1865), the Spanish-American War (1898), the Philippine War (1899–1902), the Great War or World War I (1914–1918), World War II (1941–1945), the Korean War (1950–1953), the Vietnam War (1964–1975), the Persian Gulf War (1991), the war in Afghanistan (which began in 2002), and the present war in Iraq (which began in 2003). Of course, other mid-western and eastern cities might claim even longer records of involvement, but Decatur can proudly boast of many unique accomplishments, beginning with its connections to Lincoln, which tie the city to the Civil War in special ways—five Civil War generals hailed from Decatur and surrounding Macon County, including Richard J. Oglesby who was the last person to touch Lincoln while he was alive and who later spearheaded the work on the Lincoln Tomb in Springfield. A Decatur native, Richard Gatling, invented the machine gun during that conflict, a tool that would change history and the whole pattern of warfare forever. After the Civil War, the Grand Army of the Republic (GAR) was founded in Decatur, and it provided a model for subsequent organizations like the American Legion, the Veterans of Foreign Wars, and the Veterans Administration.

Because Decatur was situated at the crossroads of the Illinois Central and Wabash Railroads, it became a natural hub for soldiers returning from the South during the Civil War or passing through during World Wars I and II. In all three wars, Decatur initiated a canteen service that provided food, medical aid, and other services to the troops. This "home front" service began during the Civil War and continued until the surrender of the Japanese in August 1945. In both World Wars, Decatur consistently exceeded its quota for every single Liberty Loan or War Bond campaign. The city shipped out tons of wheat, corn, and hominy to aid the war effort. Decatur citizenry—men, women, and children—did such a good job of collecting scrap metal and old cars that in 1943 the War Department produced a 12-minute film entitled *Jalopies on Parade* that was shot in Decatur and concluded with high praise for this "typical American city" that contributed heroically to the wartime effort.

Decatur has a unique story to tell because its Mueller valves kept the submarines diving and surfacing properly. Its factory workers contributed to the Manhattan Project, while victory gardens grew everywhere and even schoolchildren bought War Savings Bonds. So the story of wartime Decatur is not merely a tale of soldiers, sailors, and marines, but an enduring parable of total community involvement. The women who rolled bandages and served coffee and biscuits to the soldiers passing through the Decatur station and the families who ate war cake and war bread and rode on old tires were just as much a part of the wartime culture as the machine-gunners and bombardiers. They all deserve to be celebrated, and that is the burden of this book.

One

The Early Wars 1832–1865

Long before the World Wars of the 20th century, Decatur soldiers saw action in three critical campaigns. In 1832, for example, when the city was just established, Sac and Fox Indians under Chief Black Hawk left the Iowa Territory and returned to their native Illinois, threatening settlers in the northwestern part of the state. Militias formed up immediately, including Capt. Abraham Lincoln's company from New Salem and Capt. James Johnson's Fifth Regiment, including 44 Decatur men. William Warnick, Macon County's first sheriff, and Lincoln's neighbor from the spring of 1830 to the spring of 1831, served as first lieutenant. Warnick's Tavern became a familiar stop for Lincoln in his later years on the Eighth Judicial Circuit, but in 1832 Warnick rallied the Decatur troops by brandishing his whip and shouting, "I can whip every Indian with this whip that comes down the Sangamon River." Lincoln's relatives, John and William Hanks, were also part of the regiment. Isaac C. Pugh served as second lieutenant. Chief Black Hawk was defeated at the Battle of Bad Axe on the Mississippi River in Wisconsin. Lincoln quipped that he lost more blood from mosquitoes than from actual combat with the Indians.

The name of Isaac C. Pugh surfaced again in 1846, when he volunteered for service in the Mexican War, a conflict that involved territorial expansion as a direct issue and slavery as an indirect issue. U.S. congressman Lincoln was diametrically opposed to the war, but the troops went into battle under the general leadership of Winfield Scott, "Old Fuss and Feathers." Pugh served as a captain in Company C, and this Decatur group fought at Vera Cruz and Cerro Gordo (now a street name in Decatur and the name of a nearby town). Richard J. Oglesby, later three-time governor of Illinois, served as the first lieutenant. John Post served as second lieutenant, suffered a nearly-mortal chest wound, and later became the first mayor of Decatur in 1856. Company C is credited with capturing the famous cork leg of Gen. Santa Anna, the victor of the Alamo. However, 13 of the 80 Decatur volunteers making up Company C died in Mexico.

Pugh and Oglesby figure prominently in the Civil War also. These two men were part of an illustrious group of soldiers who were all eventually promoted to the rank of general. The others included Gustavus Smith, whose skull was crushed at the Battle of Pea Ridge in Arkansas; Jesse Moore, a former Methodist minister, who was known as the "Fighting Parson;" and Herman Lieb, who commanded three African-American regiments for whom he provided basic education as well as military training. Oglesby was shot in the chest during the Battle of Corinth, Mississippi, and he would probably have died were it not for the services of Dr. Silas T. Trowbridge, one of Decatur's illustrious Army surgeons. His colleagues included Dr. H. C. Johns (founder of the Decatur Sanitary Commission—an early form of the Red Cross—and husband of Jane Martin Johns who wrote a memoir of the period) and Dr. Ira N. Barnes, a member of one of the leading families of Decatur. Lawyers Nathan and Ansel Tupper also served with distinction, as did John Post, the former mayor. This roll call begins to suggest the community-wide surge of support for the Union. The women of Decatur quickly joined in the patriotic spirit of the times as well. When Oglesby—still a Colonel—recruited men in front of Michel's Cigar Store on April 15, 1861, the day after Fort Sumter fell, women presented each volunteer with a tiny hand-sewn flag to attach to his lapel. These same women also sewed a regimental flag for the 8th Illinois Infantry, which like the 41st, and the 116th, were primarily Decatur units. Some 3,690 Decaturites went to war; many were wounded, and at least 56 were killed.

After the Battle of Shiloh, wounded Union troops began moving up the Illinois Central line, stopping at Decatur. Jane Martin Johns organized the Sick and Wounded Soldiers Aid Society in November 1861. Known as the "Basket Brigade," these women volunteers provided socks, pickles, biscuits, and hot coffee for the grateful troops. This local initiative became the model for the later Decatur Canteen. The women also helped Army widows and children, a task taken up formally by the Grand Army of the Republic, founded in Decatur on April 6, 1866. Not surprisingly, Gen. Isaac C. Pugh was one of the founding members. In gratitude, the city named Pugh Street and Pugh School after this singular man who truly embodied the spirit of service and patriotism.

BUST OF CHIEF BLACK HAWK. During the Black Hawk War of 1832, Chief Black Hawk sent some of his men to negotiate with the Illinois militiamen, but the Native Americans were attacked by Maj. Isaiah Stillman's undisciplined troops, thus needlessly prolonging the war. (Courtesy John McClarey.)

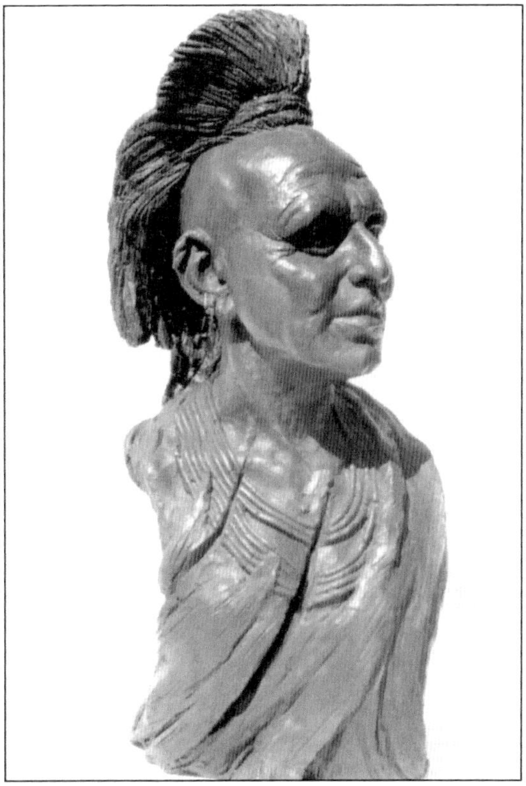

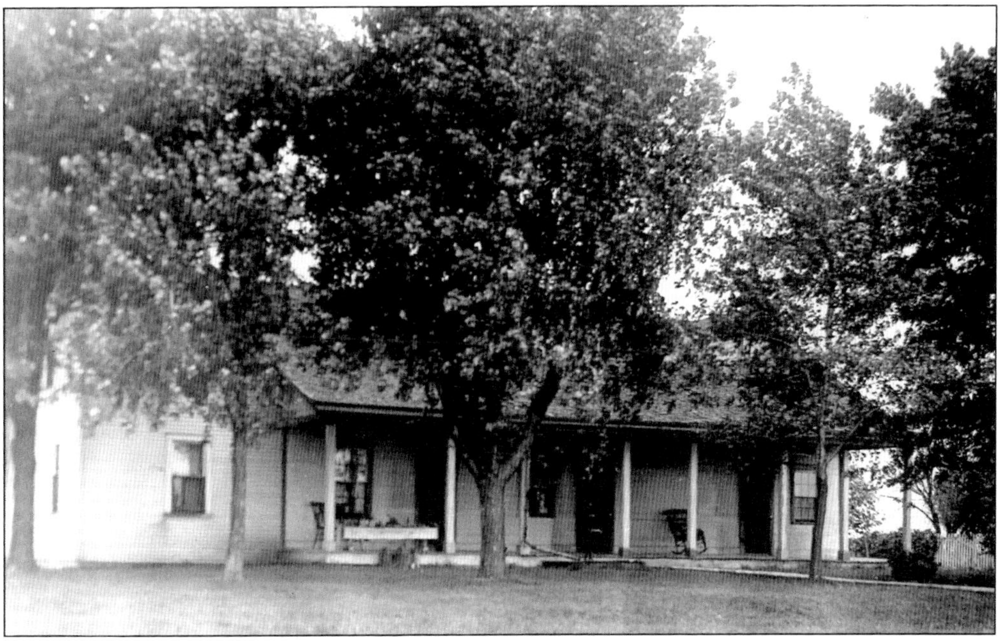

THE WARNICK TAVERN. This structure was built in 1833 by William Warnick, first sheriff of Macon County, Abraham Lincoln's first neighbor in Illinois, and a major in the Black Hawk War. The house was later sold to John Eckle, who ran a tavern there which Lincoln frequented in the 1840s and 1850s. (Courtesy Decatur Public Library.)

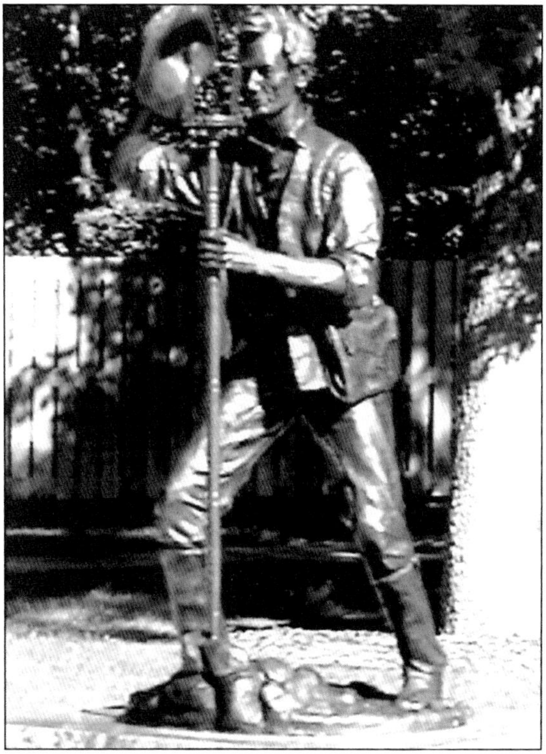

BRONZE STATUE OF LINCOLN AT NEW SALEM. Lincoln is depicted during his surveying days at New Salem. In fact, the statue stands at the entrance to New Salem Village, where Lincoln was elected captain of a company of volunteers for the Black Hawk War. (Courtesy John McClarey.)

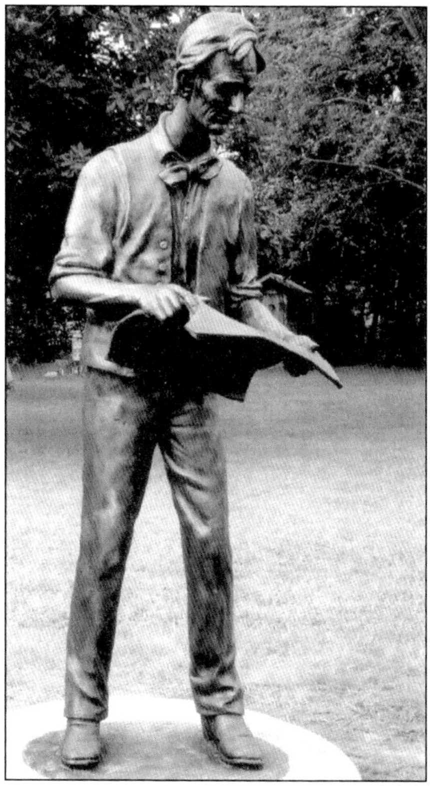

LINCOLN IN DECATUR. In this statue, Lincoln is shown a few years after the Black Hawk War, during the peaceful years of the mid-1830s. The future president is studying a map of Illinois, imagining all the possibilities for growth on the prairie frontier. The Civil War lay far in the future. (Courtesy John McClarey.)

GENERAL RICHARD J. OGLESBY. Looking handsome in his uniform, General Oglesby posed for this carte de visite in 1862. It is a rare image. Oglesby went on to serve as governor of Illinois three times before retiring to Oglehurst, his final home in Elkhart, Illinois. (Courtesy Lincoln Library Sangamon Valley Collection.)

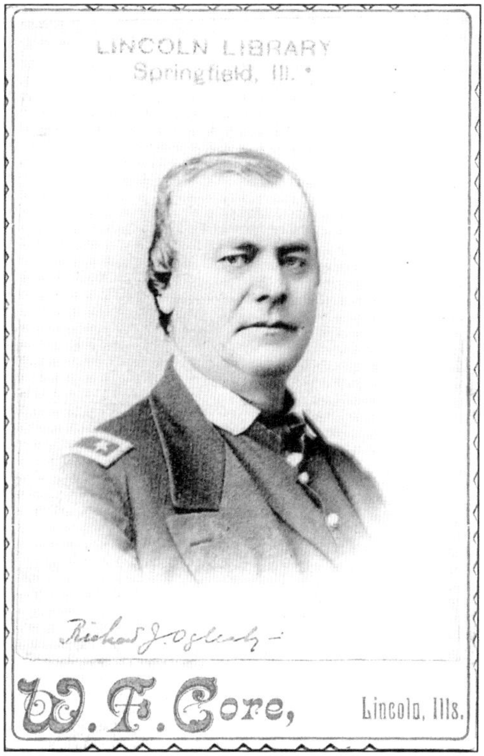

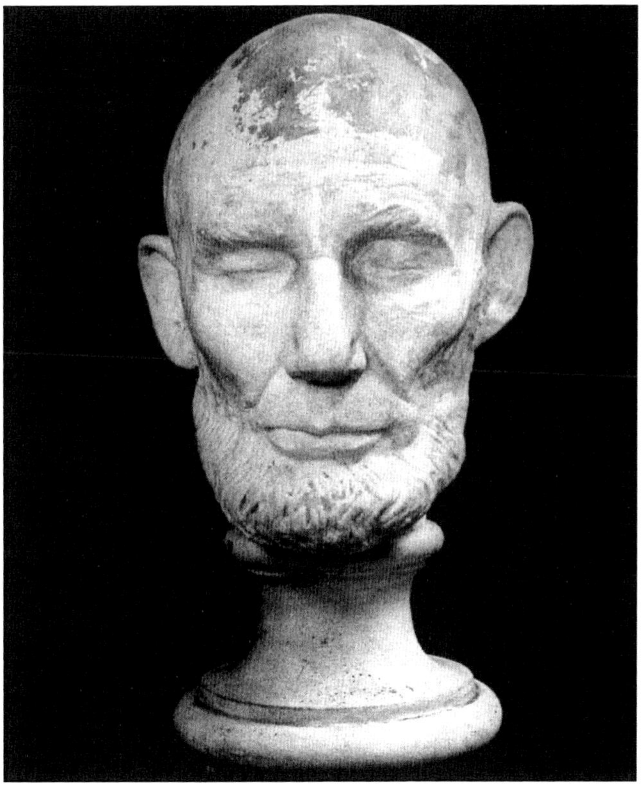

ABRAHAM LINCOLN LIFE MASK. Molded by sculptor Clark Mills in February 1865, this life mask shows a hollow-cheeked and war-weary President Lincoln about two months before he was assassinated. Lincoln aged dramatically during the four years of a bitter Civil War. (Courtesy Macon County Historical Society Museum.)

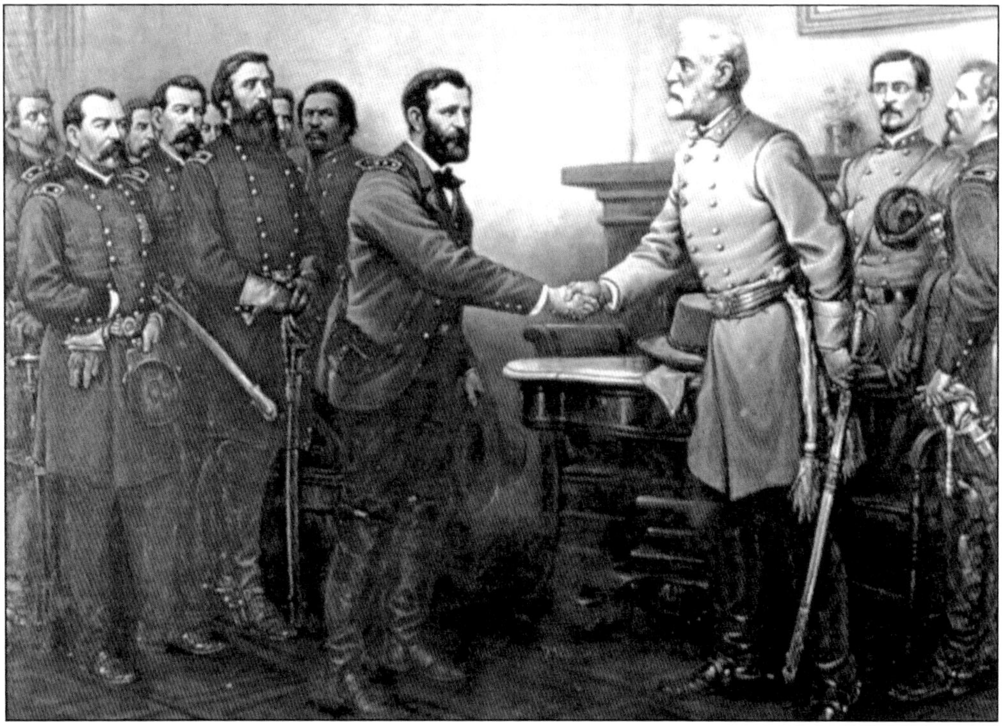

LEE SURRENDERING TO GRANT AT APPOMATTOX. In this reproduction of Thomas Nast's painting, Gen. Robert E. Lee shakes hands with Gen. Ulysses S. Grant on April 9, 1865. John Wilkes Booth shot Lincoln in the head at Ford's Theater only five days later. (Courtesy Macon County Historical Society Museum.)

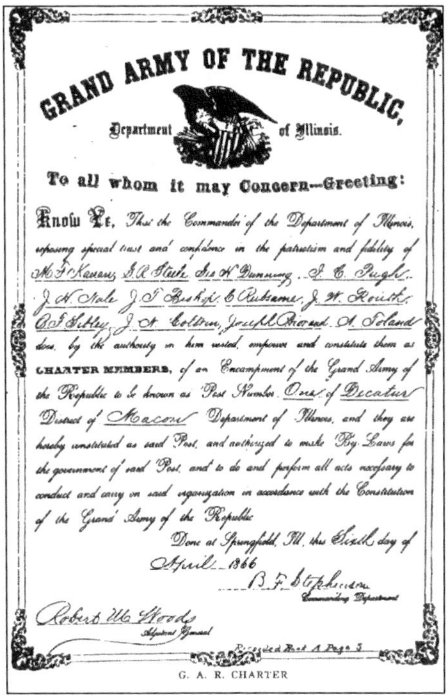

GRAND ARMY OF THE REPUBLIC,

Department of Illinois.

To all whom it may Concern—Greeting:

Know Ye, That the Commander of the Department of Illinois, reposing special trust and confidence in the patriotism and fidelity of M. F. Kanan, G. R. Steele, Geo. H. Dunning, I. C. Pugh, J. H. Nale, J. T. Bishop, C. Rubsame, J. W. Routh, B. F. Sibley, J. H. Coltrin, Joseph Prorand, A. Toland does, by the authority in him vested, empower and constitute them as CHARTER MEMBERS, of an Encampment of the Grand Army of the Republic to be known as Post Number One of Decatur District of Macon Department of Illinois, and they are hereby constituted as said Post, and authorized to make By-Laws for the government of said Post, and to do and perform all acts necessary to conduct and carry on said organization in accordance with the Constitution of the Grand Army of the Republic

Done at Springfield, Ill, this Sixth day of April 1866

B. F. Stephenson
Commanding Department

Robert M. Woods
Adjutant General

Recorded Book A Page 3

G. A. R. CHARTER

GRAND ARMY OF THE REPUBLIC CHARTER. Dated April 6, 1866, the Grand Army of the Republic (GAR) Charter contains the signature of General Isaac C. Pugh, on the right-hand side, six lines down. This copy of the original document faithfully recreates the 19th-century love of graphic embellishment and florid rhetoric. (Courtesy Decatur Genealogical Society.)

BIRTHPLACE OF THE GRAND ARMY OF THE REPUBLIC. In this building at 253 South Park Street, near the very spot where Lincoln was first nominated for the presidency, 13 men met on April 6, 1866, under the leadership of Maj. B. F. Stephenson, and founded the GAR. The last member of the Decatur GAR post died on March 16, 1942. (Courtesy Decatur Public Library.)

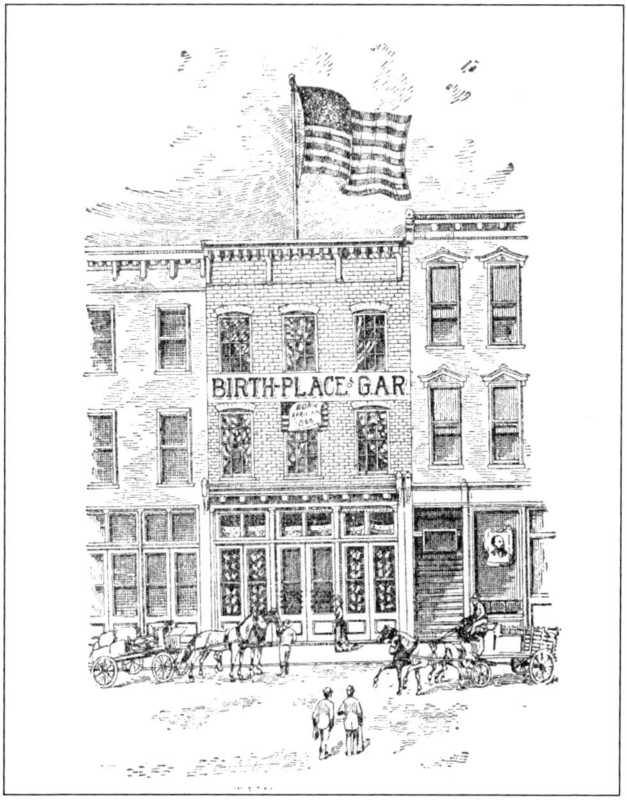

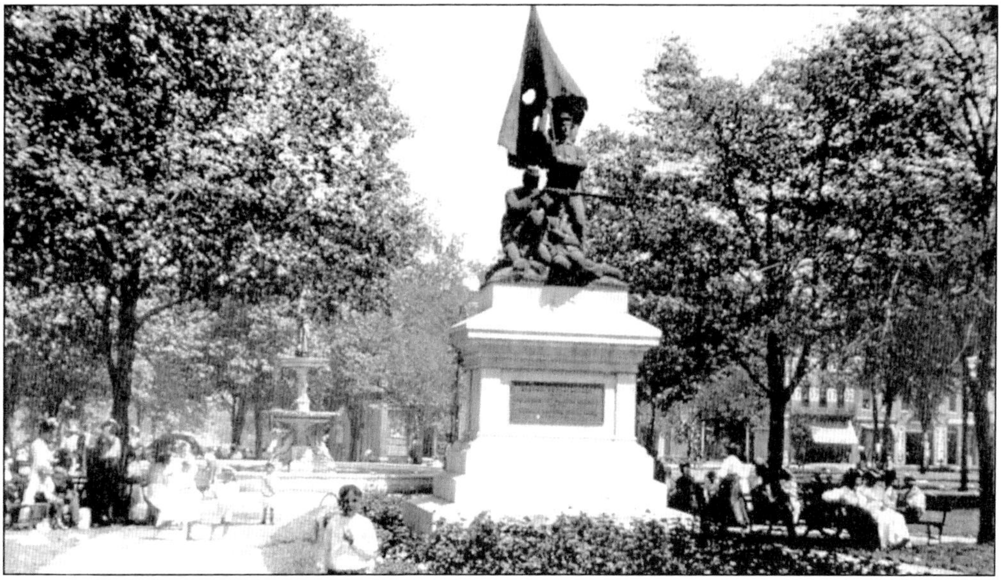

CIVIL WAR STATUE, CENTRAL PARK. Erected in 1904 through funds collected by various organizations, this group of bronze Union soldiers rallying beneath a tattered flag is perhaps the finest piece of statuary in Decatur. It has served as a downtown landmark for over a century. (Courtesy Pat Riley.)

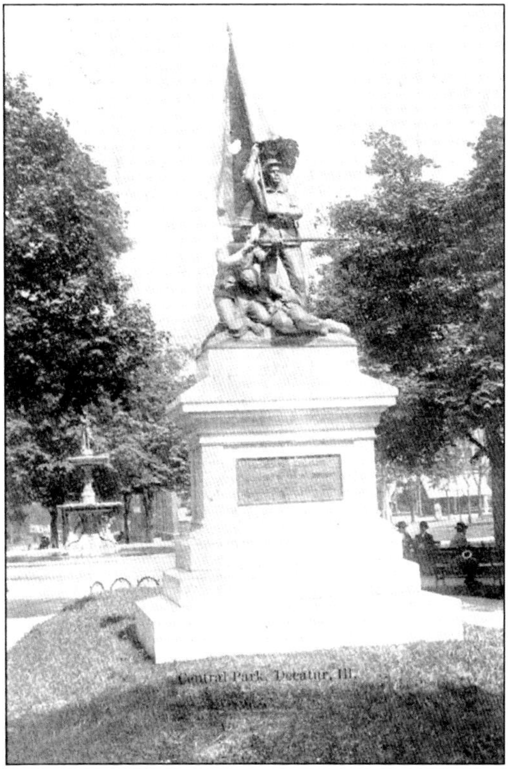

CIVIL WAR STATUE ON A SUMMER DAY. This postcard shows another view of the Civil War statue, with the old Decatur fountain clearly visible on the left and three gentlemen sitting on a park bench enjoying the air. They were probably old enough to remember the war. (Courtesy Pat Riley.)

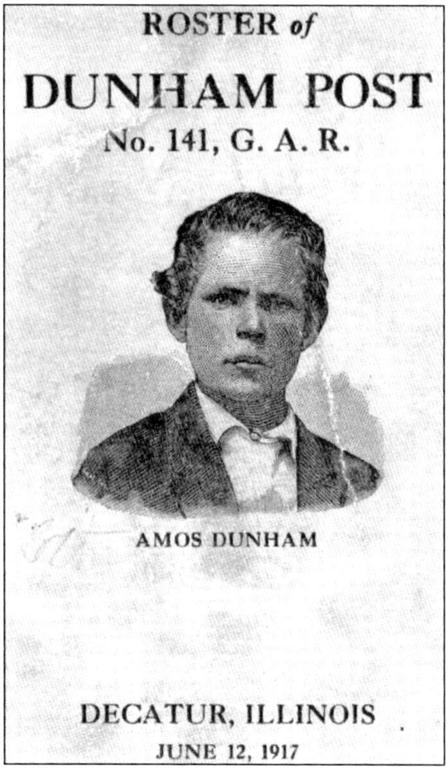
ROSTER *of*
DUNHAM POST
No. 141, G. A. R.
AMOS DUNHAM
DECATUR, ILLINOIS
JUNE 12, 1917

PVT. AMOS DUNHAM, U.S. ARMY. Amos was killed in 1862, the first casualty from Decatur or Macon County. In a letter home he explained his reason for volunteering, "Dear old Decatur, as well as every city in the United States, was in grief and danger." (Courtesy Decatur Public Library.)

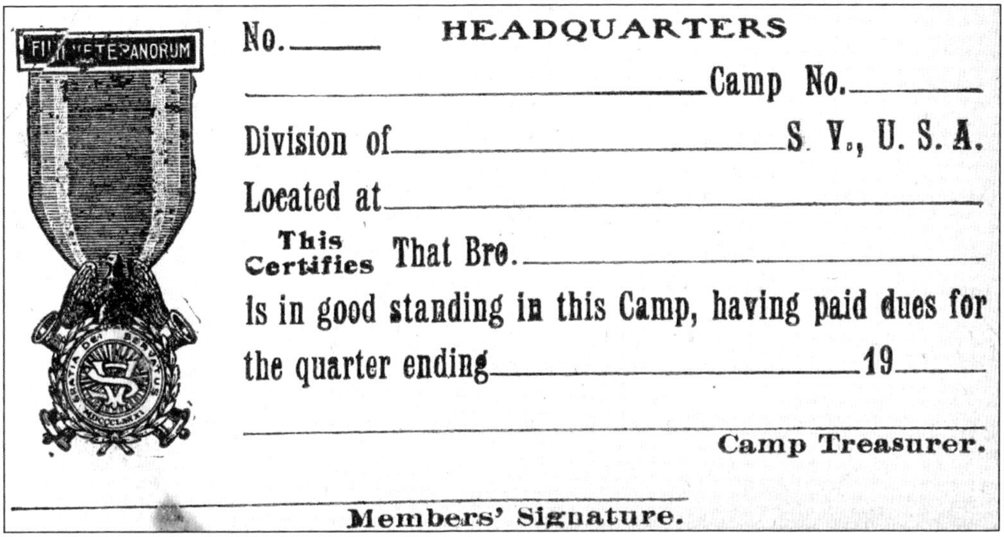

No._____ HEADQUARTERS

____________________ Camp No.______

Division of____________________ S. V., U. S. A.

Located at____________________________

This Certifies That Bro.________________________

is in good standing in this Camp, having paid dues for the quarter ending________________19____

____
Camp Treasurer.

____
Members' Signature.

SONS OF VETERANS MEMBERSHIP CARD. A spin-off from the GAR, the Sons of Veterans, was also founded in Decatur with the sponsorship of Isaac Pugh. The Latin inscriptions read "*Filii Veteranorum*" (sons of veterans) and "*Gratia Dei Servatus*" (having served by the grace of God). This batch of cards was printed off-center. (Courtesy Macon County Historical Society Museum.)

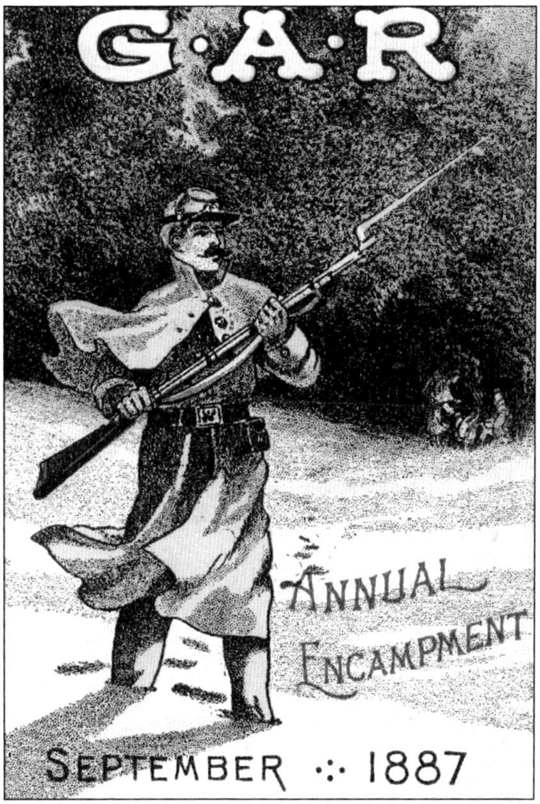

GAR SOUVENIR CARD, 1887. This souvenir card was printed by the GAR to commemorate the annual "encampment" or convention held that September of 1887 in St. Louis. The soldier is depicted romantically with bayonet and fluttering cape. (Courtesy Pat Riley.)

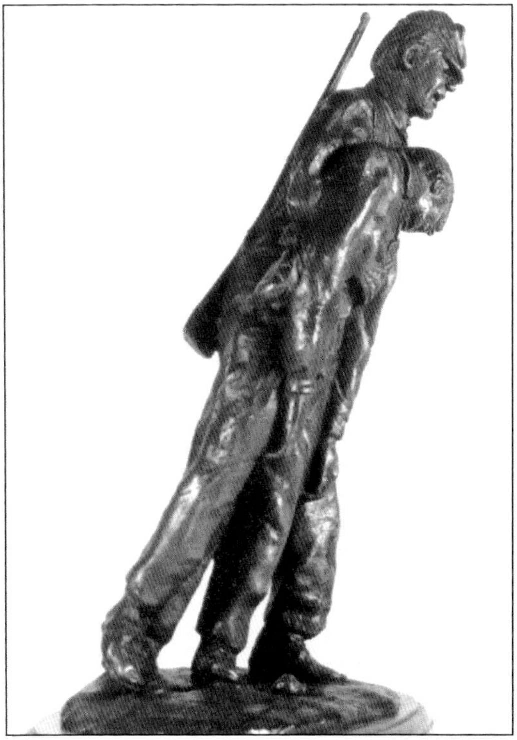

UNION SOLDIER AIDING A WOUNDED COMRADE. This statuette by Decatur sculptor and historian John McClarey eloquently describes the close bonding of soldiers under fire. Many soldiers died from subsequent infections rather than the actual wounds. (Courtesy John McClarey.)

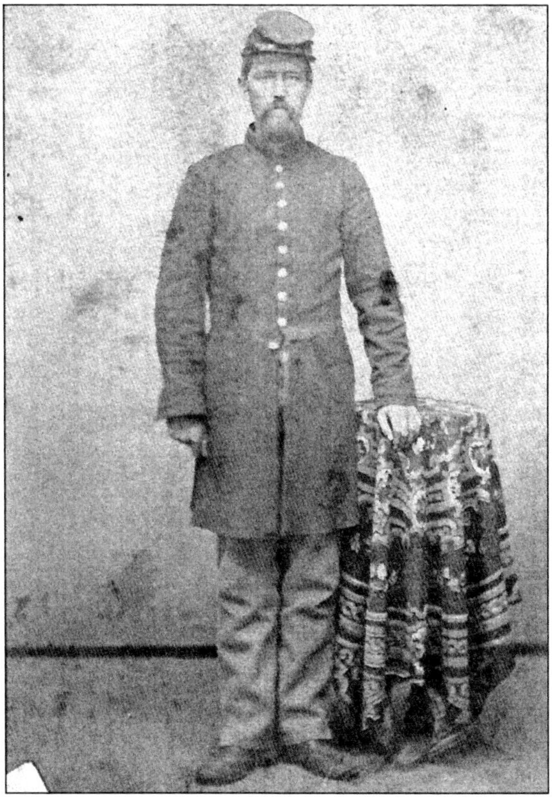

PRIVATE WILLIAM DICKERSON. In this carte de visite, made about 1864, Private William Dickerson, Company E, 116th Regiment, wears the standard forage cap, frock coat, and baggy trousers. (Courtesy Decatur Historical Society Museum.)

COL. NATHAN W. TUPPER. Buried in Greenwood Cemetery, Colonel Tupper is the hero of the 116th Regiment, having fought at Chickasaw Bayou, Vicksburg, Jackson, and Mission Ridge. He died in Decatur on March 10, 1864 from exposure on the march from Chattanooga to Knoxville. His brother, Ansel Tupper, also died in the war. (Courtesy Decatur Historical Society Museum.)

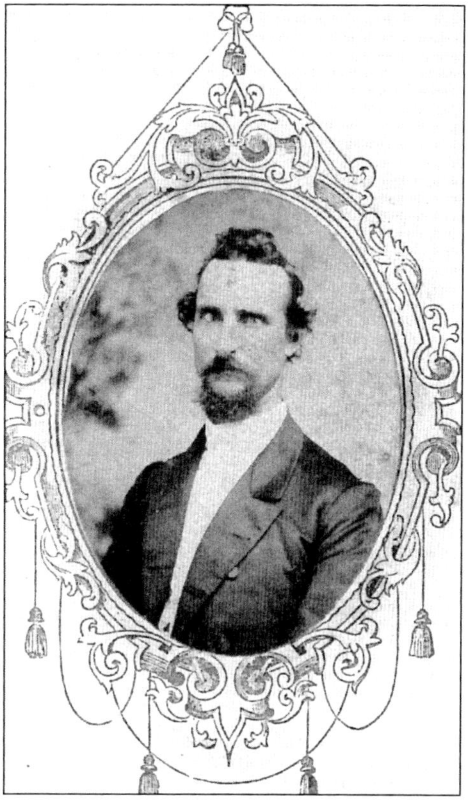

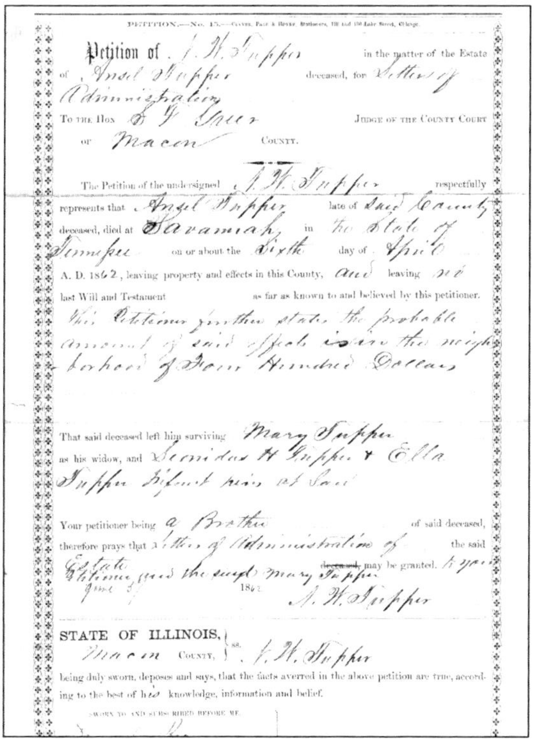

Petition of N. W. Tupper in the matter of the Estate of Ansel Tupper deceased, for Letters of Administration

To the Hon. D. F. Greer Judge of the County Court of Macon County.

The Petition of the undersigned N. W. Tupper respectfully represents that Ansel Tupper late of said County deceased, died at Savannah in the State of Tennessee on or about the Sixth day of April A. D. 1862, leaving property and effects in this County, and leaving no last Will and Testament as far as known to and believed by this petitioner.

That said deceased left him surviving Mary Tupper as his widow, and Leonidas H. Tupper & Ella Tupper Infant heirs at Law

Your petitioner being a Brother of said deceased, therefore prays that Letters of Administration of the said Estate may be granted.

N. W. Tupper

STATE OF ILLINOIS, Macon County, ss. N. W. Tupper being duly sworn, deposes and says, that the facts averred in the above petition are true, according to the best of his knowledge, information and belief.

SWORN TO AND SUBSCRIBED BEFORE ME.

PROBATE DOCUMENT OF ANSEL TUPPER. This probate document, which helped to settle the estate of Ansel Tupper after his wartime death, was signed by his brother, Nathan, on April 6, 1862. (Courtesy Decatur Genealogical Society.)

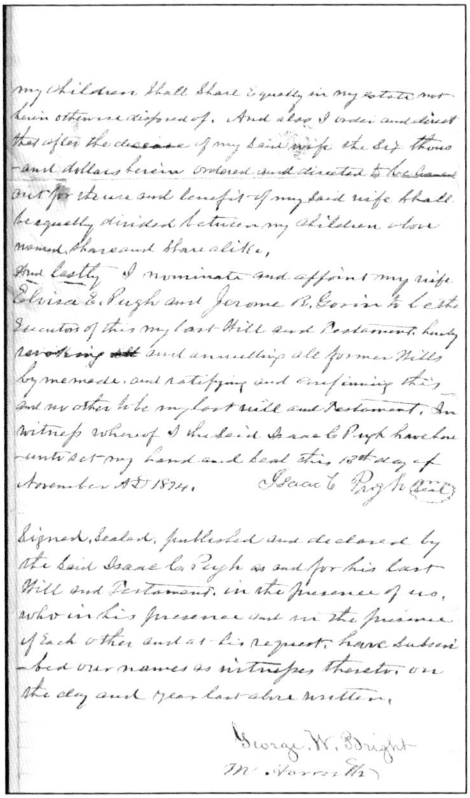

my children shall share equally in my estate not
herein otherwise disposed of. And also I order and direct
that after the decease of my said wife the six thous
-and dollars herein ordered and directed to be loaned
out for the use and benefit of my said wife shall
be equally divided between my children above
named share and share alike,
And lastly I nominate and appoint my wife
Elvira E. Pugh and Jerome R. Gorin to be the
Executors of this my last Will and Testament hereby
revoking all and annulling all former Wills
by me made, and ratifying and confirming this
and no other to be my last will and Testament. In
witness whereof I the said Isaac C Pugh have here
-unto set my hand and seal this 18th day of
November AD 1874. Isaac C Pugh (Seal)

Signed, sealed, published and declared by
the said Isaac C. Pugh as and for his last
Will and Testament, in the presence of us,
who in his presence and in the presence
of each other and at his request, have subscri
-bed our names as witnesses thereto on
the day and year last above written.

George W. Bright
[illegible]

ELVIRA PUGH BANKING DOCUMENT. This note, signed by Pugh's widow Elvira, was handled by the Millikin Banking Company on April 29, 1874. During the war, James Millikin was part of a vigilante group keeping an eye on "Copperheads" (Southern sympathizers) like the Knights of the Golden Circle, which was active in Decatur. (Courtesy Decatur Genealogical Society.)

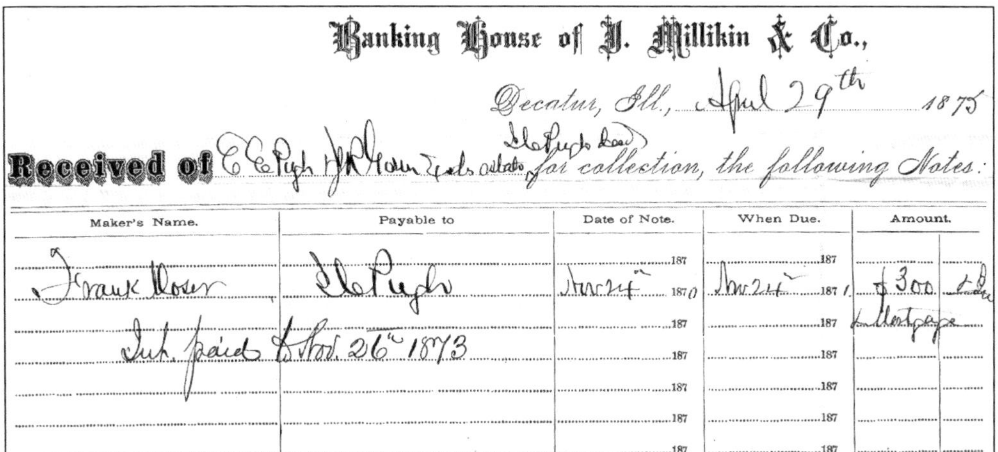

Banking House of J. Millikin & Co.,

Decatur, Ill., April 29th 1875

Received of E. C. Pugh [illegible] for collection, the following Notes:

Maker's Name.	Payable to	Date of Note.	When Due.	Amount.
		187	187	
Frank Moser	I. C. Pugh	Nov 24 1870	Nov 24 1871	$300 [illegible]
		187	187	Mortgage
Int. paid	to Nov. 26th 1873	187	187	
		187	187	
		187	187	
		187	187	

Orea C Ewing

CODICIL TO ISAAC PUGH'S WILL. Pugh's signature appears on the middle right of this document. In addition to being a veteran of three wars and a retired general, Pugh also served as postmaster of Decatur and as commissioner of Macon County. His farm bordered the present Grand and Water Street area. (Courtesy Decatur Genealogical Society.)

CAVALRYMAN AMERICUS PATRICK. In this studio shot, probably taken during the Civil War, Americus Patrick wears the beret-style cap and the snug-fitting cavalry jacket of a cavalry soldier. His descendants still live in Decatur today. (Courtesy Dayle Cochran Irwin.)

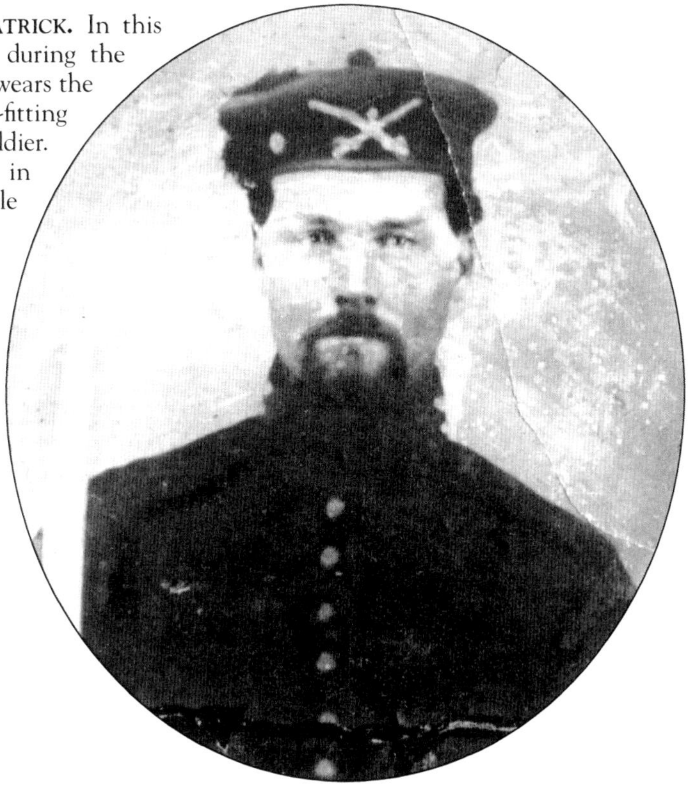

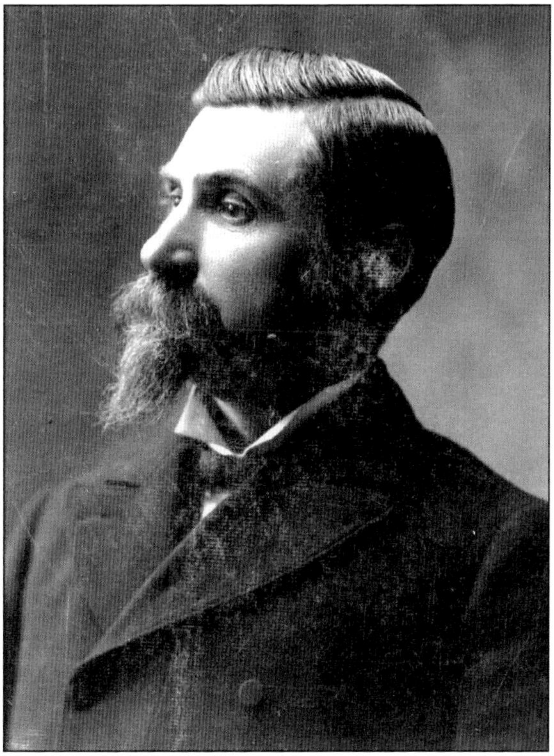

SAMUEL M. LUTZ. This formal photograph, taken December 12, 1903, shows Samuel Lutz who was famous as a singer and a local dealer in musical instruments. Many of his original hymns and war songs were performed during the Civil War. (Courtesy Decatur Public Library.)

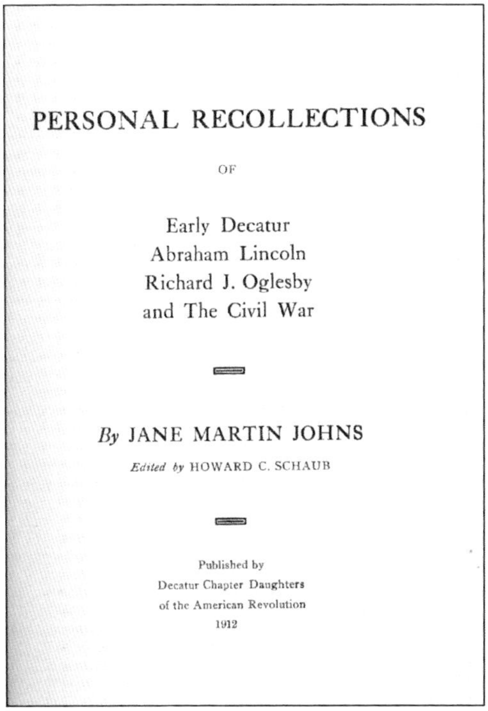
PERSONAL RECOLLECTIONS

OF

Early Decatur
Abraham Lincoln
Richard J. Oglesby
and The Civil War

By JANE MARTIN JOHNS

Edited by HOWARD C. SCHAUB

Published by
Decatur Chapter Daughters
of the American Revolution
1912

PERSONAL RECOLLECTIONS. This candid memoir is one of the best primary sources for early Decatur and Civil War era history. Among other stories, Jane Martin Johns tells the tale of dirty, unruly, and ungrateful Southern civilians that she handed over to county authorities. Her husband, an Army surgeon, was almost shot in his own neighborhood by a Copperhead. (Courtesy Dan Guillory.)

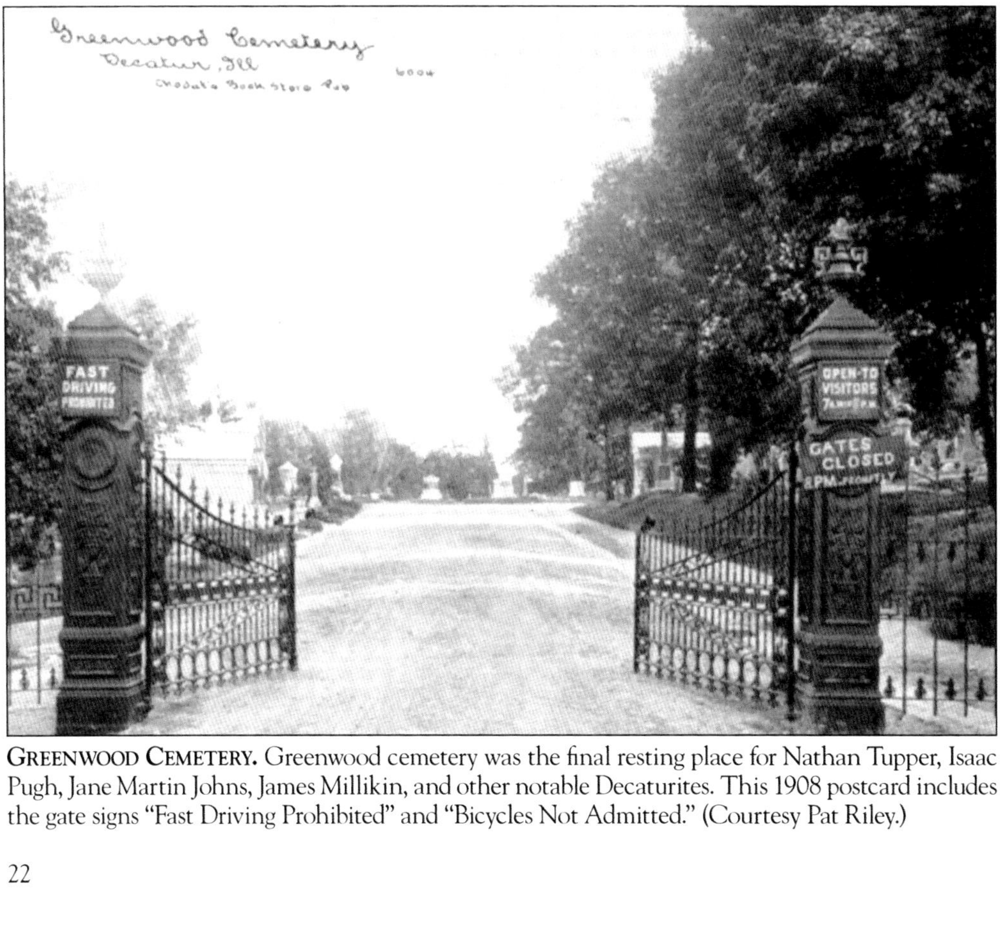

GREENWOOD CEMETERY. Greenwood cemetery was the final resting place for Nathan Tupper, Isaac Pugh, Jane Martin Johns, James Millikin, and other notable Decaturites. This 1908 postcard includes the gate signs "Fast Driving Prohibited" and "Bicycles Not Admitted." (Courtesy Pat Riley.)

Two

The Great War 1914–1918

World War I is often called the Great War because, before it ended in November 1918, the conflict involved England, France, Germany, Italy, Hungary, Austria, Russia, and—finally—the United States. It is also "great" by virtue of its ferocity, the use of aerial bombardment, tanks, submarines, machine guns, land mines, heavy artillery, and poison gas. It was fought on a great scale, all along the border of France and Germany, with a "no man's land" in-between. Although America was staunchly isolationist, the country enthusiastically supported the war once the American Expeditionary Force (AEF) was sent to France in 1917.

Decatur, Illinois consistently exceeded its quota on the five Liberty Loan (war bond) campaigns as well as the two Red Cross drives. It is interesting that the U.S. Government was not fully prepared—financially or militarily—for this conflict, and the citizens were expected to take up the slack by rationing themselves on food (especially wheat, beef, sugar, and coffee) and fuel (especially coal). They were expected to contribute to the coffers by buying bonds and savings stamps (which could be converted into bonds). Despite a great deal of publicity designed to convince the populace that a genuine food shortage existed, there was in fact, no shortage during the war period of 1917–1918. America was already an incredibly rich country with many new immigrants and vast agricultural and technological resources. If the United States had been in for the long haul, say, four or five years, then a labor shortage would have reduced agricultural and industrial output. But the war ended before any of these deleterious effects could occur. Since World War I had begun in 1914, America entered it rather late but still contributed mightily in terms of national treasure and human lives. American "doughboys" participated in some of the bloodiest encounters of the whole war, and they faced battle-hardened German troops.

On the home front, women were bombarded with pamphlets and billboards under the auspices of the National Defense Council, making it clear that they, too, were expected to volunteer, usually as Red Cross volunteers or salespersons for war bonds. Men who hadn't volunteered were expected to work in agriculture or in defense industries, and factory owners had to justify their work force and their products in terms of the war effort. In the midst of all these governmental imperatives, the Red Cross Canteen arose between the Wabash and Illinois Central train stations, aiding soldiers in much the same way as Jane Martin Johns and the "basket brigade" had done 50 years earlier. Women also volunteered throughout the city to make surgical dressings, knitted garments, hospital garments, and clothing for refugees.

In the spring of 1918, a kind of war hysteria swept through Decatur, and a great deal of pressure was put on ordinary citizens to achieve various food and bond quotas. Lists were kept of everyone who bought war bonds, or did not. Neighbors denounced neighbors who dared to express any doubts, however slight, about the wisdom of going to war. Any man driving his car on Sunday and squandering precious fuel usually found the vehicle painted yellow on Monday morning. Fortunately, these excesses were short-lived.

Some 3,586 Decatur men went to France, and about 100 died overseas. Most of the troops served in Company A of the 124th Machine Gun Battalion. They landed at Brest, France, on May 24, 1918, serving under Capt. W. Lutz Krigbaum, who was promoted to major and awarded the Croix de Guerre and the Distinguished Service Cross. One of his men, Sgt. Castle Williams, was the first Decatur man to die in France. Company A returned home on May 31, 1919, and in July a huge military funeral and parade occurred to honor Sergeant Williams, whose name is still attached to the local American Legion Post.

The doughboys came back to a different world, one defined by jazz, flapper girls, bathtub gin, tin lizzies, radio jingles, and unregulated stock speculation. The whole nation partied for a decade, but the high times came to a sudden halt with the collapse of the stock market in 1929 and the ensuing Great Depression, a grim experience that lasted until the very eve of World War II.

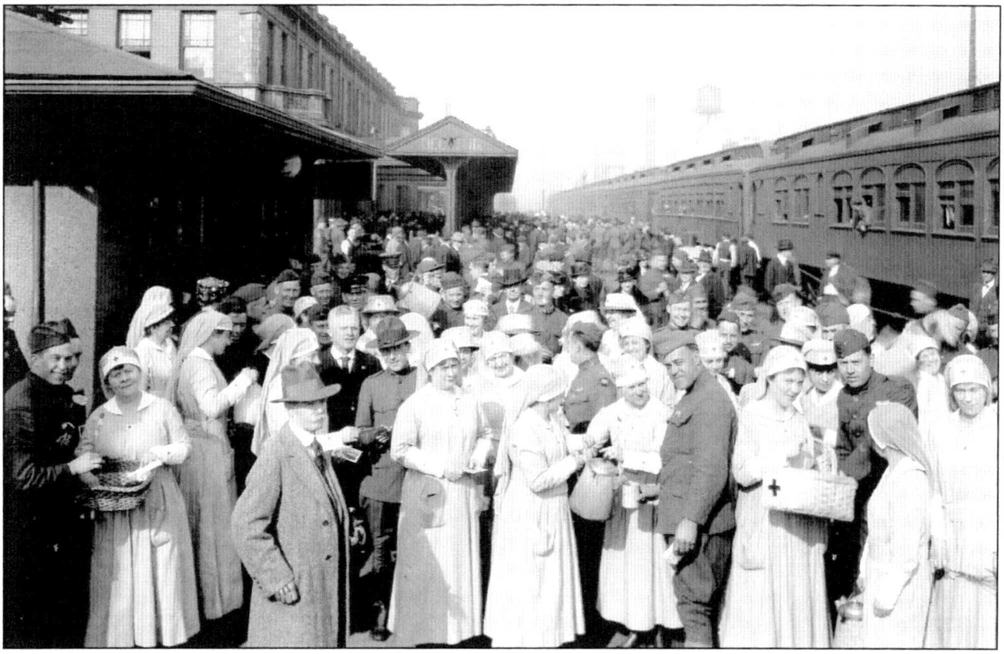

DECATUR CANTEEN VOLUNTEERS, 1917. These women worked throughout the war to dispense coffee, biscuits, newspapers, and cake to the appreciative servicemen. Decatur actually earned a nationwide reputation for hospitality and friendly service. The man in the overcoat is John Culver, the manager. (Courtesy Decatur Public Library.)

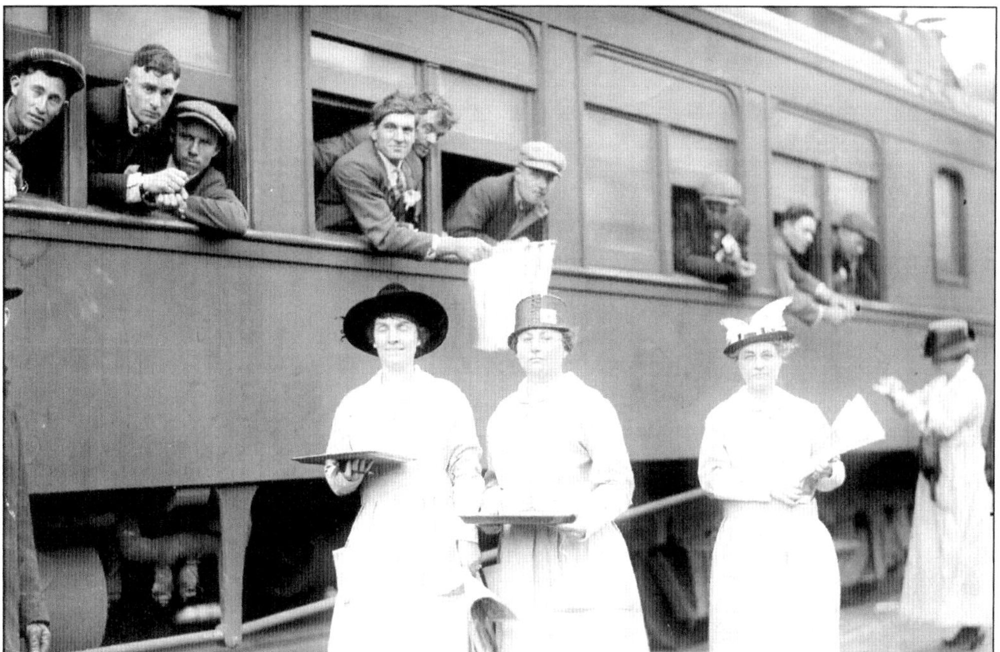

DRAFTEES SERVED AT THE CANTEEN. These flag-waving young men are recent draftees en route to a processing center. Four canteen volunteers have just passed out food and newspapers, which explains their smiling faces in this spring 1918 photograph. (Courtesy Decatur Public Library.)

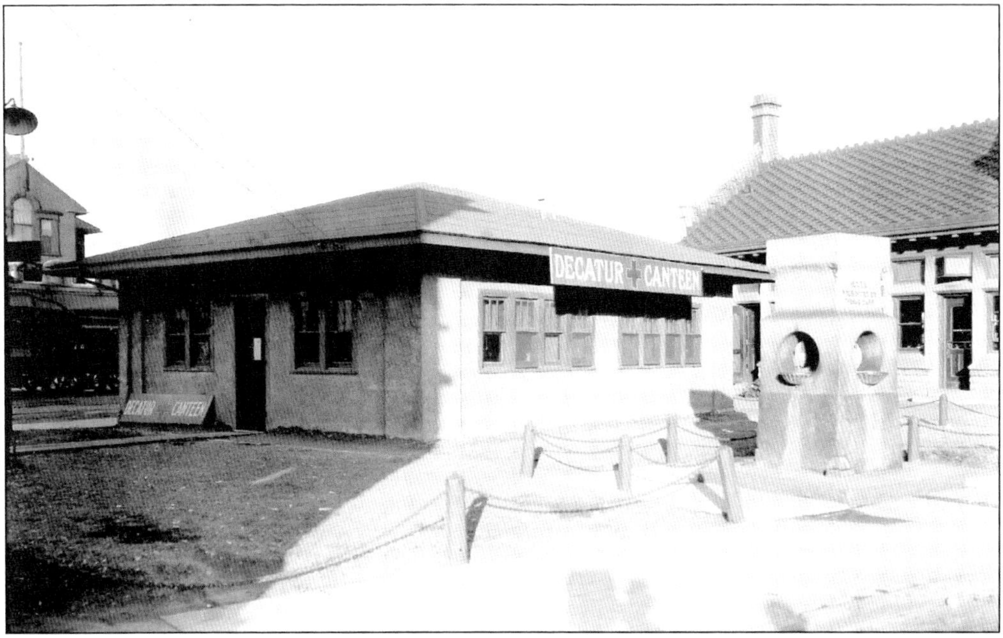

DECATUR RED CROSS CANTEEN HUT. This building served as the focal point for the volunteer work directed toward transient soldiers. It met the needs of servicemen in both World War I and II. Note the Women's Christian Temperance Union (W.C.T.U.) water fountain, which was meant to encourage sobriety. (Courtesy Decatur Public Library.)

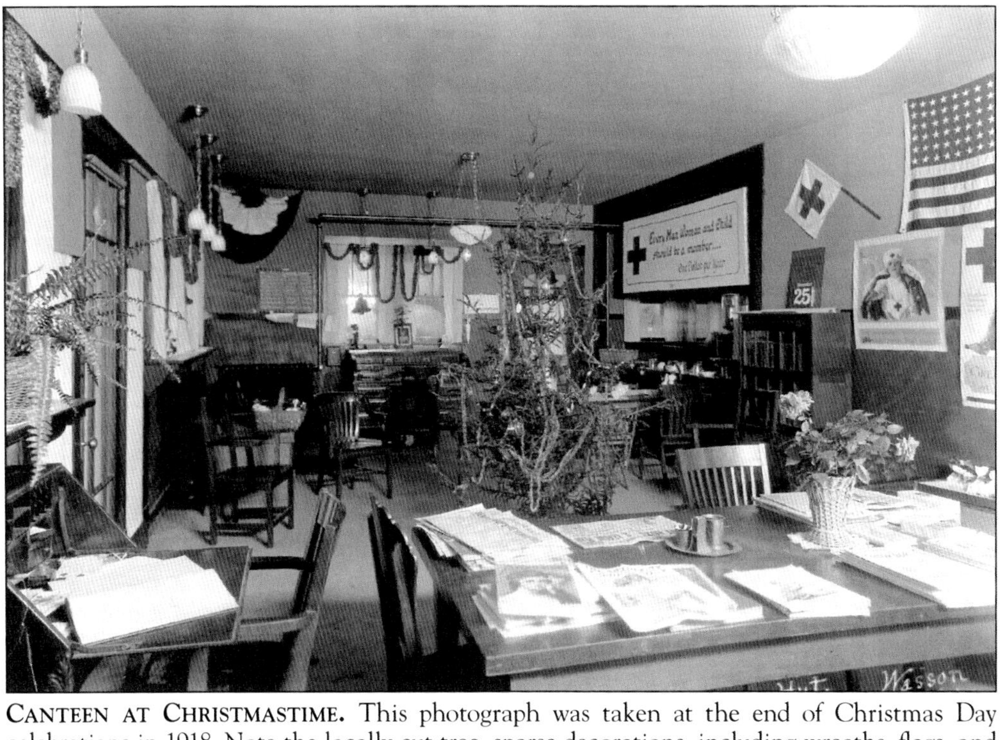

CANTEEN AT CHRISTMASTIME. This photograph was taken at the end of Christmas Day celebrations in 1918. Note the locally cut tree, sparse decorations, including wreaths, flags, and bunting. There is an unmistakable air of efficiency. (Courtesy Decatur Public Library.)

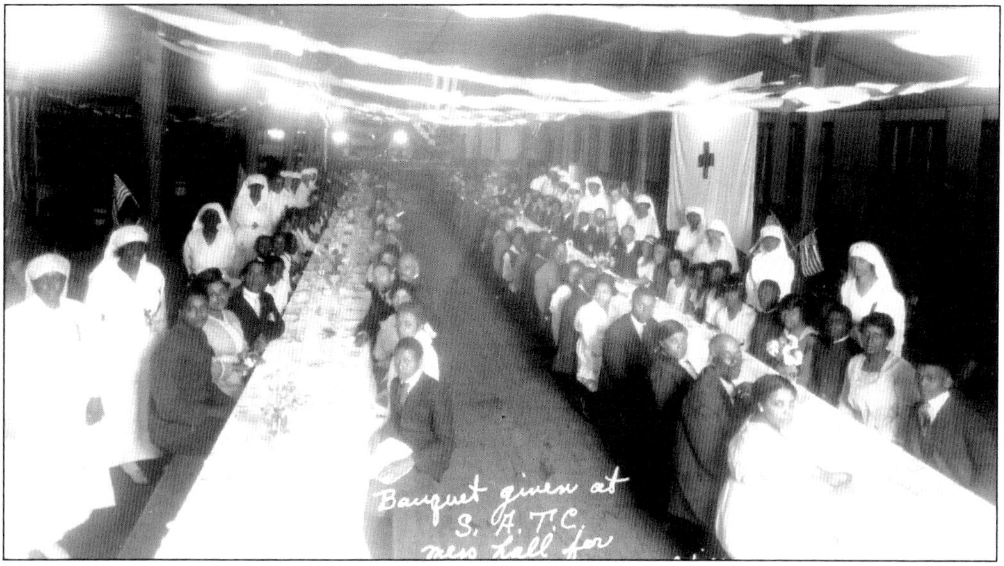

Banquet for African-American Soldiers. Taken in the summer of 1919, this photograph suggests that racial barriers were still present in Decatur as the African-Americans, who had served in the Transportation Corps, were given a separate banquet from the Caucasian returnees. (Courtesy Decatur Public Library.)

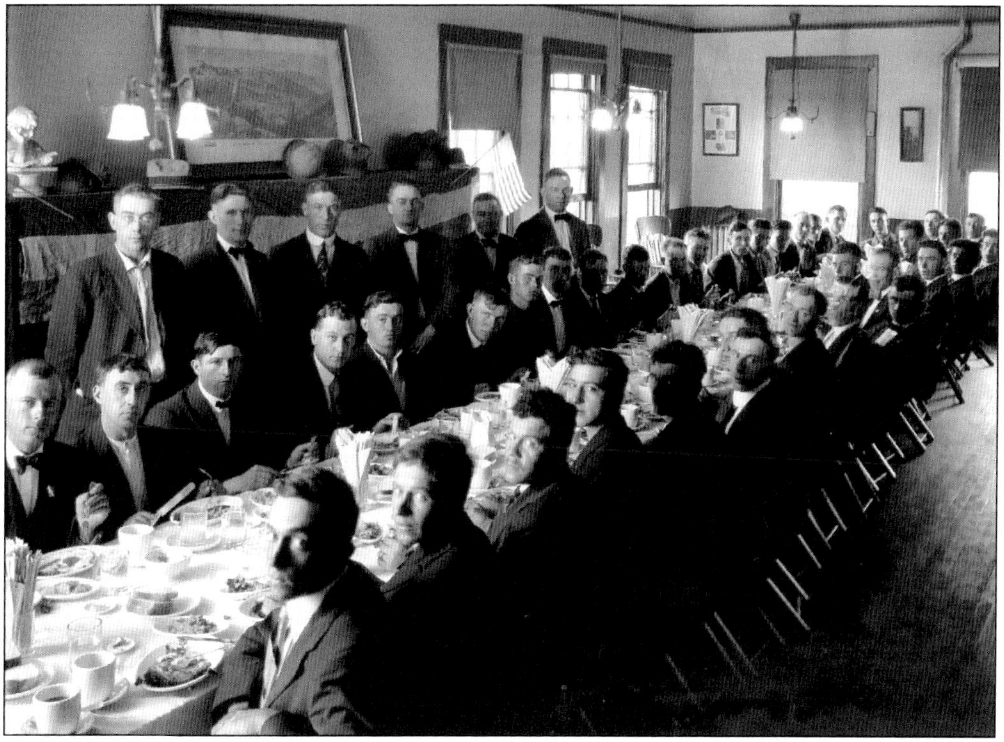

Banquet for Company A. These soldiers were the mainstay of the Decatur-based Company A. They had just recently honored their fallen comrade, Sgt. Castle Williams, with an elaborate parade and military funeral. The photograph was taken in the summer of 1919. (Courtesy Decatur Public Library.)

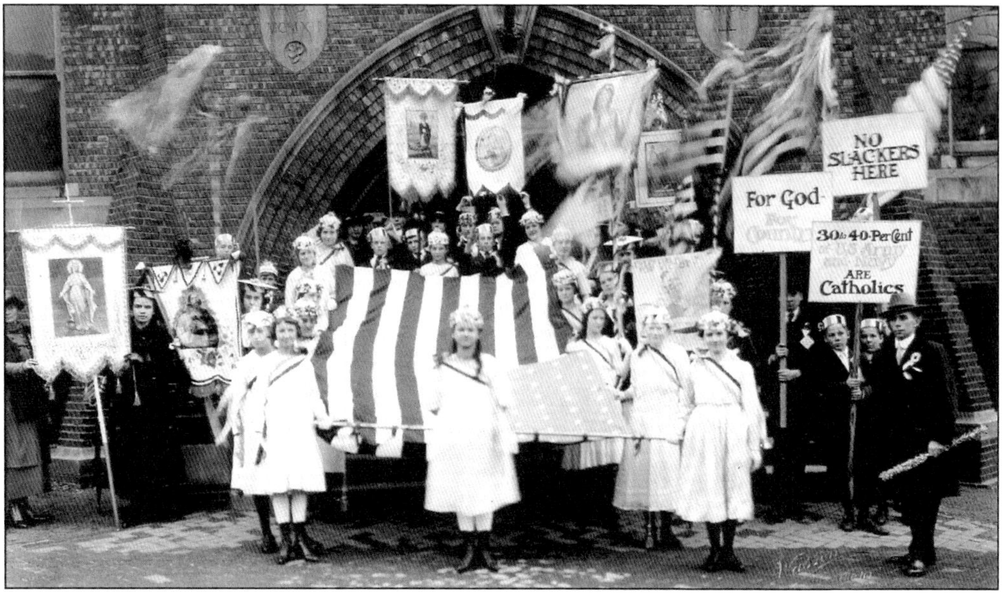

ST. PATRICK'S SCHOOL. Anti-Irish and anti-Catholic feelings were still part of Decatur's generally Protestant, German, and Anglo-Saxon culture. Hence, the felt need of these Catholic students to express their patriotism in this 1918 photograph. "No Slackers Here" proclaims the sign. The building in the background was rather new, having been constructed in 1912. It still stands today. (Courtesy Decatur Public Library.)

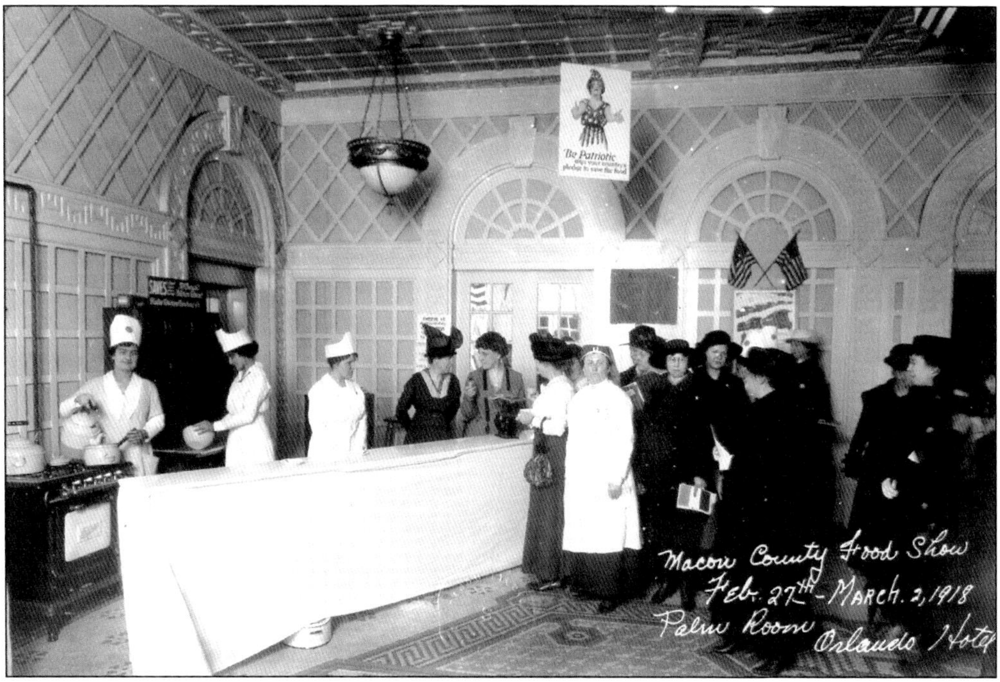

MACON COUNTY PATRIOTIC FOOD SHOW. Held from February 27 to March 2, 1918, at the Palm Room of the Orlando Hotel, the Patriotic Food Show was essentially a mixture of home economics and patriotism. In this picture, University of Illinois "food experts" are putting on a demonstration. (Courtesy Decatur Public Library; original photograph by Bijou Studios.)

UNITED STATES FOOD ADMINISTRATION. This window placard verified that the household was in compliance with the food austerity program of the U.S. Government. Actually, there was no food shortage in 1917 or 1918, but Decatur did its duty and avoided coffee, chocolate, sugar, butter, and beef. (Courtesy Decatur Public Library.)

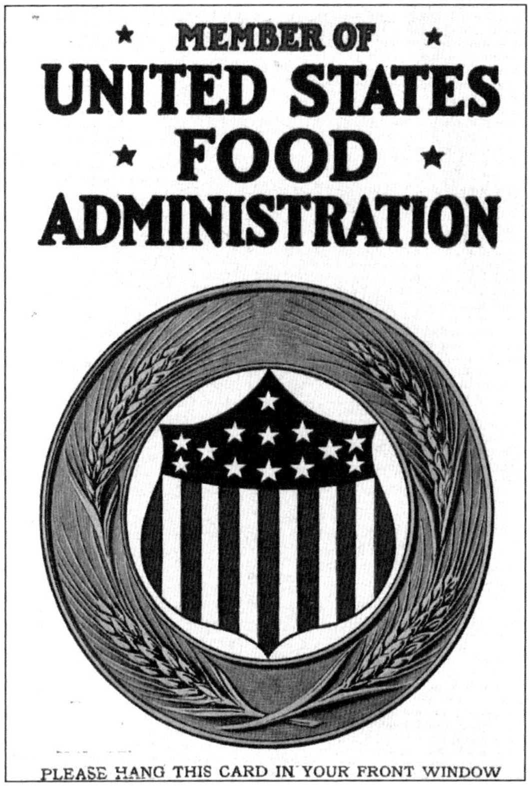

PRIZES FOR WAR BREAD, CAKE AND COOKIES

Prizes for war bread, cake and cookies are offered by the Patriotic Food Show at Hotel Orlando building, Decatur, Feb. 27, 28, March 1 and 2.

The prizes and conditions are:

No. 243 Potato Bread

For bread from Recipe No. 243 in official Recipe Book of the show, as follows:

1¼ cups mashed potato (solidly packed)
1½ teaspoons salt
1 tablespoon sugar
1 tablespoon fat
2¼ cups flour
¼ cake compressed yeast softened in 1 tablespoon luke warm water.

Prizes—First, $4; second, $3; third, $1.

Original Bread Recipe

For bread from original recipe by exhibitor, using not more than one half wheat flour. Prizes—First, $4; second, $3; third, $1.

Honey Cake, No. 296

Honey cake from Recipe No. 296 in official Recipe Book, as follows:

1 cup rice flour
2 cups pastry flour
½ cup fat
½ cup water
2 eggs
2-3 cup glucose
1-3 cup honey
5 teaspoons baking powder
1 teaspoon vanilla.

Prizes—First, $3; second, $2; third, $1.

Cut Out Sugar

Owing to the fact that Recipe No. 299 had sugar in it, the Devil's Food Cake is cut out and only one cake prize is offered, Recipe No. 296, above, a real war cake.

WAR BREAD AND WAR CAKE. These partial recipes—cooking times are not stated—were part of a contest sponsored by the Decatur *Herald* as part of the Patriotic Food Show of 1918. Many homemakers attempted to bake creatively, and many versions of war bread and war cake were submitted to the judges. (Courtesy Decatur Public Library.)

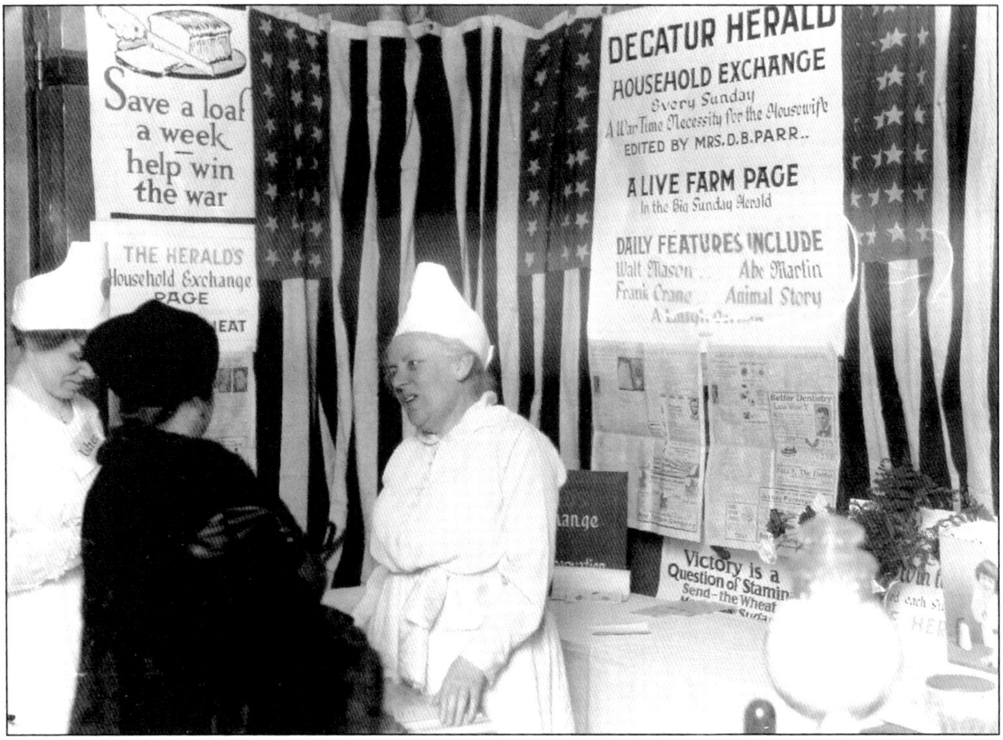

DECATUR *HERALD* FOOD BOOTH. The local newspaper published recipes and food tips, as well as slogans like, "Save a loaf a week—help win the war." The English, French, and Germans were the ones suffering from food shortages, but the war did change the way Americans cooked, raising consciousness about fats and sugar. (Courtesy Decatur Public Library.)

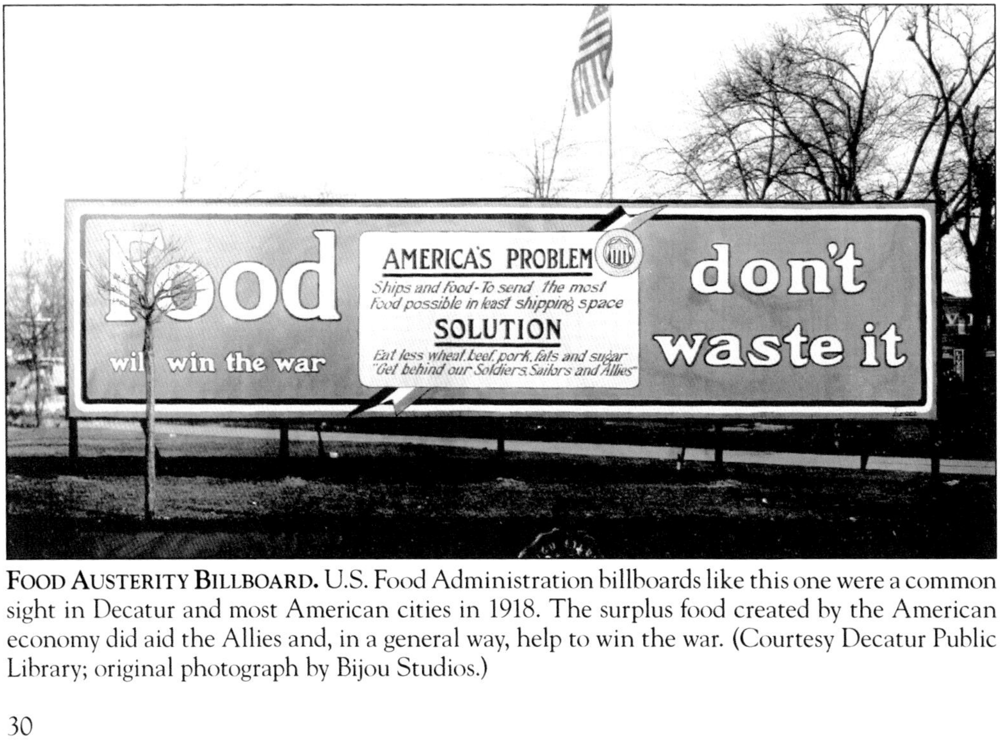

FOOD AUSTERITY BILLBOARD. U.S. Food Administration billboards like this one were a common sight in Decatur and most American cities in 1918. The surplus food created by the American economy did aid the Allies and, in a general way, help to win the war. (Courtesy Decatur Public Library; original photograph by Bijou Studios.)

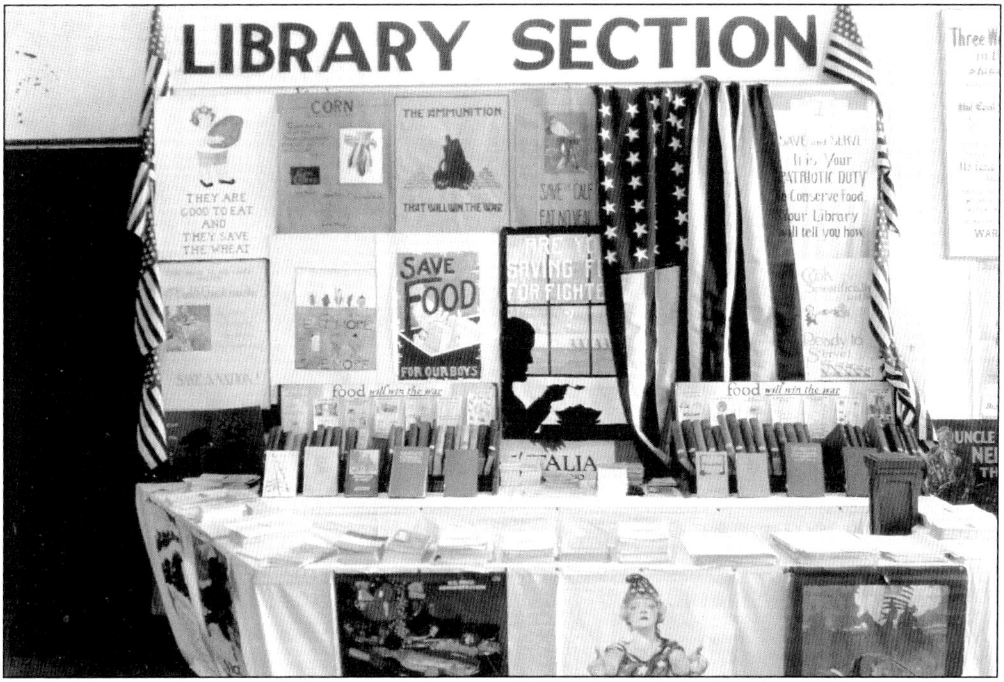

LIBRARY FOOD DISPLAY. As part of the Patriotic Food Show, the Decatur Public Library exhibited food books and posters, like the one with the little chubby girl holding an oversized potato. The slogan reads, "They are good to eat and save the wheat." (Courtesy Decatur Public Library.)

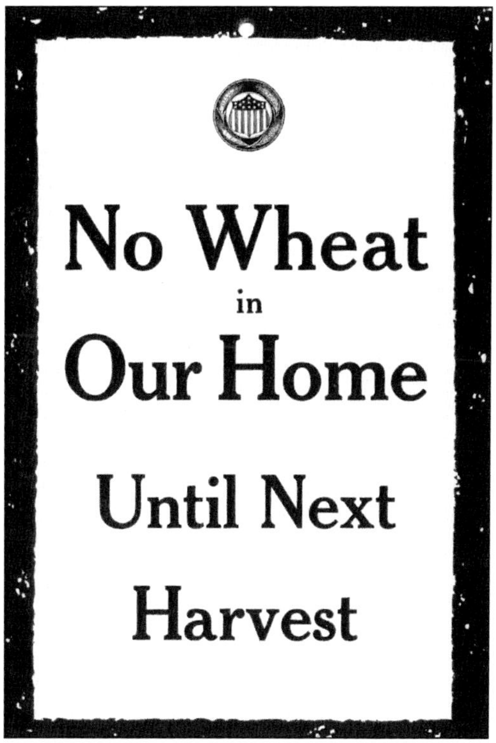

WHEAT RATIONING WINDOW DISPLAY. This cardboard window display, provided to consumers by the U.S. Food Administration, attached to the window shade pull. Thousands of these placards were visible throughout the city of Decatur. (Courtesy Decatur Public Library.)

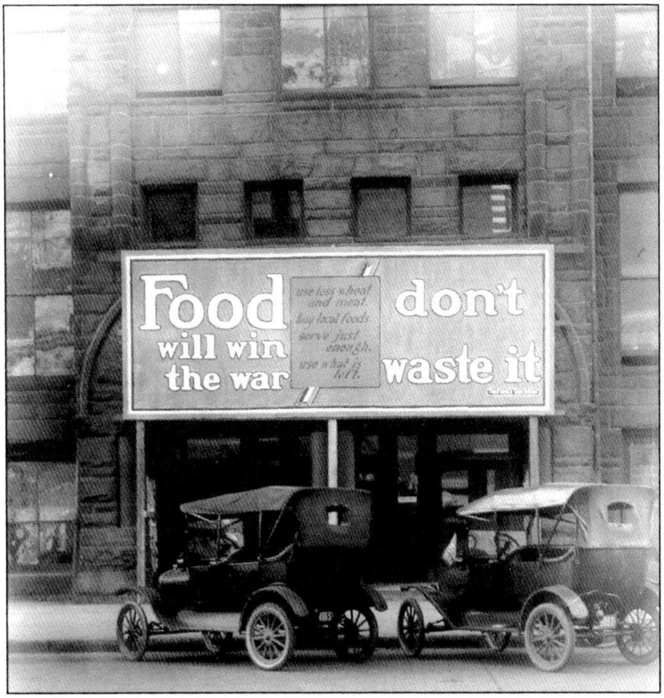

FOOD BILLBOARD ON OLD COURT HOUSE. This billboard, with Ford Model Ts parked beneath, adorns the front wall of the Old Court House, which served Decatur until the 1930s. It was impossible to walk anywhere in the city without some reminder of the food austerity program. (Courtesy Decatur Public Library.)

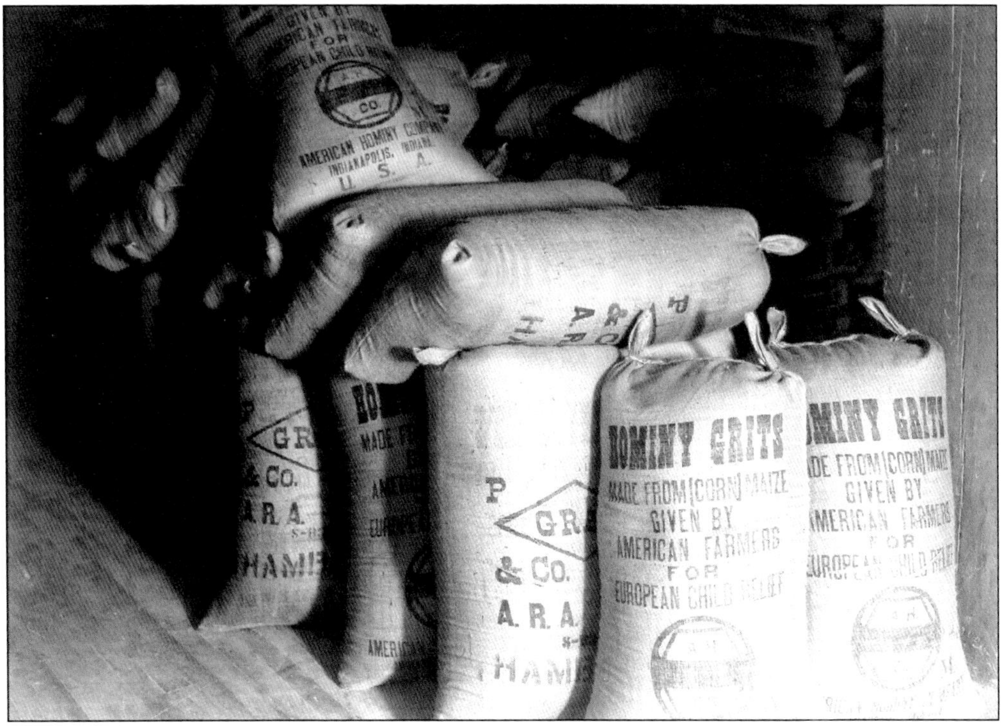

HOMINY GRITS. These sacks of grits are piled in the warehouse of the American Hominy Company Processing Plant in Decatur in 1918, and destined for a trip overseas to feed French children, among others. This kind of food diplomacy was the lynchpin of the Marshall Plan three decades later. (Courtesy Decatur Public Library.)

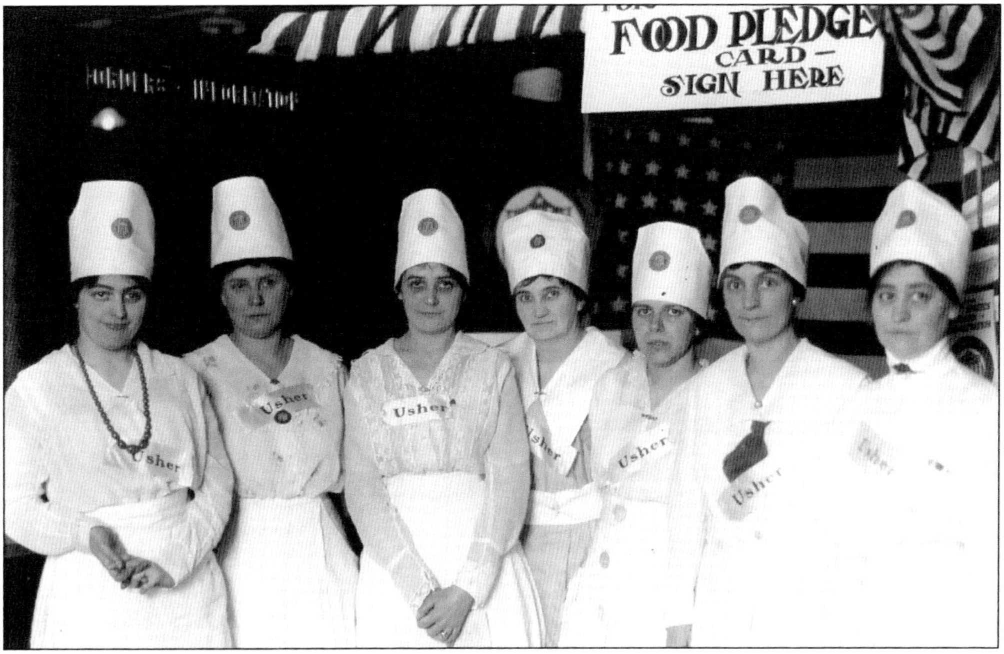

FOOD USHERS. These women were serving as food ushers in the Patriotic Food Show. Their outfits, replete with badges, pins, sashes, and insignia, are typical of the period. The fact that seven ushers were needed was a sign of the show's success. (Courtesy Decatur Public Library.)

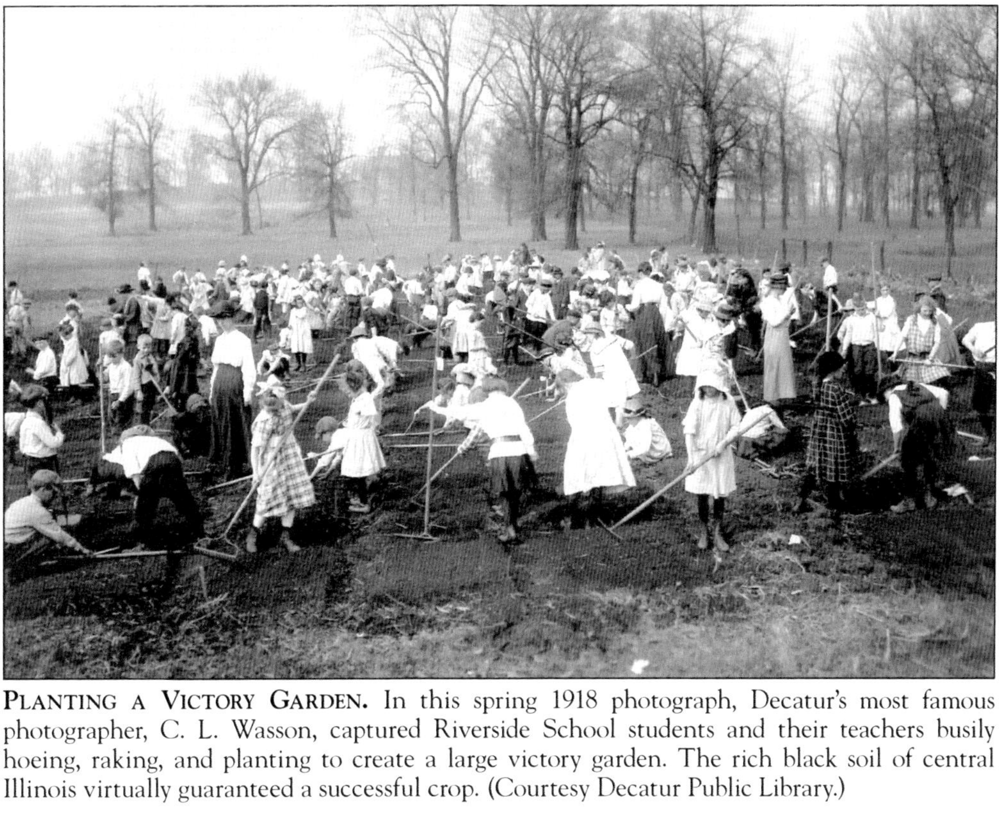

PLANTING A VICTORY GARDEN. In this spring 1918 photograph, Decatur's most famous photographer, C. L. Wasson, captured Riverside School students and their teachers busily hoeing, raking, and planting to create a large victory garden. The rich black soil of central Illinois virtually guaranteed a successful crop. (Courtesy Decatur Public Library.)

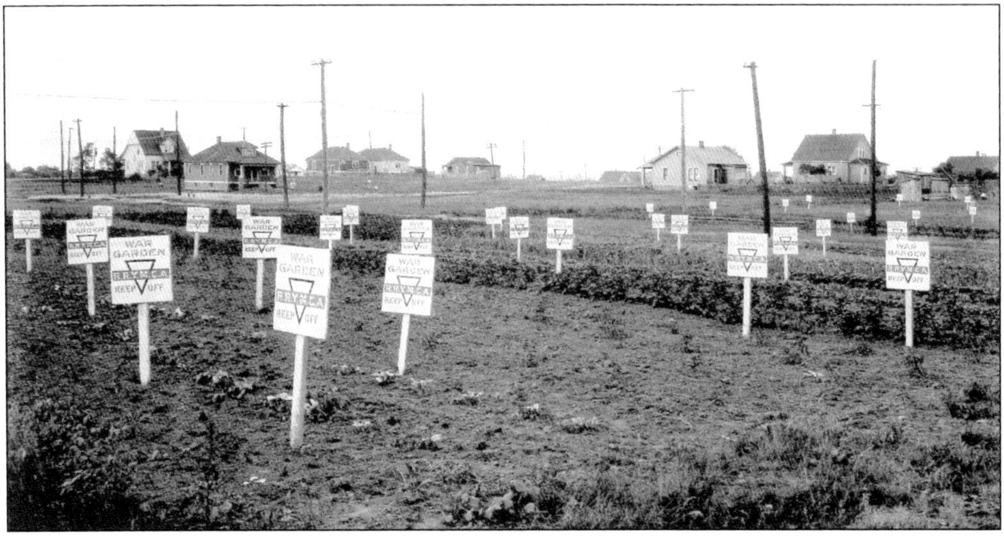

WAR GARDEN. These garden plots, somewhere on Decatur's northeast side, were planted by the Rural Route YMCA in 1918, another example of broadly-based citizen involvement in the wartime effort. Of course, many people would have had vegetable gardens regardless. (Courtesy Decatur Public Library.)

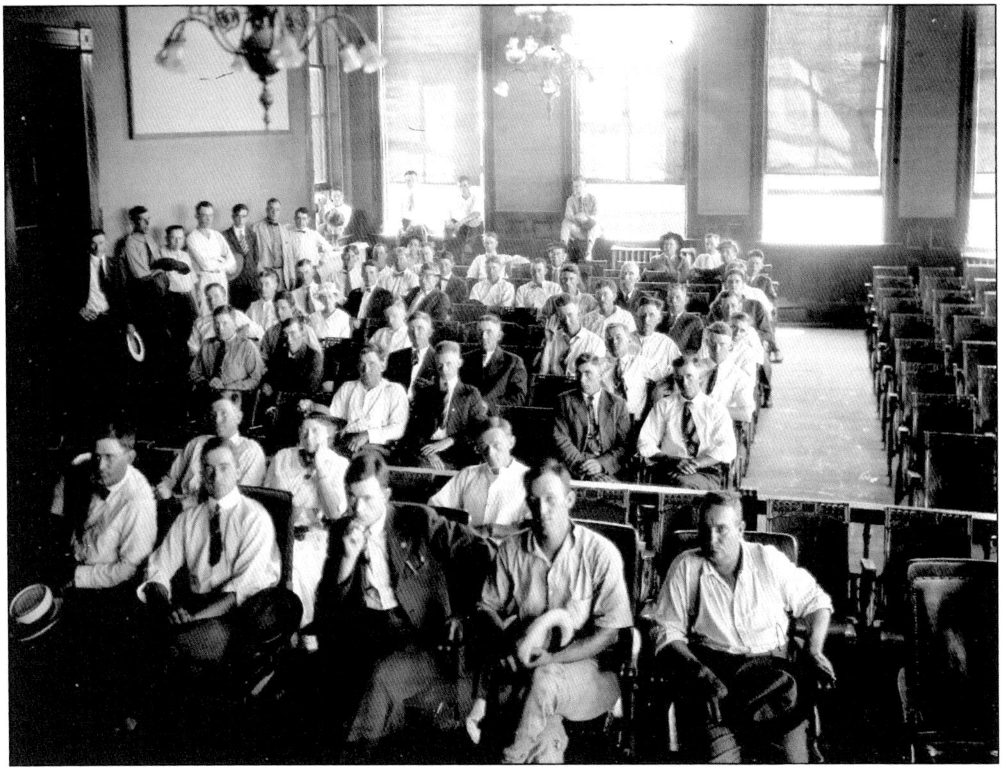

DRAFTEES WAITING FOR EXAMINATIONS. Decatur draftees and some family members are waiting for physical and written examinations on a hot afternoon in August 1917. There is a woman on the left, presumably a wife, sister, or sweetheart of one of the draftees. (Courtesy Decatur Public Library.)

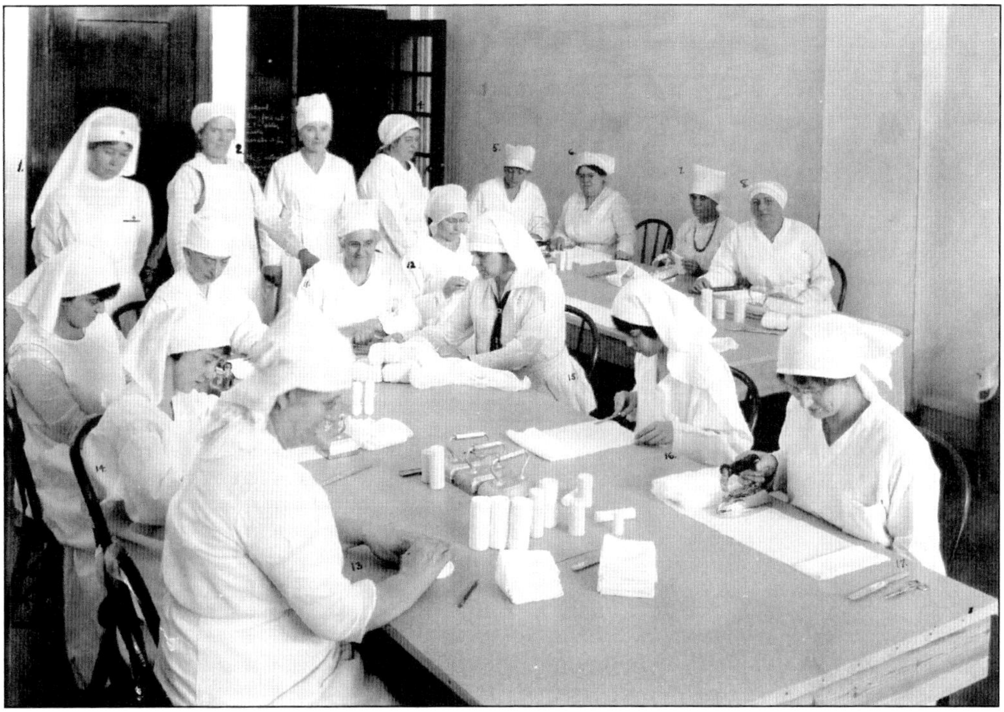

ROLLING BANDAGES. Under the watchful eye of Mrs. L. M. Lindsey (upper left hand corner), volunteers in homemade uniforms roll, press, and package bandages and field dressings for American and Allied troops. These bandages were part of the much improved medical treatment for the average soldier at the front. (Courtesy Decatur Public Library.)

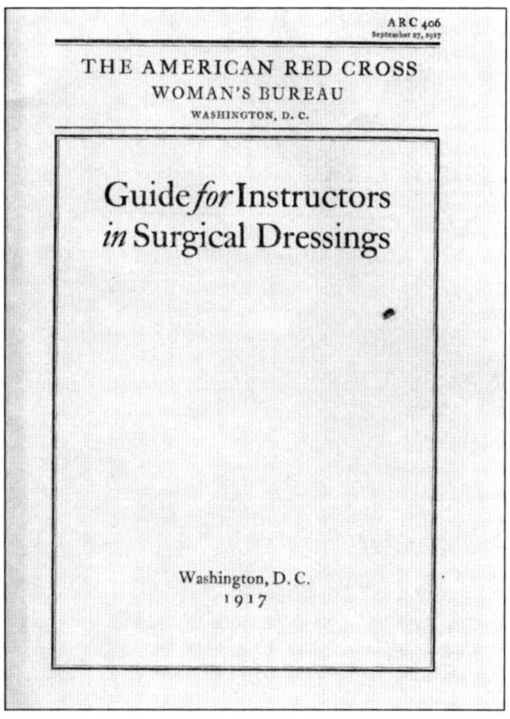

ARC 406
September 27, 1917

THE AMERICAN RED CROSS
WOMAN'S BUREAU
WASHINGTON, D. C.

Guide *for* Instructors
in Surgical Dressings

Washington, D. C.
1917

AMERICAN RED CROSS BOOKLET. The *Guide for Instructors in Surgical Dressings*, published in 1917, was the basic handbook for American Red Cross volunteers who made hundreds of thousands of bandages. They literally saved the lives of countless soldiers, American and Allied. (Courtesy Decatur Public Library.)

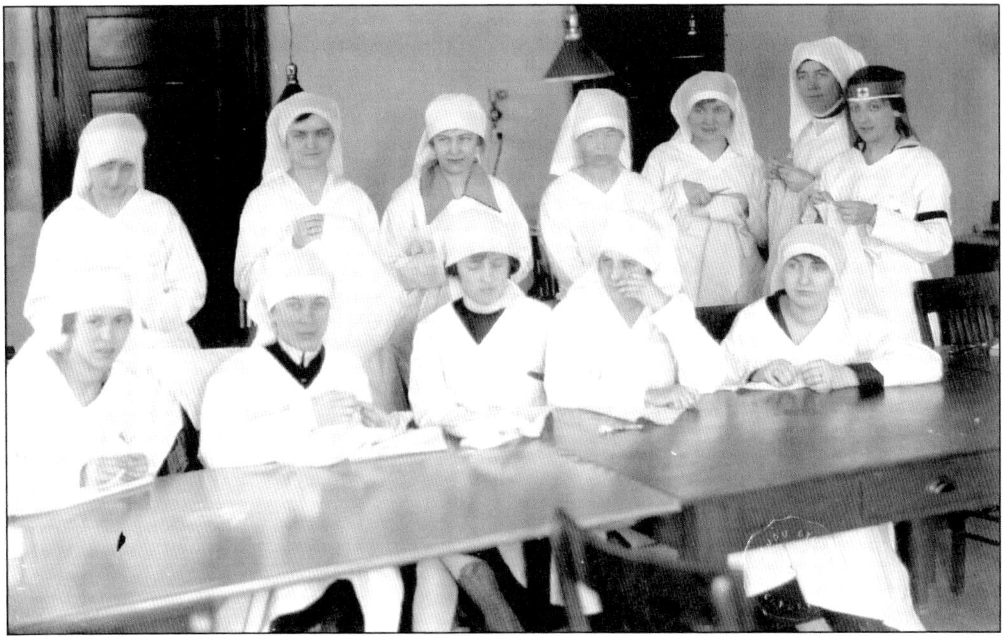

MILLIKIN STUDENTS IN SURGICAL DRESSING CLASS. These Millikin coeds are learning to prepare various kinds of surgical dressings and bandages. Women were allowed to volunteer for duty as nurses, but not on the front line. This photograph was produced by the renowned Bijou Studios of Decatur in 1918. (Courtesy Decatur Public Library.)

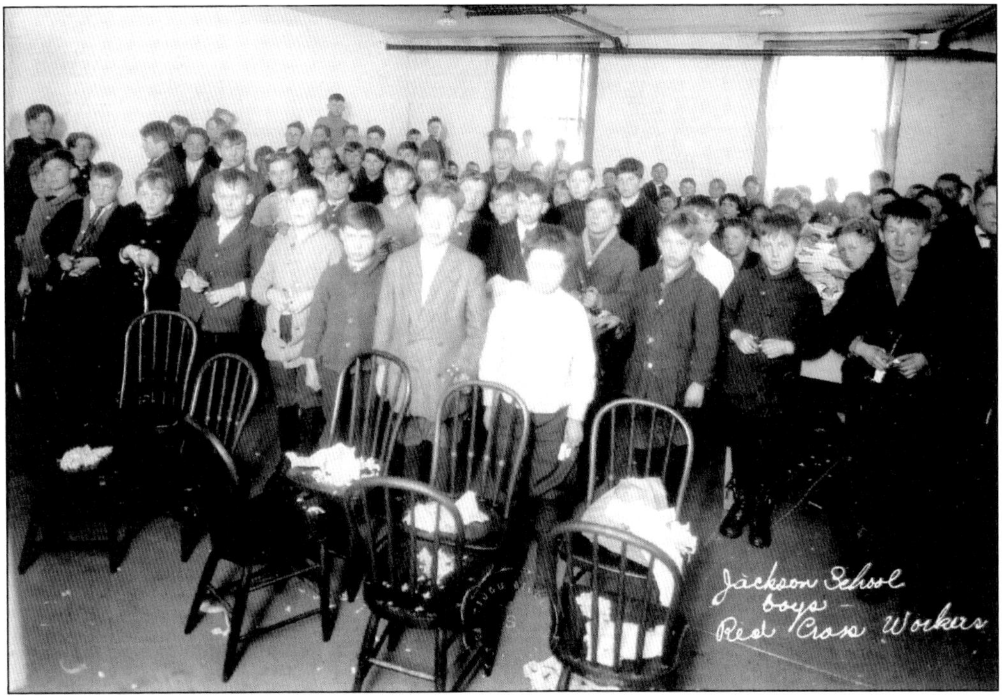

JACKSON SCHOOL BOYS. These young male students are learning basic Red Cross bandaging techniques as part of their school day at Jackson School in late 1917. Everyone was expected to participate in the war effort. (Courtesy Decatur Public Library.)

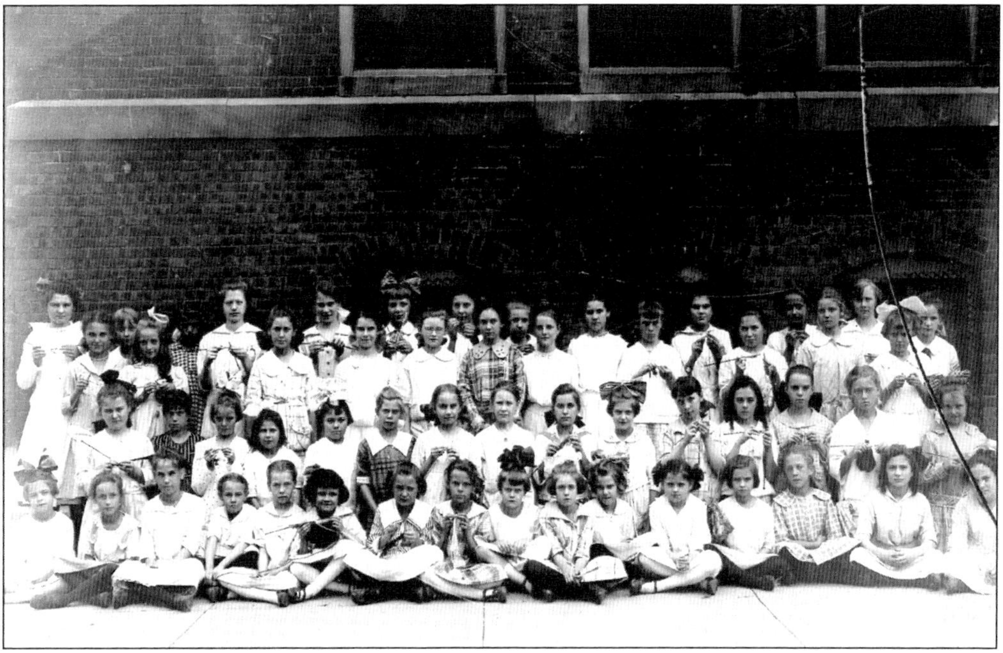

THE KNITTING CLUB. These girls from Warren School organized themselves into a Knitting Club to produce needed articles for troops going overseas. The photograph, taken by Bijou Studios in September 1917, shows how people at every level of society volunteered to help win the war. (Courtesy Decatur Public Library.)

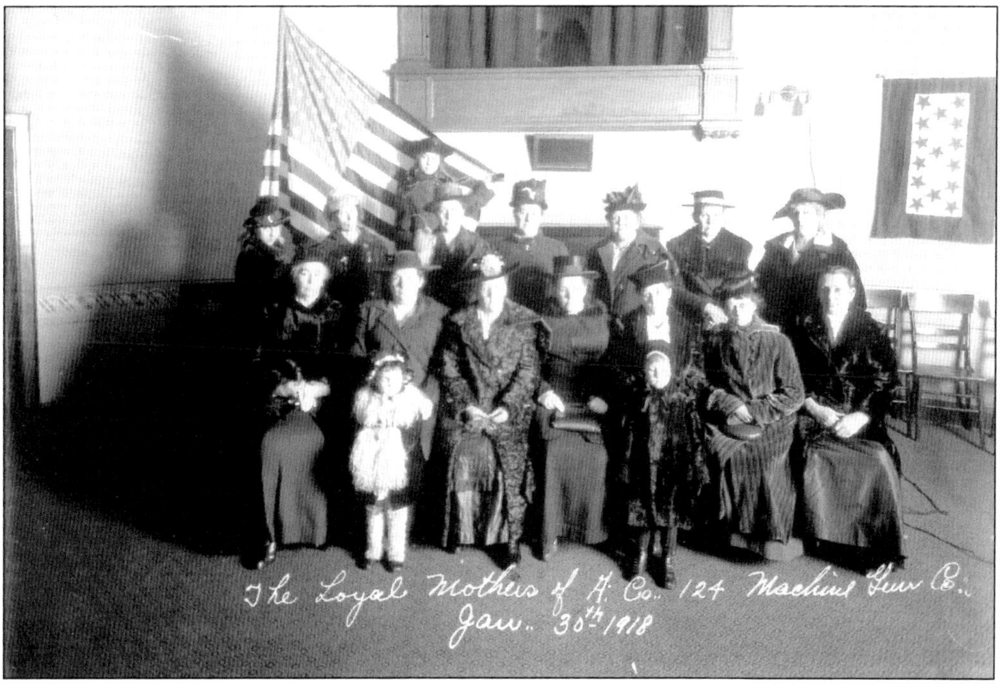

LOYAL MOTHERS OF COMPANY A. It is clear from the style and quality of the clothing that these mothers, gathered for a group portrait by Bijou Studios on January 30, 1918, represented many social classes in Decatur, as did their sons in Company A. (Courtesy Decatur Public Library.)

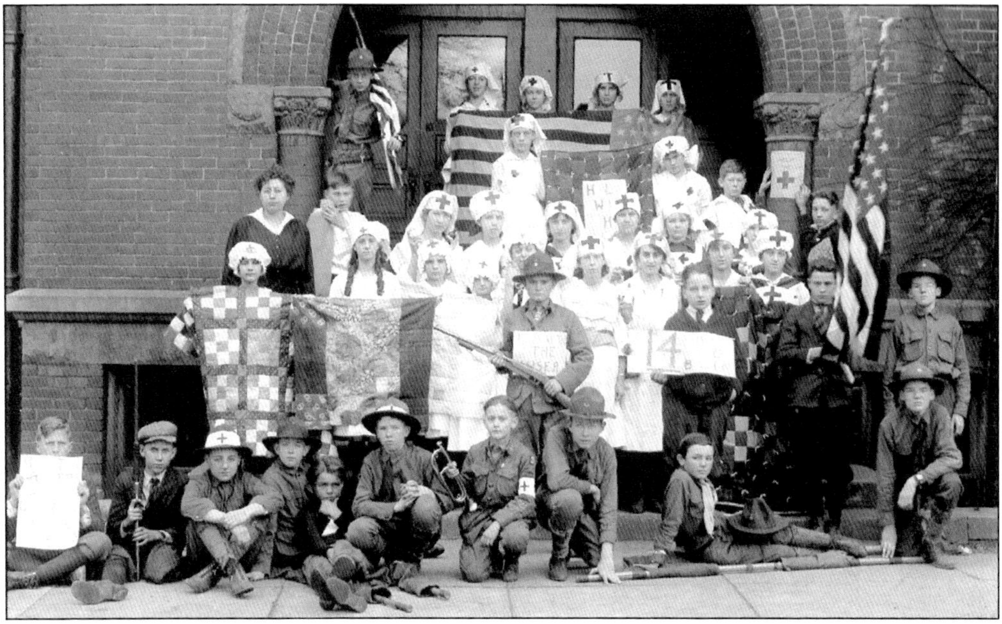

DECATUR JUNIOR HIGH SCHOOL. These junior high students (dressed as nurses and soldiers) are holding knives, bugles, guns, quilts, medicine bottle, flags, and even a stretcher to suggest the items needed by the doughboys fighting in France. The group photograph was taken in November 1917 by C. L. Wasson Studios. (Courtesy Decatur Public Library.)

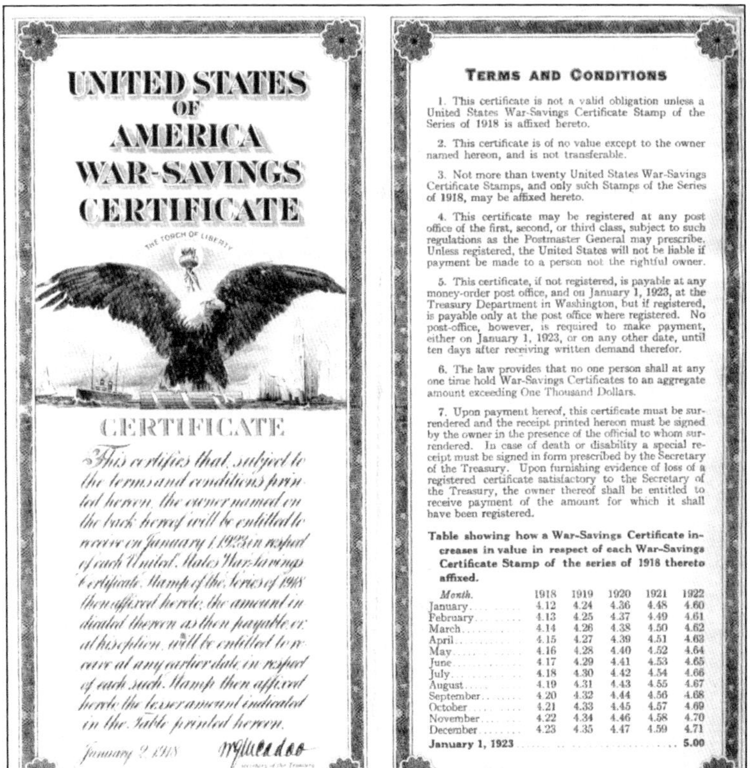

UNITED STATES OF AMERICA WAR-SAVINGS CERTIFICATE

THE TORCH OF LIBERTY

CERTIFICATE

This certifies that, subject to the terms and conditions printed hereon, the owner named on the back hereof will be entitled to receive on January 1, 1923, in respect of each United States War-Savings Certificate Stamp of the Series of 1918 then affixed hereto, the amount indicated therein as then payable, or, at his option, will be entitled to receive at any earlier date, in respect of each such Stamp then affixed hereto, the lesser amount indicated in the Table printed hereon.

January 2, 1918 W. G. McAdoo

TERMS AND CONDITIONS

1. This certificate is not a valid obligation unless a United States War-Savings Certificate Stamp of the Series of 1918 is affixed hereto.

2. This certificate is of no value except to the owner named hereon, and is not transferable.

3. Not more than twenty United States War-Savings Certificate Stamps, and only such Stamps of the Series of 1918, may be affixed hereto.

4. This certificate may be registered at any post office of the first, second, or third class, subject to such regulations as the Postmaster General may prescribe. Unless registered, the United States will not be liable if payment be made to a person not the rightful owner.

5. This certificate, if not registered, is payable at any money-order post office, and on January 1, 1923, at the Treasury Department in Washington, but if registered, is payable only at the post office where registered. No post-office, however, is required to make payment, either on January 1, 1923, or on any other date, until ten days after receiving written demand therefor.

6. The law provides that no one person shall at any one time hold War-Savings Certificates to an aggregate amount exceeding One Thousand Dollars.

7. Upon payment hereof, this certificate must be surrendered and the receipt printed hereon must be signed by the owner in the presence of the official to whom surrendered. In case of death or disability a special receipt must be signed in form prescribed by the Secretary of the Treasury. Upon furnishing evidence of loss of a registered certificate satisfactory to the Secretary of the Treasury, the owner thereof shall be entitled to receive payment of the amount for which it shall have been registered.

Table showing how a War-Savings Certificate increases in value in respect of each War-Savings Certificate Stamp of the series of 1918 thereto affixed.

Month.	1918	1919	1920	1921	1922
January	4.12	4.24	4.36	4.48	4.60
February	4.13	4.25	4.37	4.49	4.61
March	4.14	4.26	4.38	4.50	4.62
April	4.15	4.27	4.39	4.51	4.63
May	4.16	4.28	4.40	4.52	4.64
June	4.17	4.29	4.41	4.53	4.65
July	4.18	4.30	4.42	4.54	4.66
August	4.19	4.31	4.43	4.55	4.67
September	4.20	4.32	4.44	4.56	4.68
October	4.21	4.33	4.45	4.57	4.69
November	4.22	4.34	4.46	4.58	4.70
December	4.23	4.35	4.47	4.59	4.71
January 1, 1923					5.00

WAR-SAVINGS CERTIFICATE. This 1918 document shows the rate of accrued interest on War Savings Stamps purchased in 1918 and held until 1923. An investment of $4.12, for example, would yield $5.00 at maturity. That would equal over $200 in today's money. (Courtesy Decatur Public Library.)

DECATUR WAR WORKERS. This little booklet, produced by the Decatur *Review* in 1918, attempted to list all the personnel involved in war work in Macon County. Unfortunately, the roll was incomplete, and several workers complained until corrections were made. No one wanted to be ostracized or labeled a "slacker." (Courtesy Decatur Public Library.)

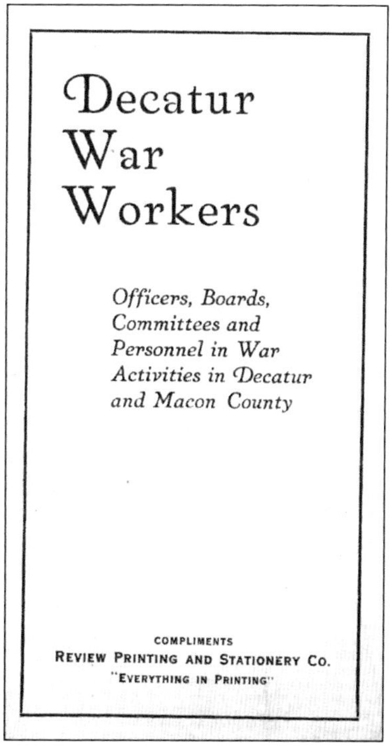

Decatur War Workers

Officers, Boards, Committees and Personnel in War Activities in Decatur and Macon County

COMPLIMENTS
REVIEW PRINTING AND STATIONERY CO.
"EVERYTHING IN PRINTING"

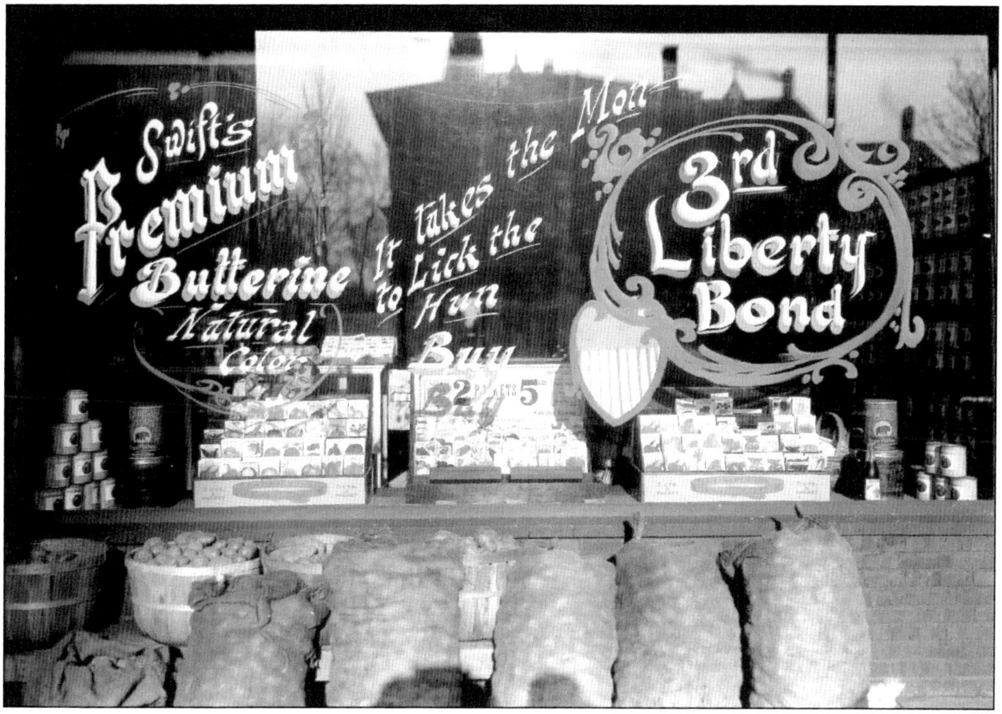

THIRD LIBERTY LOAN. There were actually five Liberty Loans or War Bond sales campaigns between 1917 and 1918 because, as the window sign proclaims, "It takes the mon to lick the hun." Note the Swift's "butterine" margarine and the 2-for-5¢ seed packets to help in planting victory gardens. (Courtesy Decatur Public Library.)

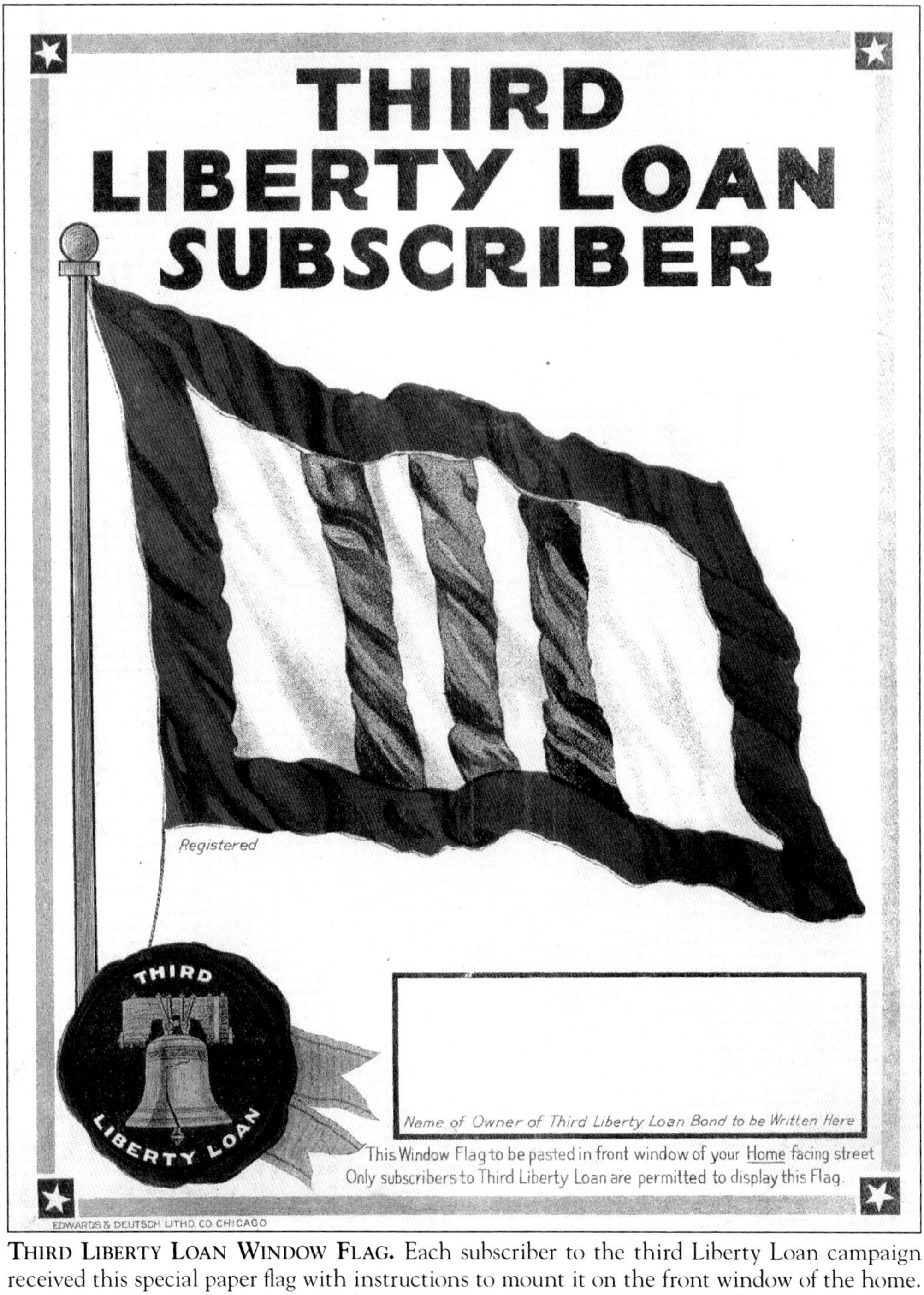

THIRD LIBERTY LOAN WINDOW FLAG. Each subscriber to the third Liberty Loan campaign received this special paper flag with instructions to mount it on the front window of the home. Non-subscribers were not permitted to use the image. There were five Liberty Loan drives, and Decatur went over-the-top all five times, easily exceeding its quota. Decatur residents also contributed generously—and exceeded their quotas—for the two Red Cross drives. In many ways, then, Decatur was an all-American city. Nationwide, that kind of enthusiasm won the war. (Courtesy Decatur Public Library.)

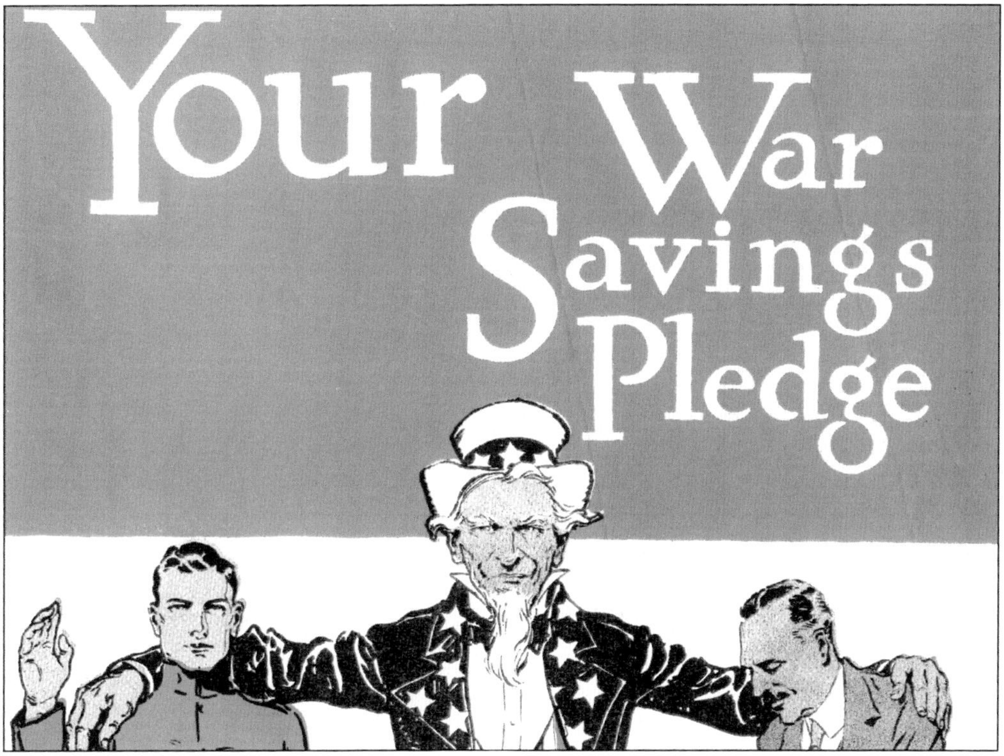

UNCLE SAM POSTER. In this Liberty Loan poster of 1918, Uncle Sam stands between a soldier and a civilian, symbolizing the unified war effort. He is encouraging Americans to pledge and buy more war bonds. People were also asked to pledge to save coal and to conserve wheat. It is clear that most Americans kept their pledge. (Courtesy Decatur Public Library.)

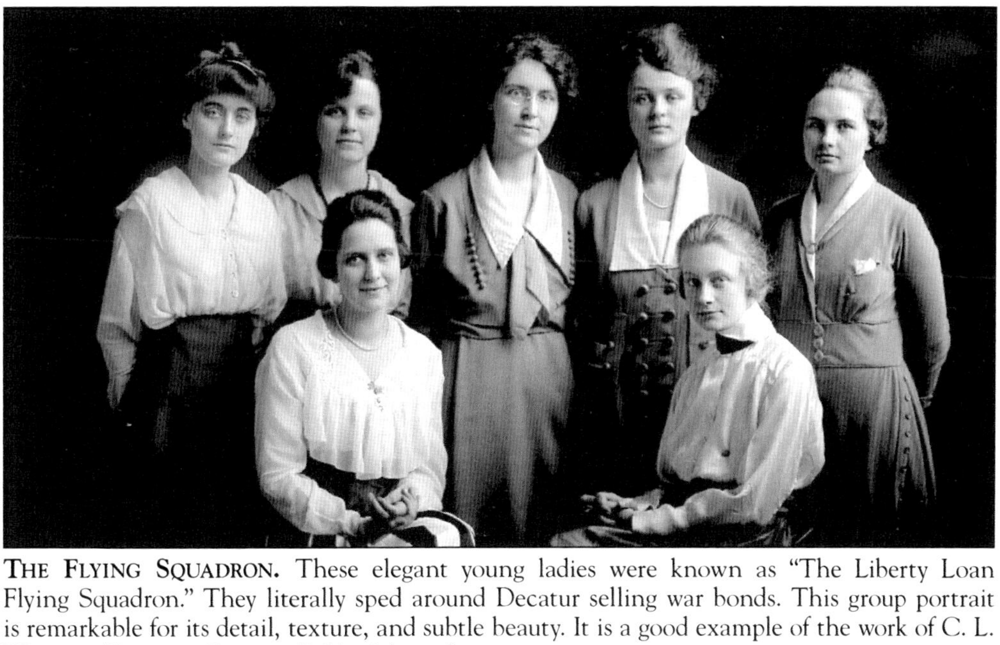

THE FLYING SQUADRON. These elegant young ladies were known as "The Liberty Loan Flying Squadron." They literally sped around Decatur selling war bonds. This group portrait is remarkable for its detail, texture, and subtle beauty. It is a good example of the work of C. L. Wasson. (Courtesy Decatur Public Library.)

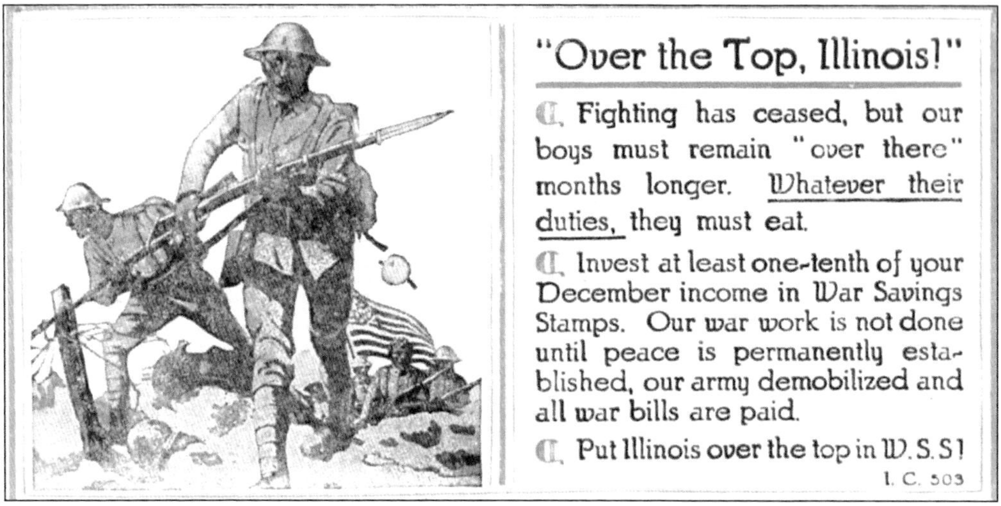
"Over the Top, Illinois!"

Fighting has ceased, but our boys must remain "over there" months longer. Whatever their duties, they must eat.

Invest at least one-tenth of your December income in War Savings Stamps. Our war work is not done until peace is permanently established, our army demobilized and all war bills are paid.

Put Illinois over the top in W. S. S!

I. C. 503

ADVERTISEMENT FOR WAR SAVINGS STAMPS. Distributed by banks and government agencies, this little flyer (printed in 1919) makes the eloquent point that, although the war was over, peace efforts and resettlements cost money, too. So Americans were still supporting the war financially almost until the start of the Roaring Twenties. (Courtesy Decatur Public Library.)

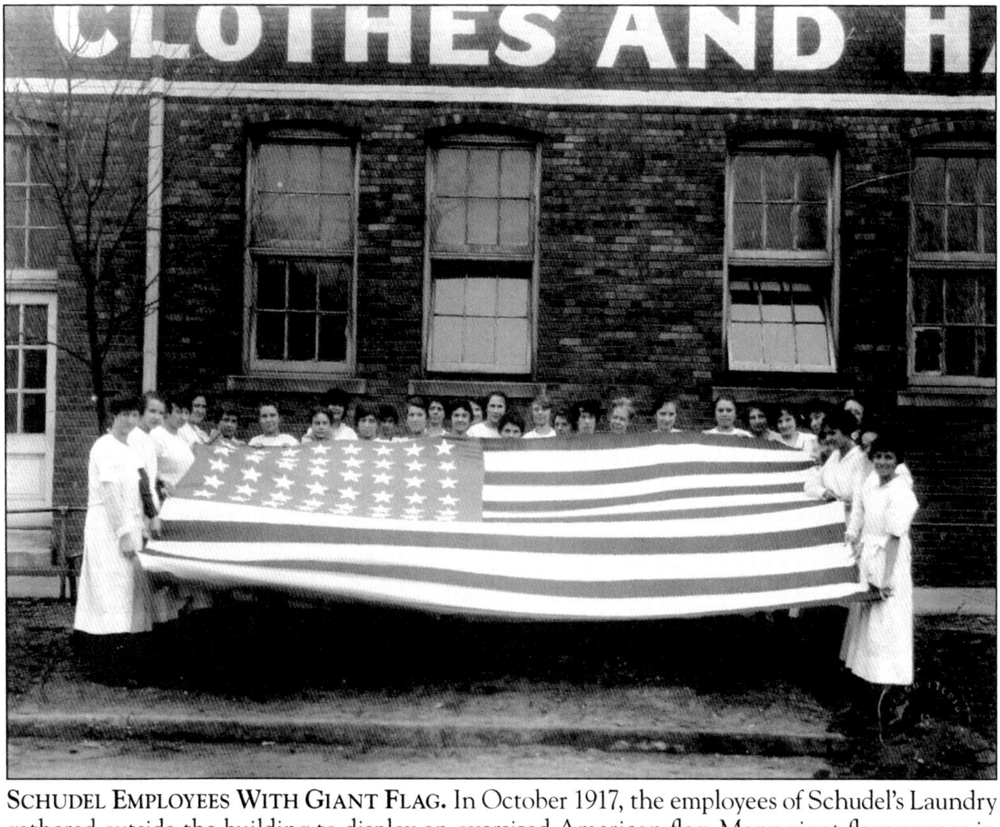

SCHUDEL EMPLOYEES WITH GIANT FLAG. In October 1917, the employees of Schudel's Laundry gathered outside the building to display an oversized American flag. Many giant flags appear in the World War I photographic record of Decatur. (Courtesy Decatur Public Library.)

SKUGIVA'S GROCERY. Neighborhood flag-raisings, like this one in front of Skugiva's Grocery Store at 1501 East Marietta Street, offered additional opportunities to display Old Glory. There are eight flags in this photograph, as well as advertisements for Procter-Gamble Naptha Soap and Senate Cigars. (Courtesy Decatur Public Library.)

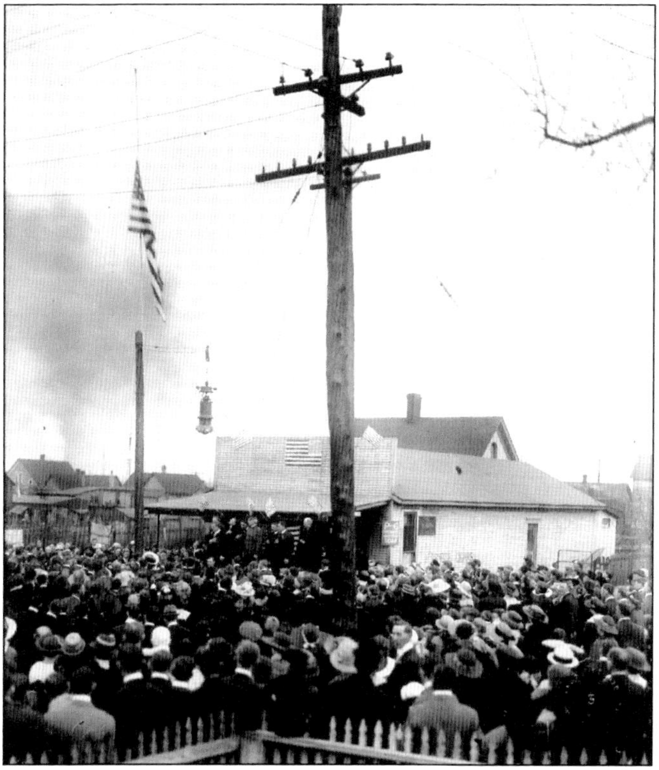

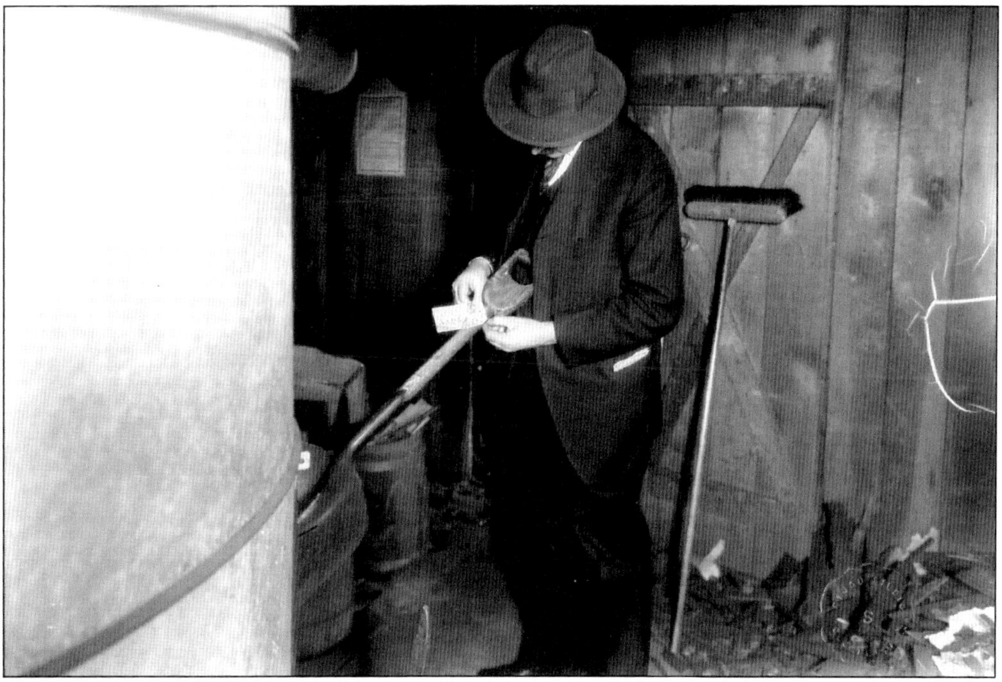

CONSERVING COAL. Superintendent of Schools James O. Engleman is seen here tagging his coal shovel. The tag reads, "Save a shovelful of coal for Uncle Sam." The large gray structure at the top left of the photograph is part of a coal-fired boiler. (Courtesy Decatur Public Library.)

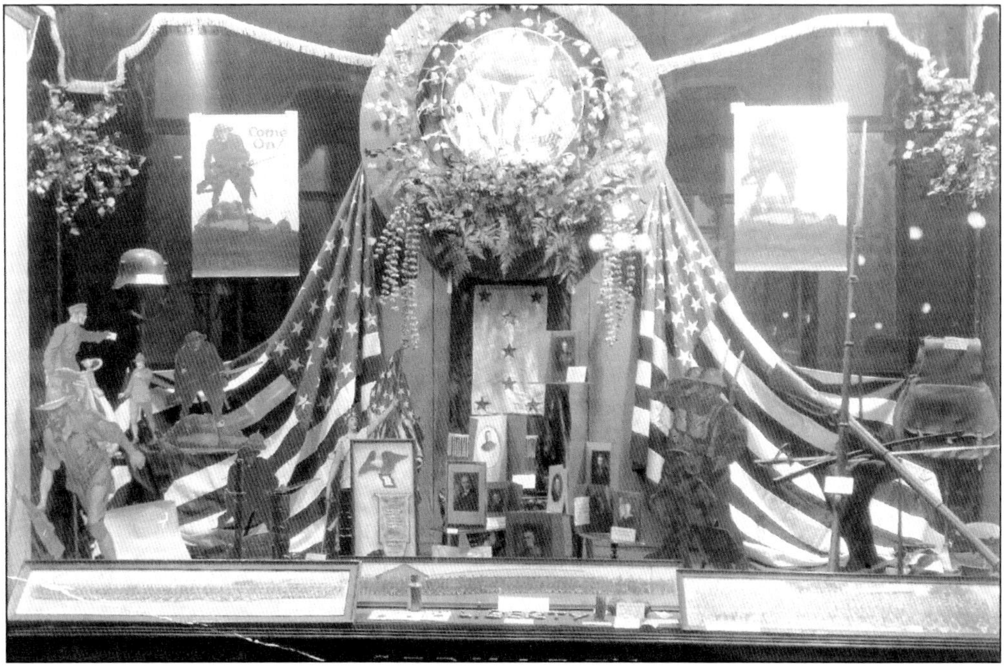

GEBHART'S WINDOW DISPLAY. Gebhart's Department Store in downtown Decatur created this patriotic exhibit in 1918. The display includes a German helmet, a Springfield rifle, flags, flowers, a wreath, and cardboard cut-out soldiers. The dark area at the top is a black velvet curtain with gold fringe. (Courtesy Decatur Public Library.)

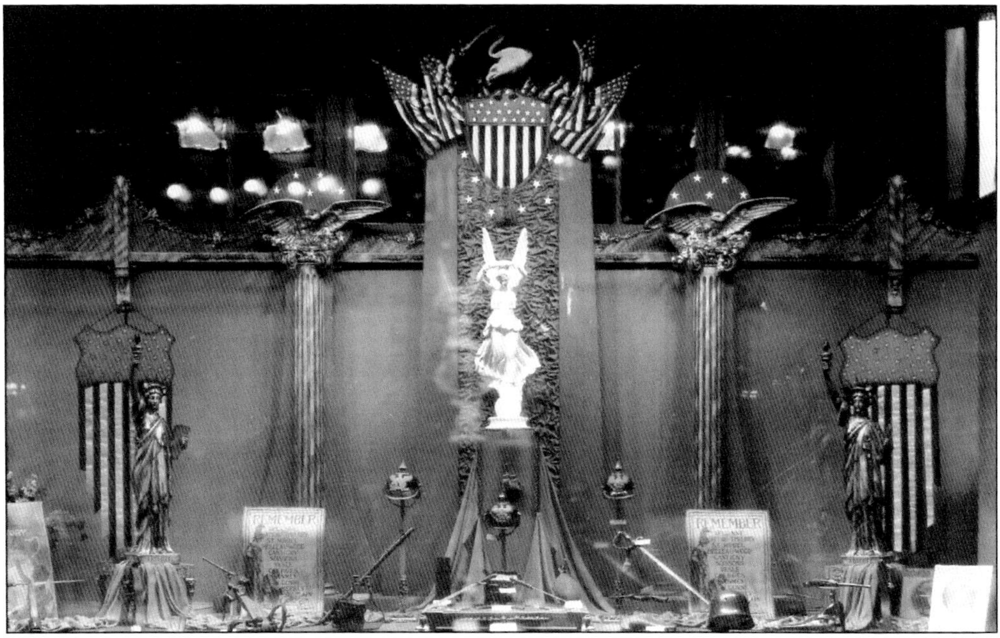

WILLIAM GUSHARD DRY GOODS COMPANY. This downtown window display of 1918 includes a Teutonic-style Imperial German Army Helmet, a modern German helmet, bayonets, swords, canteens, a Luger pistol, and a fourth Liberty Loan advertisement. These displays were extremely popular with the general public. (Courtesy Decatur Public Library.)

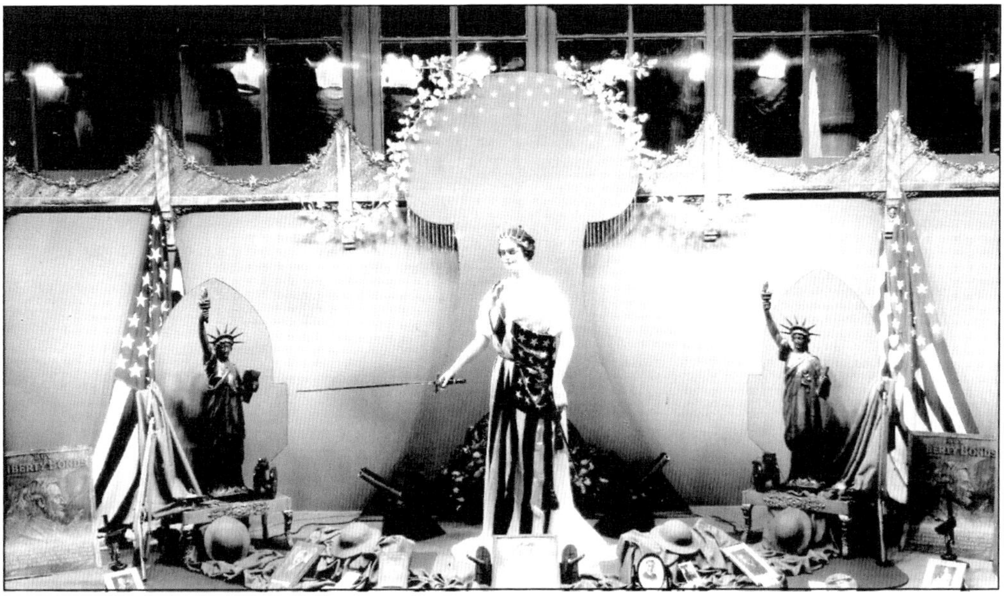

FLAG-DRAPED LADY LIBERTY. Columbia, or Lady Liberty, holds her sword against all foes in this continuation of the Gushard window exhibit containing toy cannons, wreaths of flowers, two statuettes of Liberty, American "tin pot" helmets, and another advertisement for the fourth Liberty Loan. The whole effect is shrine-like, as if the spectator were in a chapel. (Courtesy Decatur Public Library.)

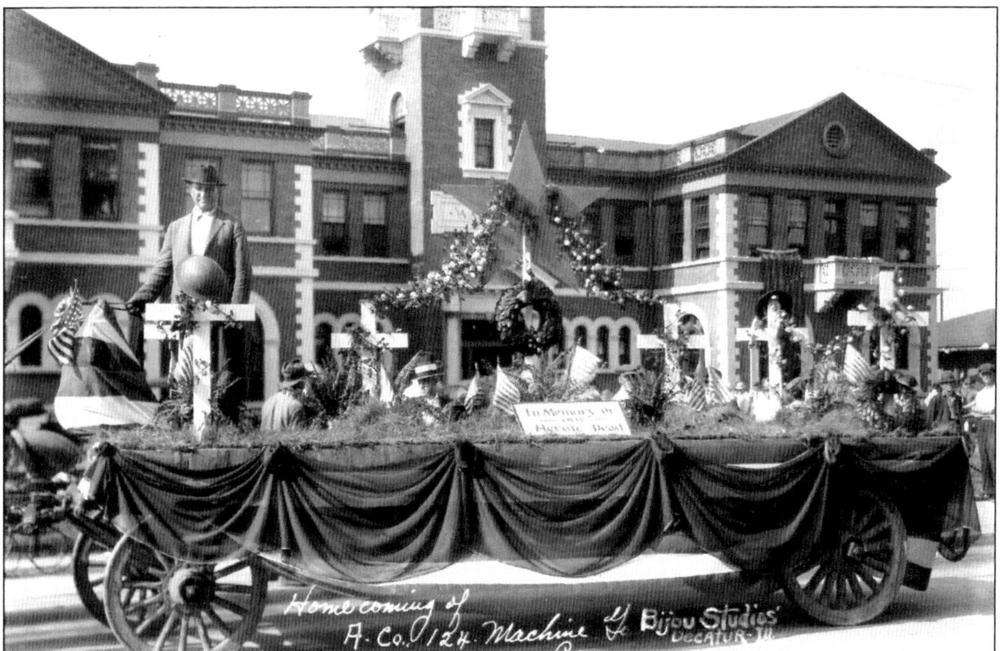

HOMECOMING PARADE. In May 1919, the city of Decatur staged a homecoming parade for the troops of Company A, 124th Machine Gun Battalion. This float, pictured in front of the Wabash Railroad Station, is designed to resemble a cemetery plot honoring the slain soldiers, which are symbolized by the white crosses. (Courtesy Decatur Public Library.)

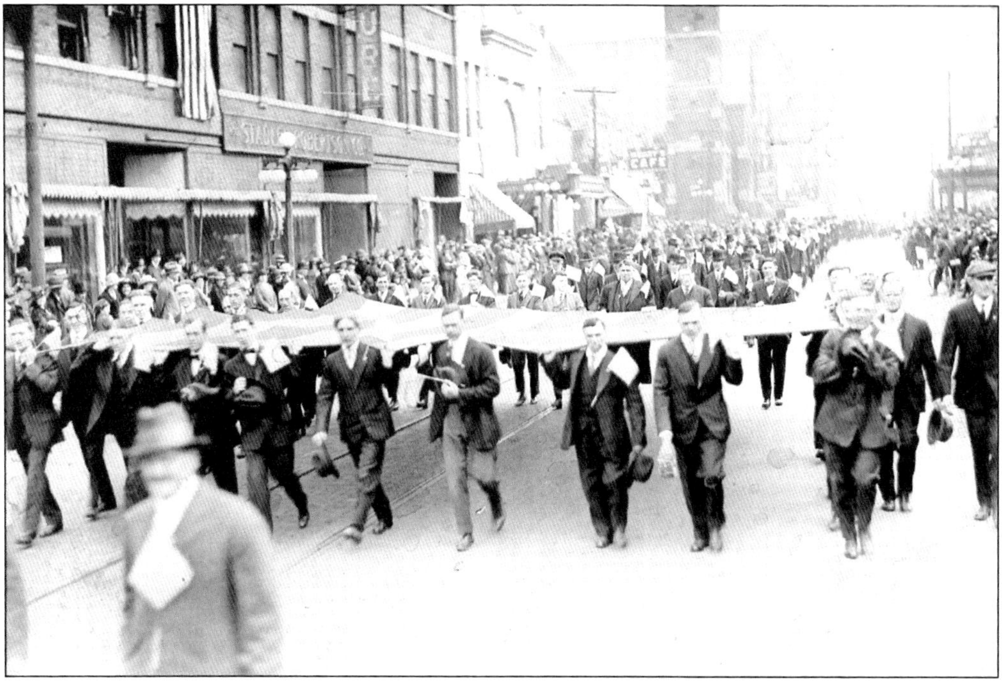

RED CROSS PARADE, 1918. These office workers are parading in front of the Stadler-Robertson Furniture Company, in the 400 block of North Water Street. People clapped loudly and threw coins onto the flag to aid the cause. (Courtesy Decatur Public Library; photograph by C. L. Wasson Studios.)

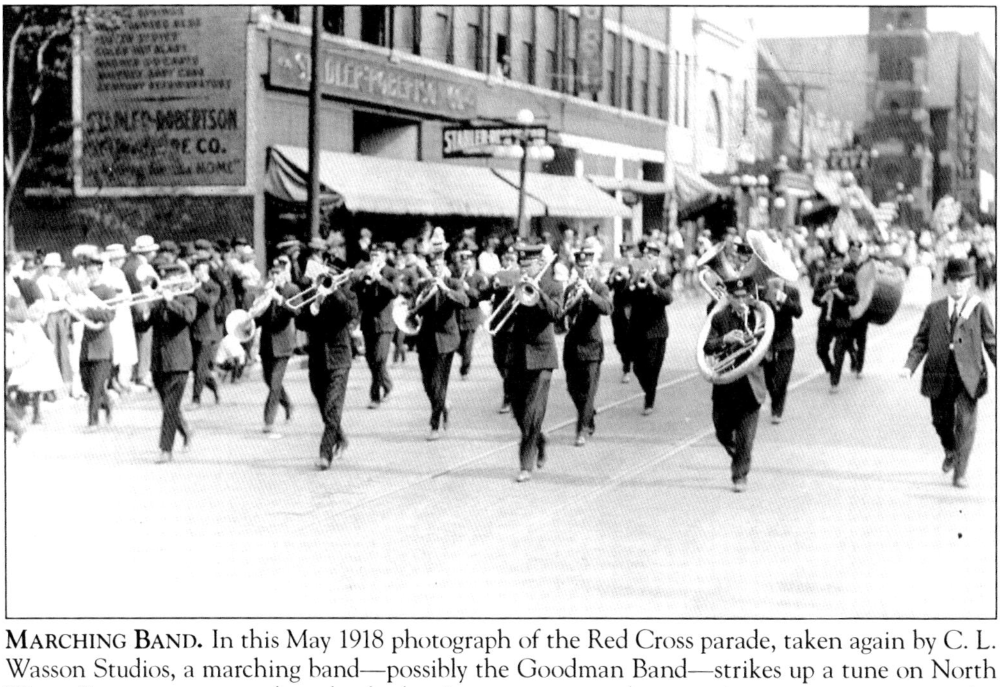

MARCHING BAND. In this May 1918 photograph of the Red Cross parade, taken again by C. L. Wasson Studios, a marching band—possibly the Goodman Band—strikes up a tune on North Water Street on a somewhat cloudy day. It was a treat to hear music; not everyone owned a phonograph or records. (Courtesy Decatur Public Library.)

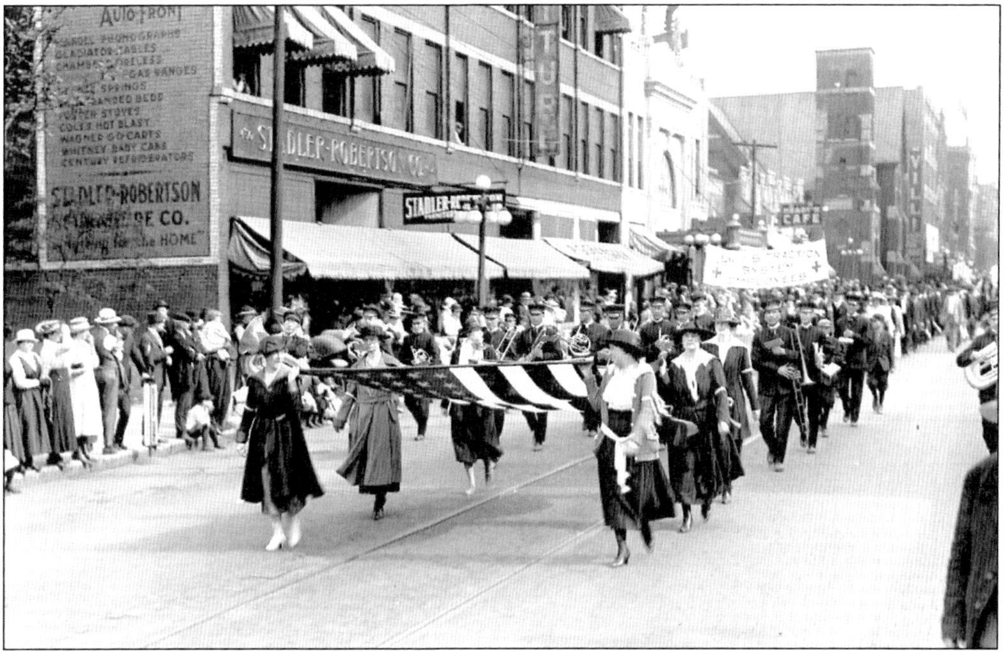

ILLINOIS TRACTION SYSTEM EMPLOYEES. Over 4,500 people marched in the Red Cross parade on May 21, 1918. There were more parades during the World War I era in Decatur than at any other time, before or since. Parades offered an emotional outlet for all and a rare chance for women to participate publicly. (Courtesy Decatur Public Library; photograph by C. L. Wasson Studios.)

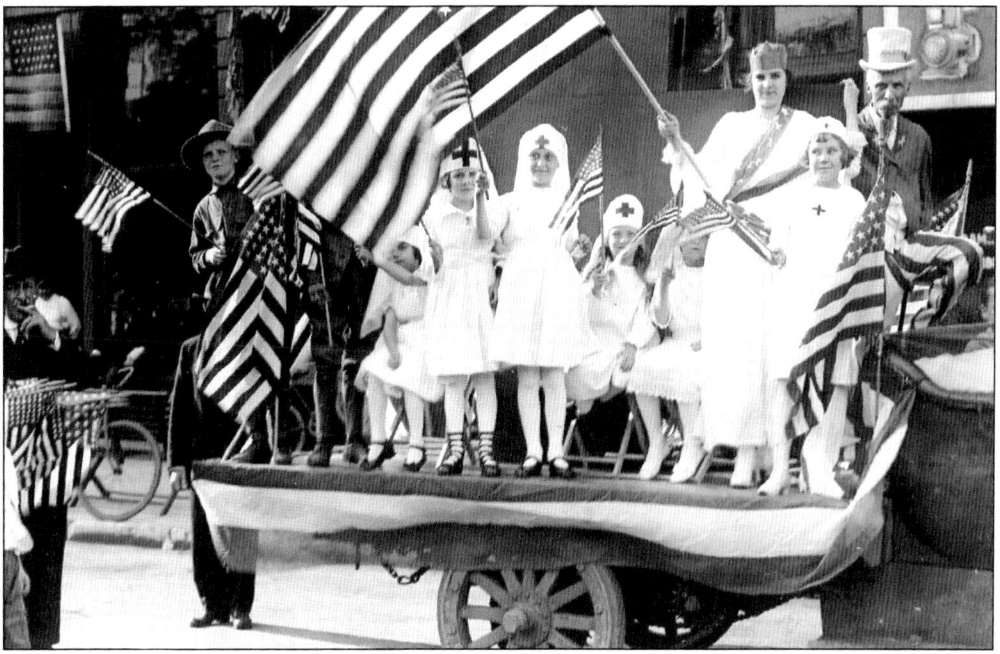

LITTLE GIRL NURSES. On this Red Cross parade float, little misses are dressed as nurses, each one waving an American flag. There is also a flag vendor in the lower left of the photograph. Americans have always had an insatiable appetite for the national icon. (Courtesy Decatur Public Library.)

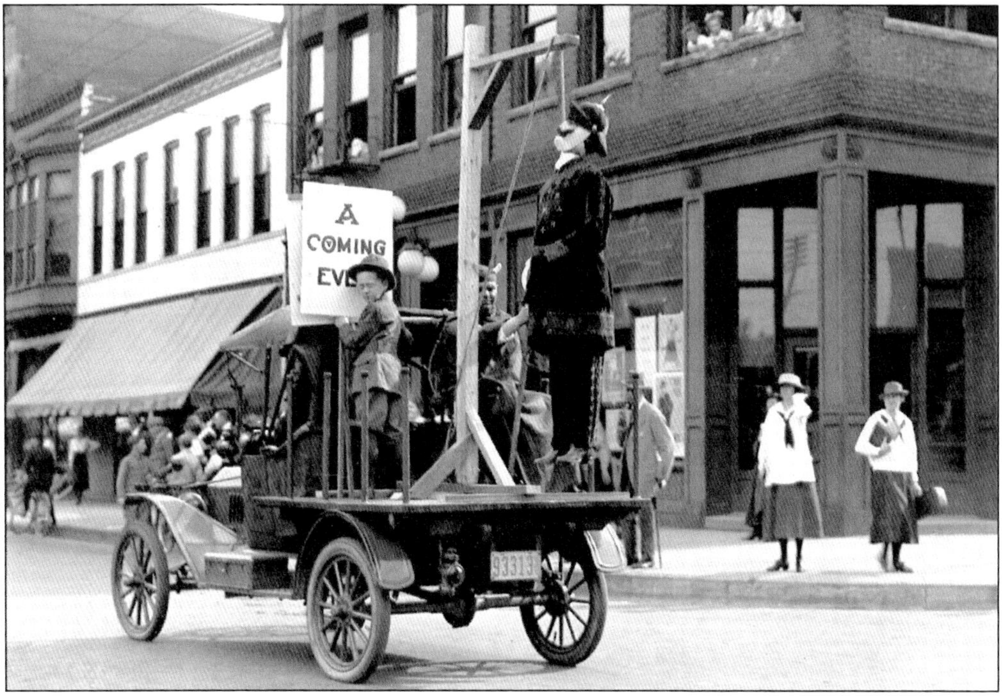

HANGING THE KAISER. This float from the 1918 Homecoming Parade shows the Kaiser being hung in effigy with the sign, "A Coming Event." The young ladies standing on the street corner in their sailor-suit outfits are sporting the latest in cutting-edge fashion. Flapper girls were just about to invade the social scene. (Courtesy Decatur Public Library.)

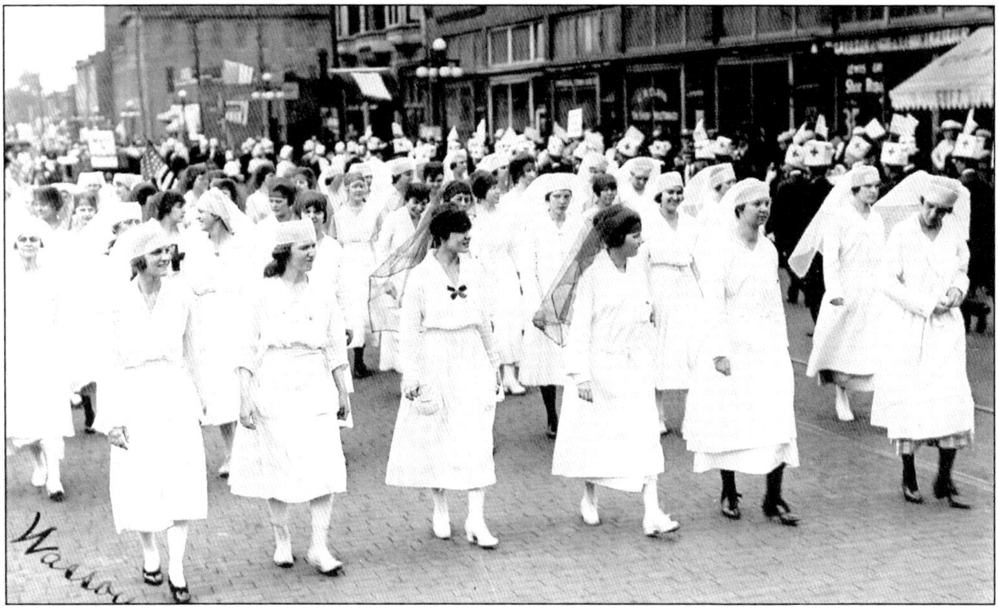

LIVING RED CROSS. When these Red Cross volunteers are viewed from above, their dark red headdresses form a large red cross. The young women are smiling and clearly enjoying the opportunity to march in the parade. (Courtesy Decatur Public Library; photograph by C. L. Wasson Studios, May 1918.)

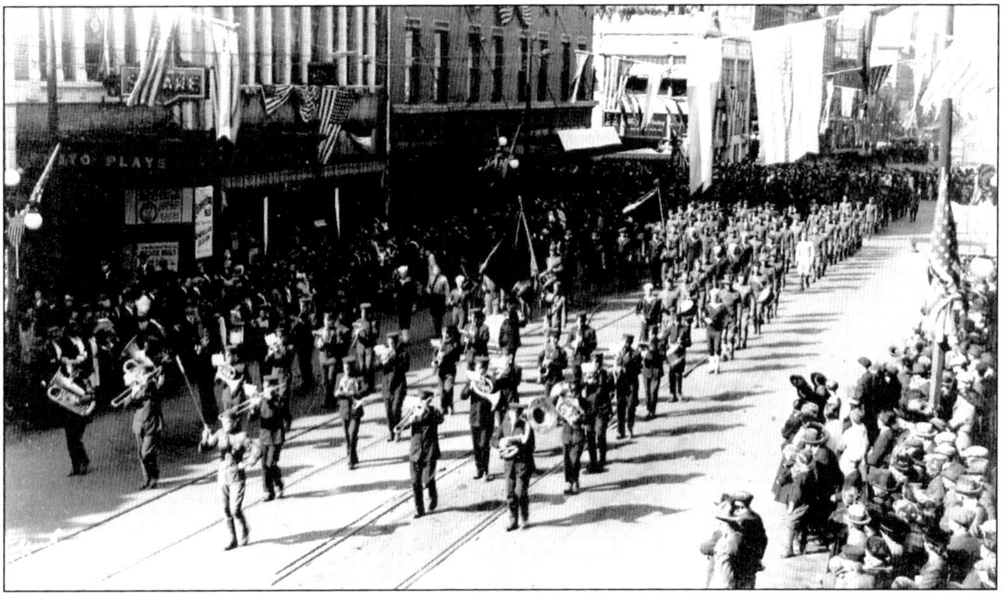

MILITARY MARCHING BAND. On this sunny day in 1918, a military band marches under fluttering flags and pennants in downtown Decatur. The crowd is large and packs both sides of the street. Parades offered free entertainment to a population that was starved for amusement or diversion. (Courtesy Decatur Public Library.)

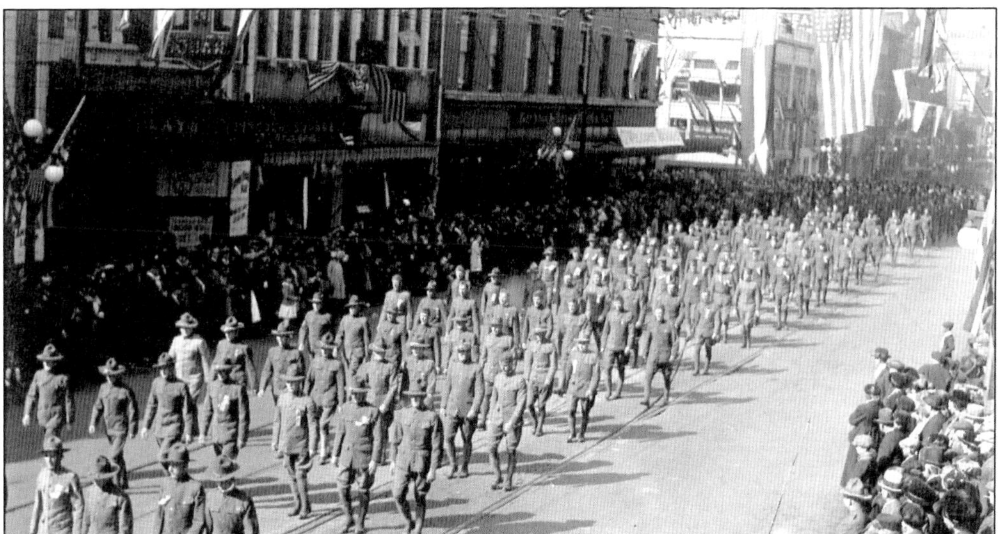

DOUGHBOYS ON PARADE. Following the military band, this contingent of doughboys marches in good order. The American Expeditionary Force was the crucial, deciding factor, in the defeat of the Kaiser, and the soldiers march with justifiable pride. (Courtesy Decatur Public Library.)

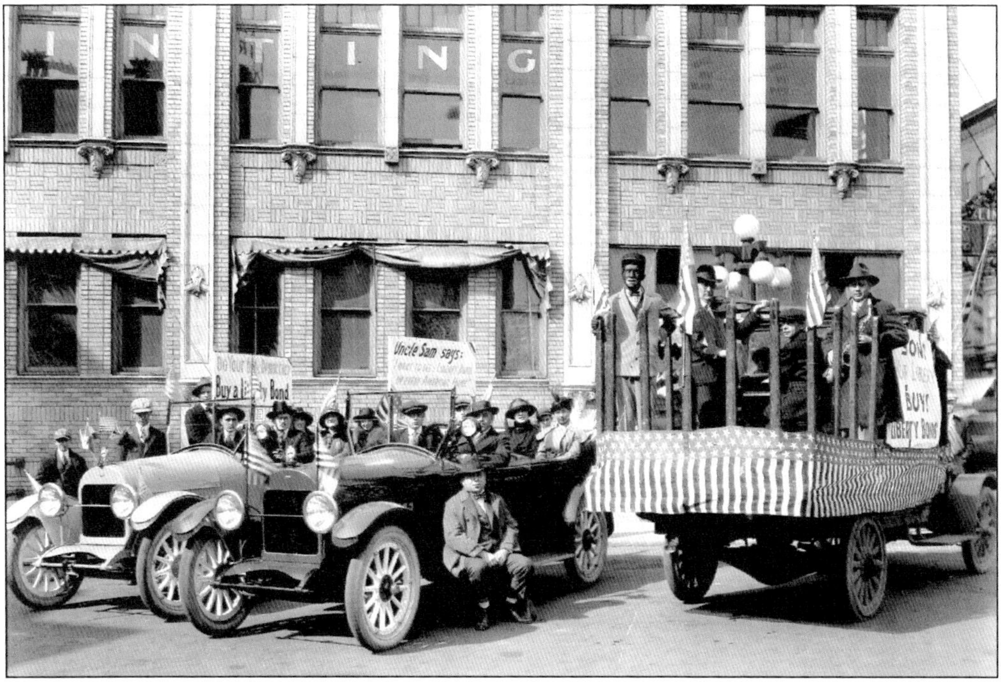

LIBERTY BOND FLOAT. As part of the Red Cross parade of May 1918, this float with musicians and a vocalist in blackface, tried to raise money for Liberty Bonds. Blackface performers were common, and the first "talkie" film, *The Jazz Singer* (1927), featured Al Jolson singing in blackface. (Courtesy Decatur Public Library.)

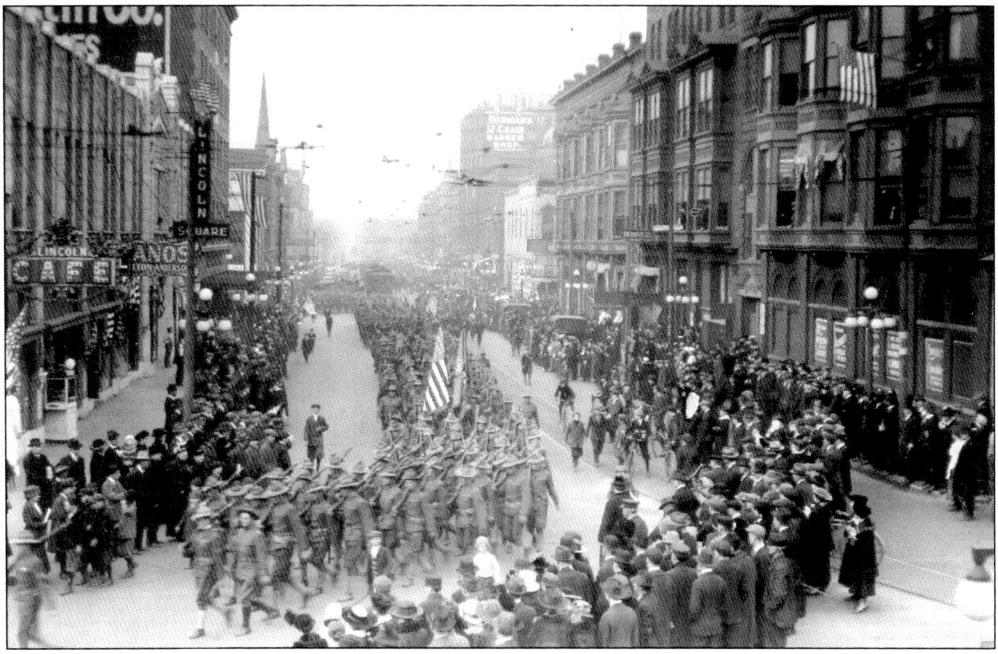

ILLINOIS MILITIA ON THE MARCH. These militia is marching down Main Street in front of the Lincoln Café in late 1917, followed by streetcars and flanked by curious bystanders. Everyone loved a parade, as this good turnout clearly demonstrates. (Courtesy Decatur Public Library.)

U.S. BOYS' WORKING RESERVE. As this 1918 flyer illustrates, the U.S. Government effectively drafted boys aged 16 to 21 to create a national labor pool of 20,000 boys for use in American agriculture. The war ended before the program could truly be established. (Courtesy Decatur Public Library.)

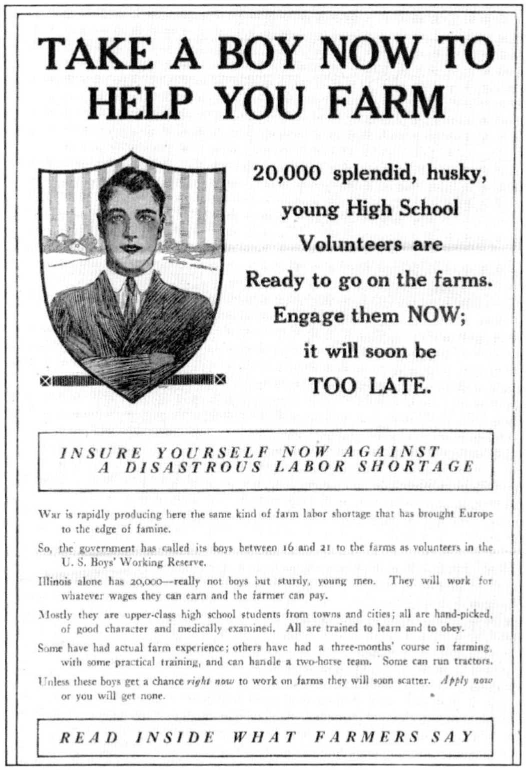

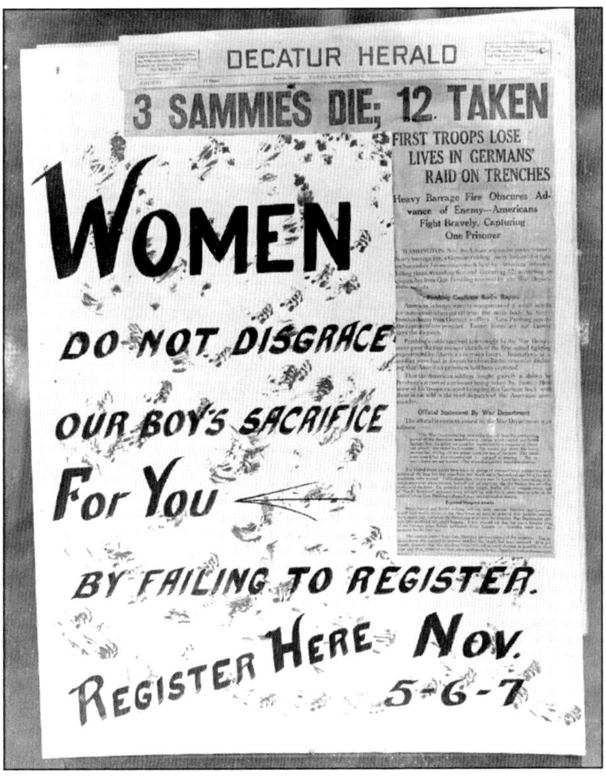

CALL FOR WOMEN'S REGISTRATION. On November 4, 1917, Decatur women were asked to register for war service as Red Cross volunteers and other occupations. Failure to do so would be a disgrace. A newspaper clipping glued to this poster tells of three Americans (called "Sammies" after Uncle Sam) killed and 12 captured. (Courtesy Decatur Public Library.)

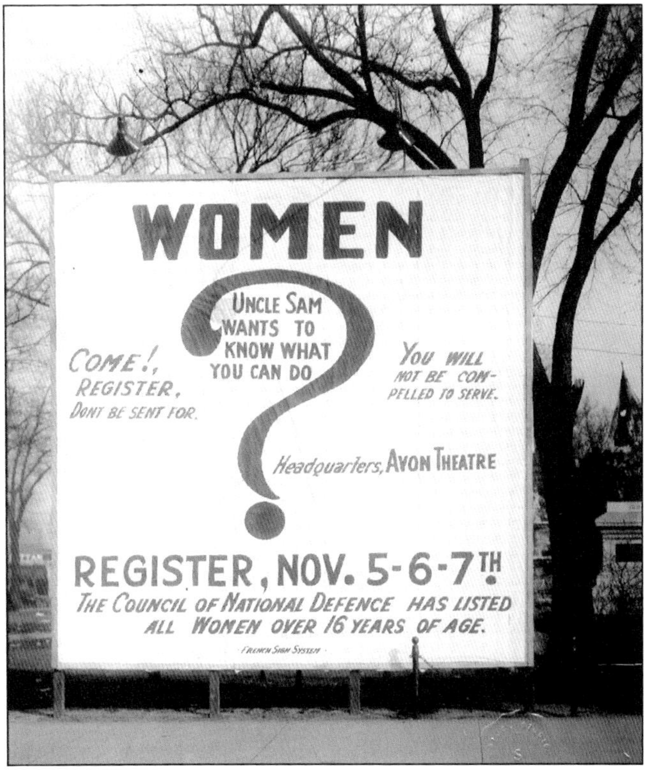

WOMEN'S BILLBOARD. During October 1917, this billboard stood prominently in Central Park, warning women to register for service or be "sent for." Although many women did volunteer work, it is not clear if there were enough jobs waiting for them. This registration was sponsored by the Decatur Woman's Committee of the Council for National Defense. (Courtesy Decatur Public Library.)

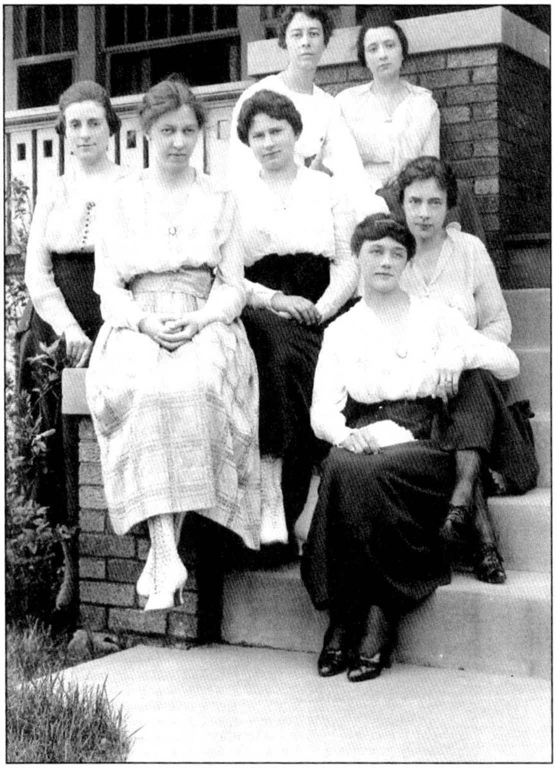

RED CROSS CLUB. Well-to-do young volunteers pose on the front steps of a residence, somewhere on Decatur's West End in the spring of 1918. Red Cross work was the most obvious way to answer the call for volunteerism. (Courtesy Decatur Public Library.)

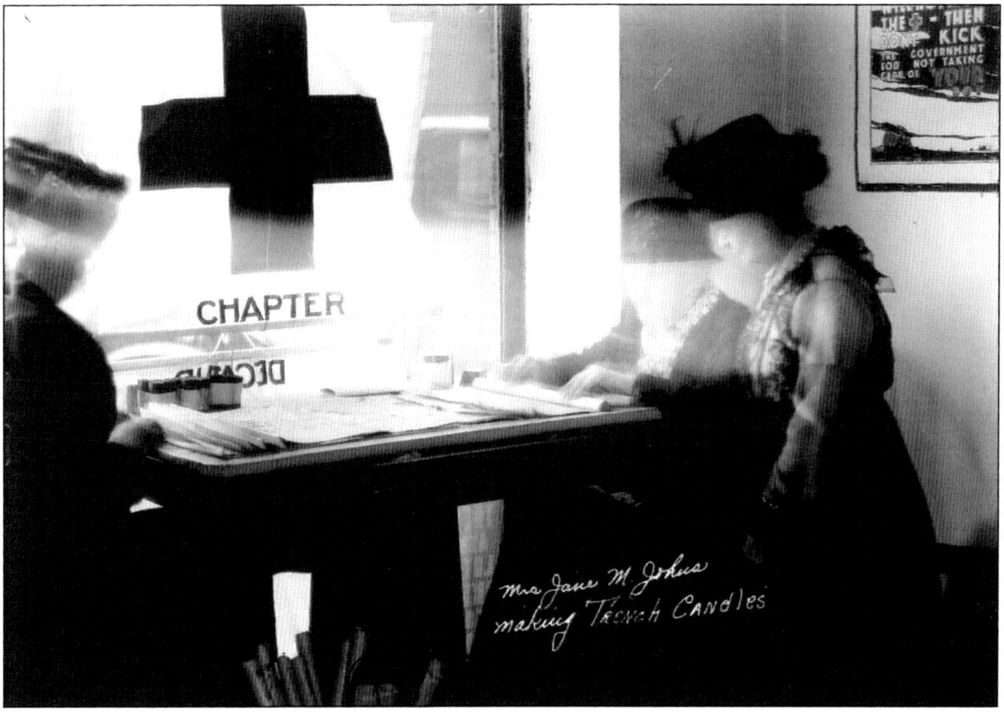

JANE MARTIN JOHNS VOLUNTEERING. Elderly Jane Martin Johns (blurry figure on the right), the author of *Personal Recollections* (1912), makes trench candles in the Red Cross office in late 1917. She was the originator of the Decatur Canteen concept during the Civil War. The poster on the wall reads, "If you will not help the Red Cross, then don't kick the Government for not taking care of your boy." (Courtesy Decatur Public Library.)

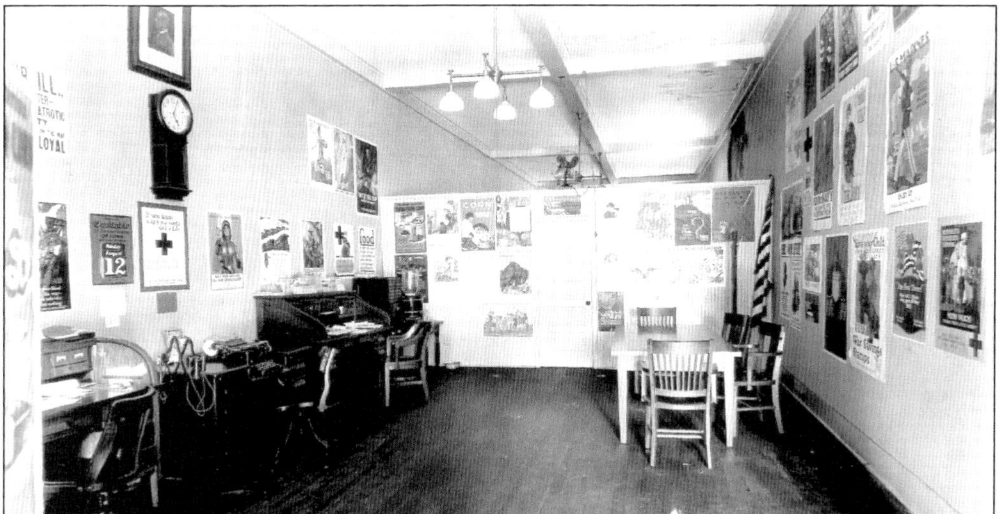

COUNCIL OF DEFENSE OFFICE. This office coordinated all the conservation and volunteer activities in Decatur with the state office in Chicago and the national office in Washington, D.C. One poster proclaims, "Corn—serve some way every meal." The photograph was taken precisely at 5:03 p.m., August 12, 1918. (Courtesy Decatur Public Library.)

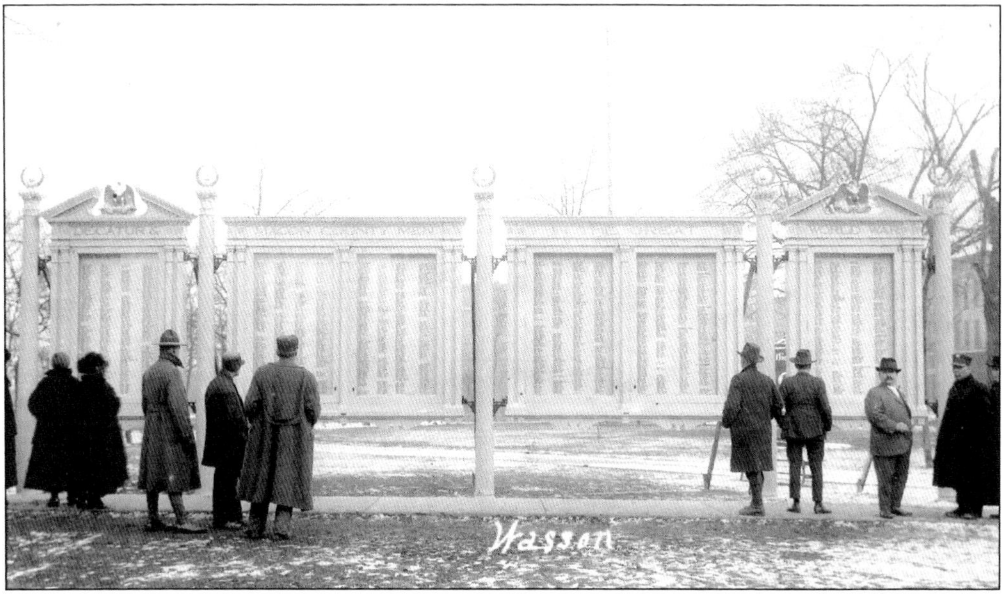

GREAT WAR HONOR ROLL. In March 1919, C. L. Wasson Studios captured this World War I marker that temporarily stood in Central Park. The listing of names on a wall foreshadows the Vietnam Memorial in Washington, D. C. (Courtesy Decatur Public Library.)

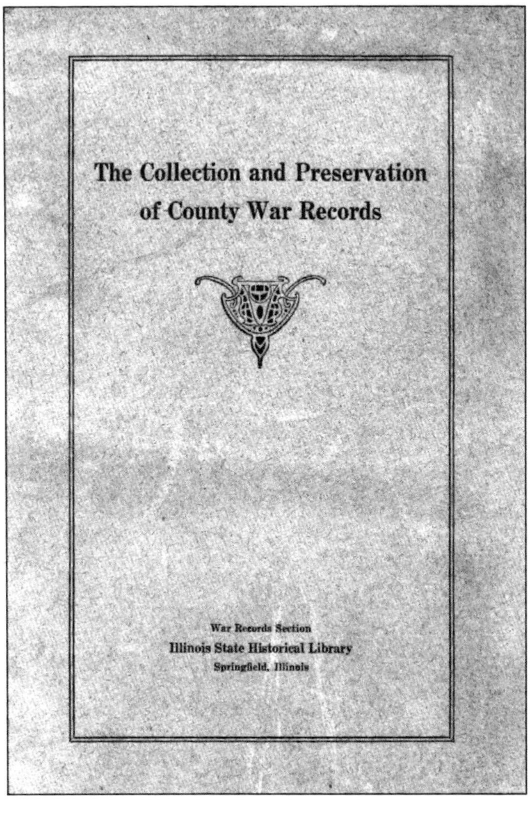
The Collection and Preservation of County War Records

War Records Section
Illinois State Historical Library
Springfield, Illinois

HISTORICAL PRESERVATION. No history of Decatur during World War I could be written without the wealth of artifacts and documents preserved locally because of this 1919 booklet by the Illinois State Historical Library: *The Collection and Preservation of County War Records.* (Courtesy Decatur Public Library.)

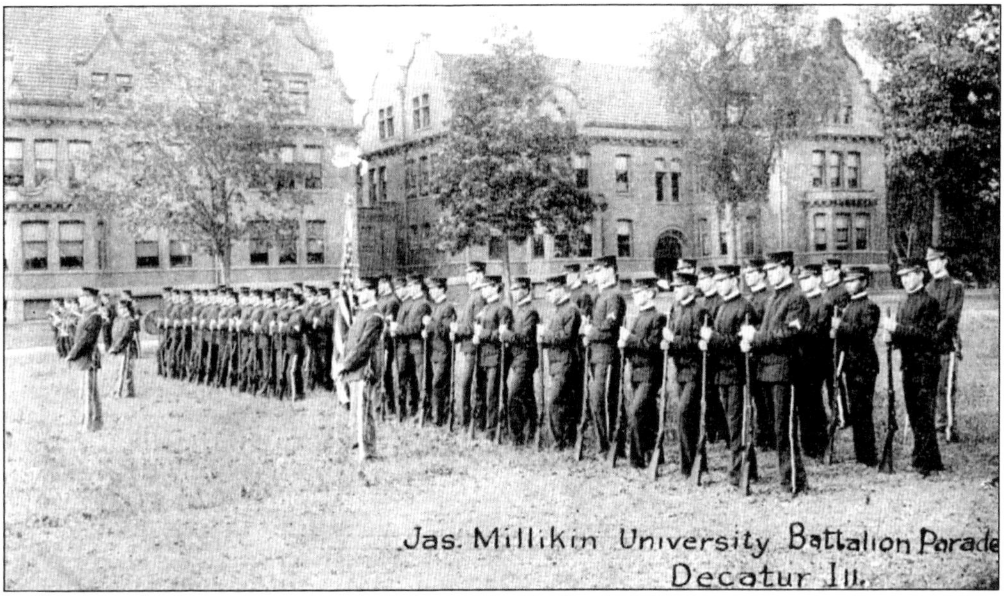

JAMES MILLIKIN UNIVERSITY BATTALION. A kind of early ROTC program, the James Millikin University Battalion is seen here on parade outside Liberal Arts Hall around 1915. Such quasi-military organizations existed all over the country and helped to form the pool of early volunteers. (Courtesy Decatur Public Library.)

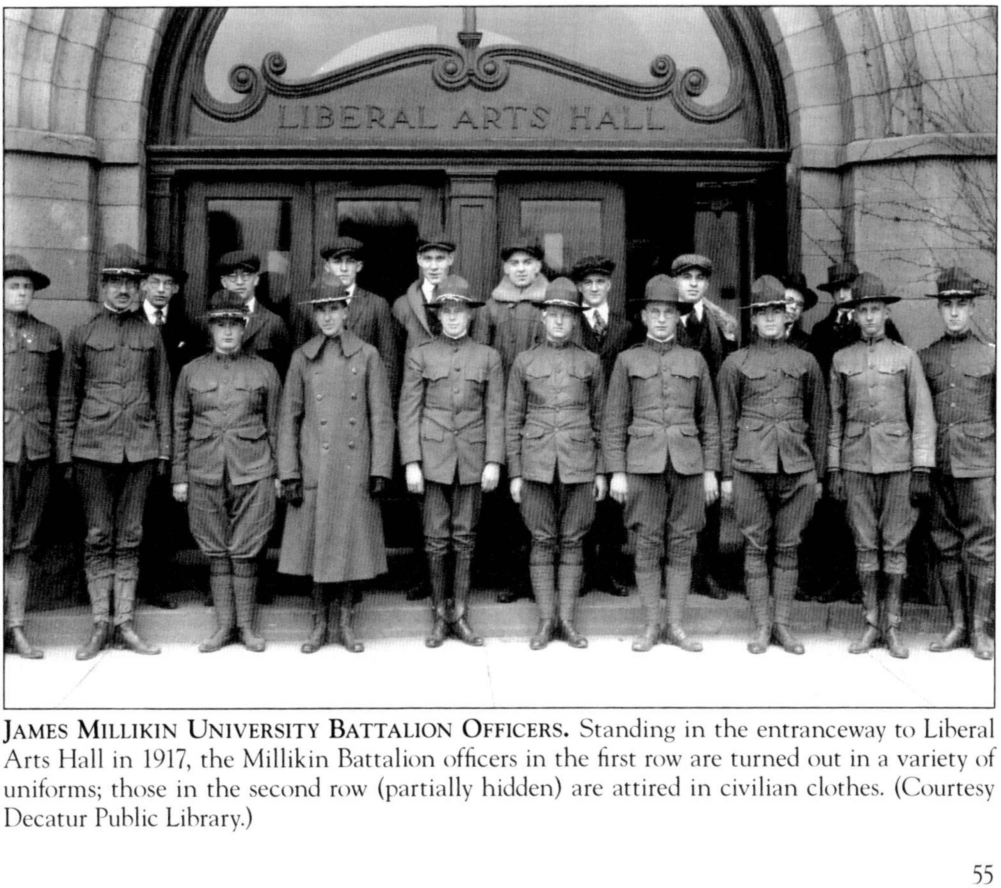

JAMES MILLIKIN UNIVERSITY BATTALION OFFICERS. Standing in the entranceway to Liberal Arts Hall in 1917, the Millikin Battalion officers in the first row are turned out in a variety of uniforms; those in the second row (partially hidden) are attired in civilian clothes. (Courtesy Decatur Public Library.)

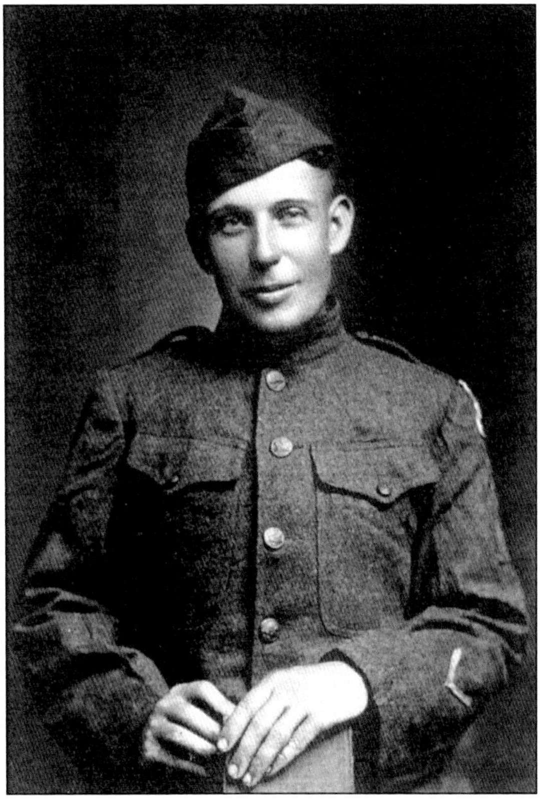

THOMAS EDWARDS. Like many other young male volunteers from Decatur, Thomas "Uncle Tom" Edwards served with Company A, 124th Machine Gun Battalion in France in 1918, and returned home in 1919. His relatives, including John and Pat Riley, still reside in Decatur. (Courtesy Pat Riley.)

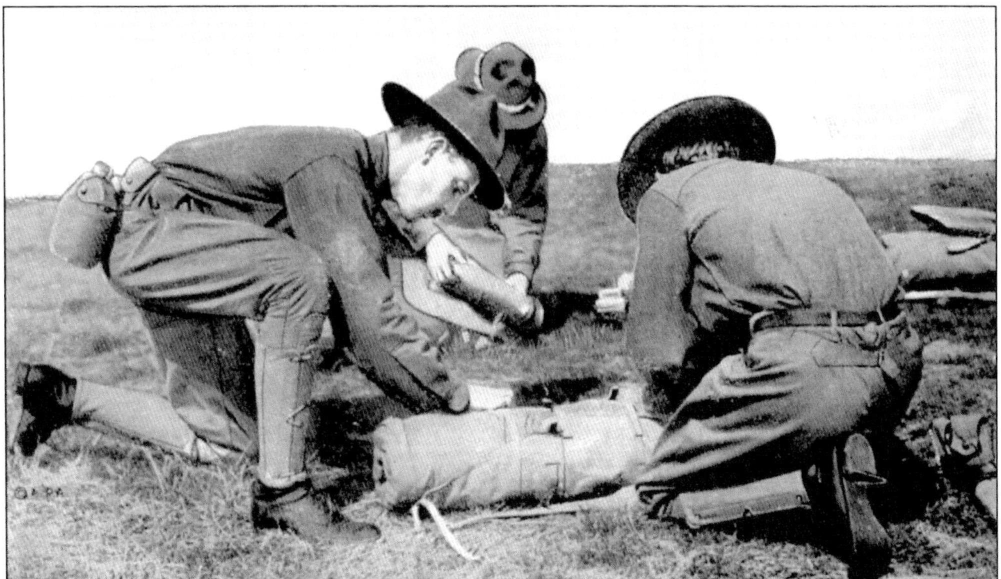

PACKING KIT. Part of a popular series of World War I Army activities, this 1917 postcard shows recent recruits tidily packing their equipment or "kit." On the whole, American soldiers were very well equipped, especially in terms of trucks, ambulances, and airplanes. (Courtesy Pat Riley.)

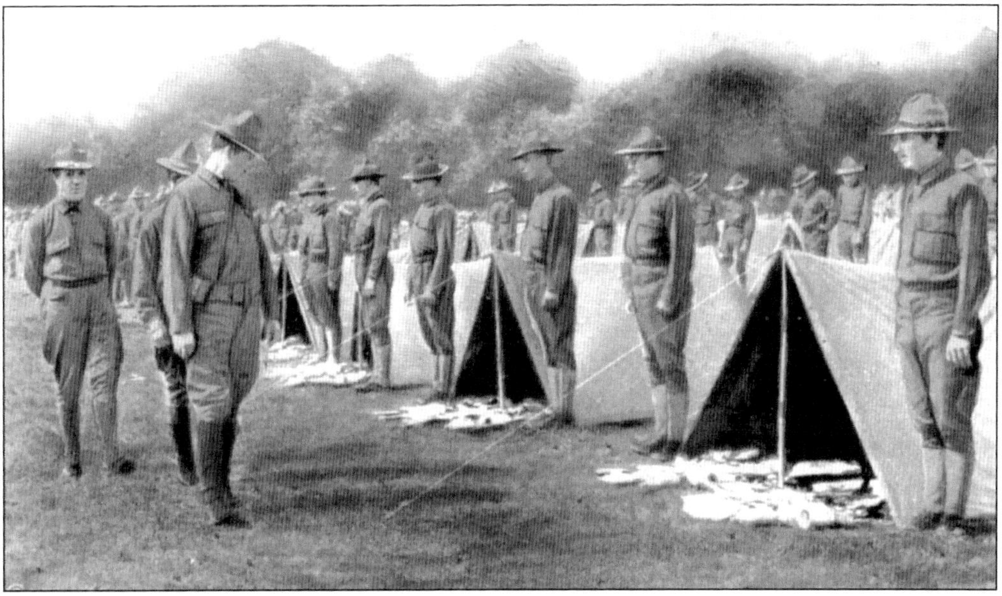

Shelter Tent Inspection. This illustrated postcard depicts the standard World War I tents, which were not very different from their Civil War counterparts. World War II tents were considerably more weatherproof, but oftentimes soldiers slept in foxholes, on the ground, or under some natural shelter, if they slept at all. (Courtesy Pat Riley.)

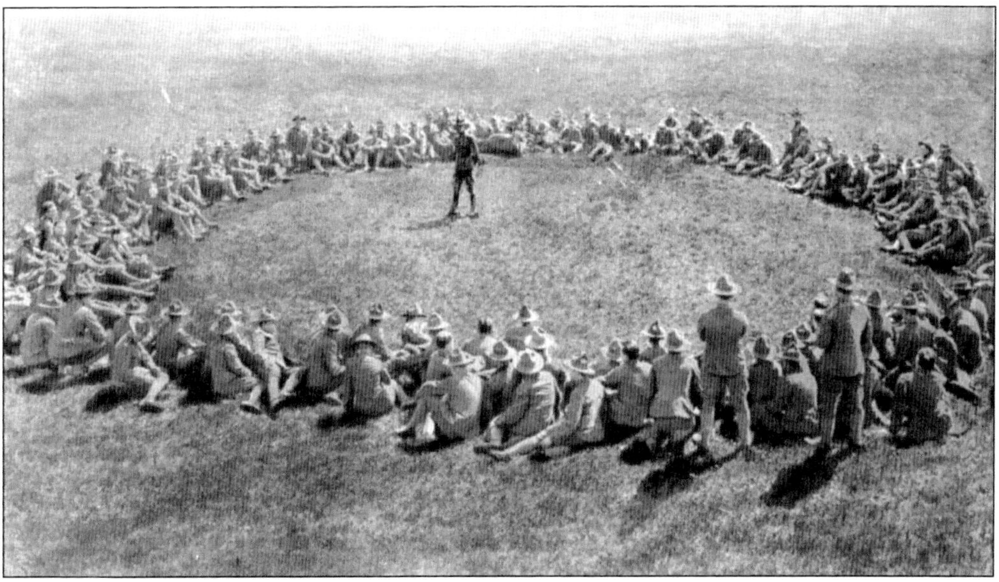

Instructions in Tactics. In this view, the doughboys are gathered in a circle, around their instructor, receiving a lesson in tactics. Actually, most of the tactical maneuvers consisted of night raids across no-man's-land in an attempt to breach the enemy's entrenchments. (Courtesy Pat Riley.)

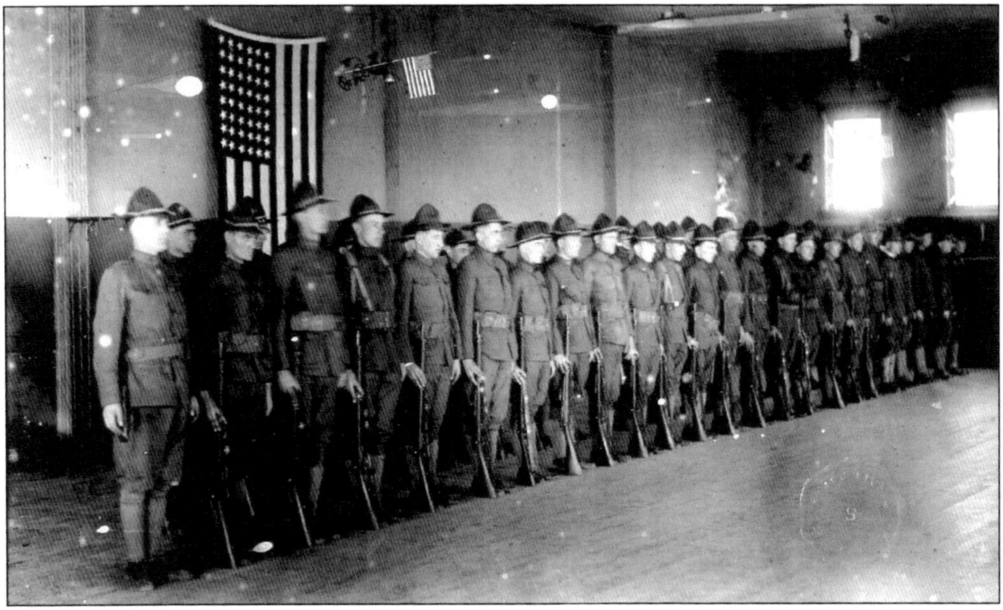

RESERVE MILITIA COMPANY. These reserve troops were training indoors during the winter of 1917–1918, having been issued their cartridge belts and Springfield 1903 rifles. The room is festooned with flags. The troops seem well equipped and well disciplined. (Courtesy Decatur Public Library.)

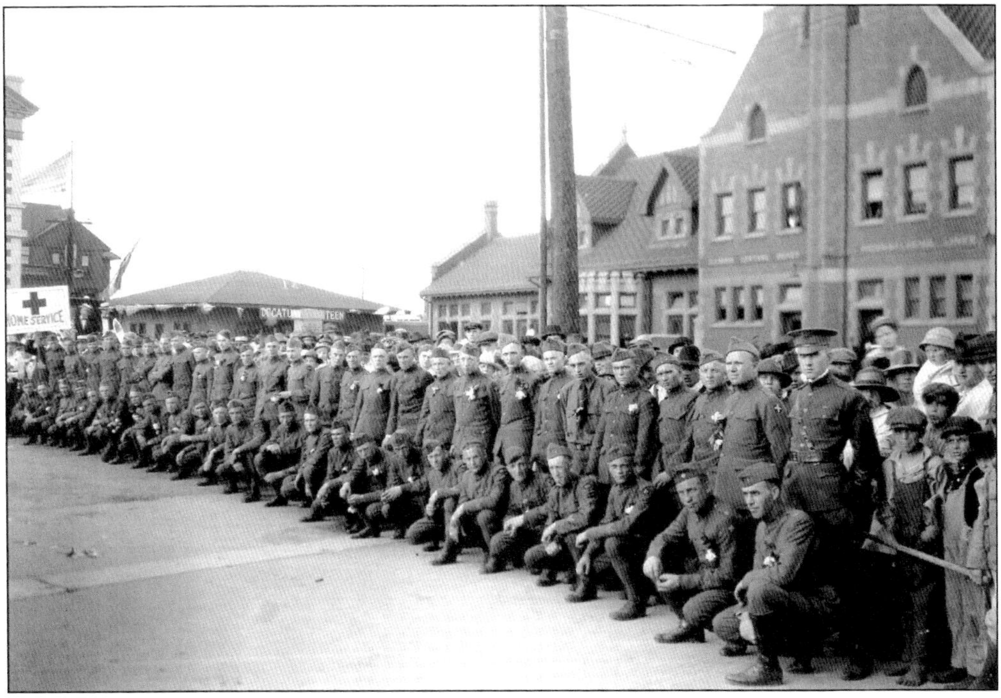

COMPANY A HOMECOMING. On May 31, 1919, the troops of Company A, Decatur's contingent in the Great War, returned home to a heroes' welcome. Officers and men are lined up between the Wabash and Illinois Central Stations, with the famous Decatur Canteen in the background and a sign for the Red Cross Home Service. (Courtesy Decatur Public Library.)

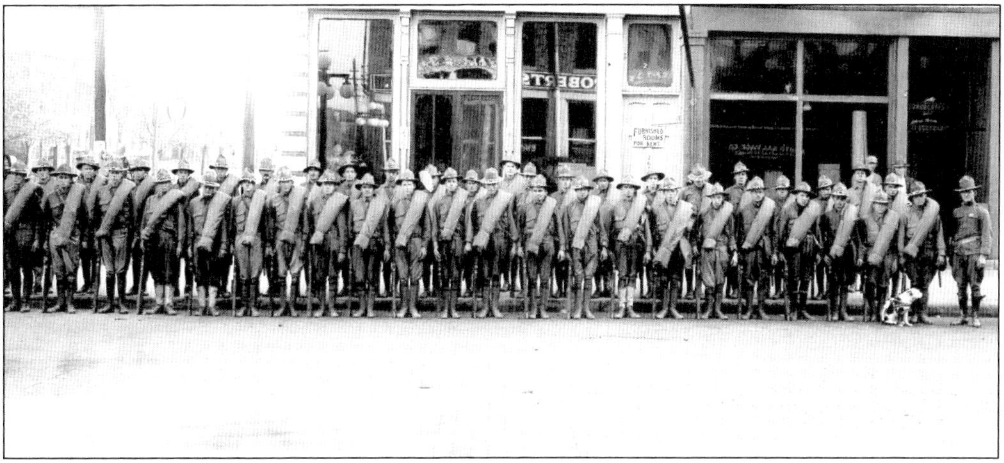

COMPANY H. Illinois National Guard troops of Company H posed in this 1917 photograph with their canine company mascot (far right). The company had just returned from drilling in Springfield. If the war had lasted longer, these men would undoubtedly have gone to France. (Courtesy Decatur Public Library; photograph by C. L. Wasson Studios.)

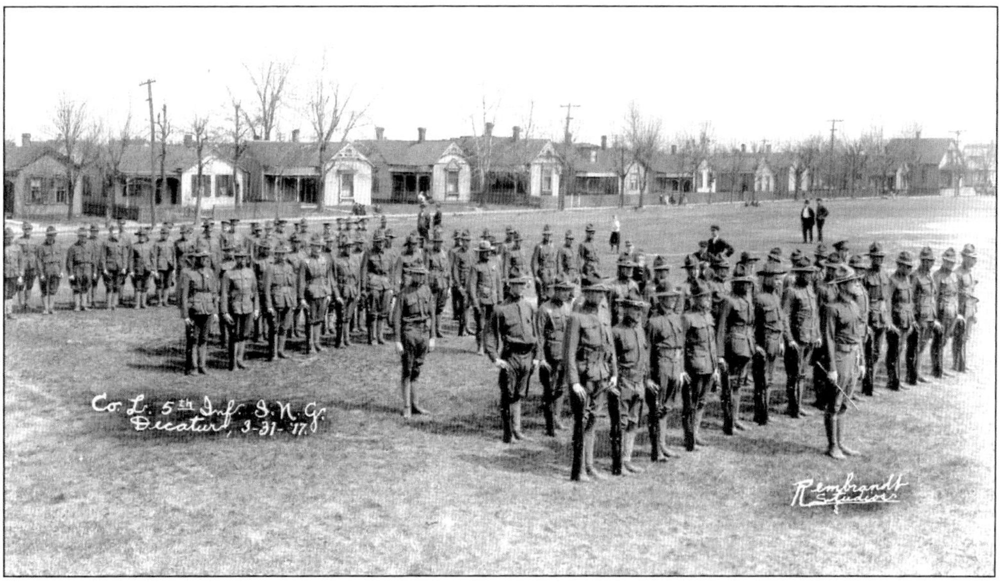

COMPANY L. On a beautiful spring day, Illinois National Guard troops of Company L were drilling on a field somewhere on the east side of Decatur. If the war had dragged on into 1919, these troops would probably have seen duty at the front. (Courtesy Decatur Public Library; photograph by Rembrandt Studios, taken March 31, 1917.)

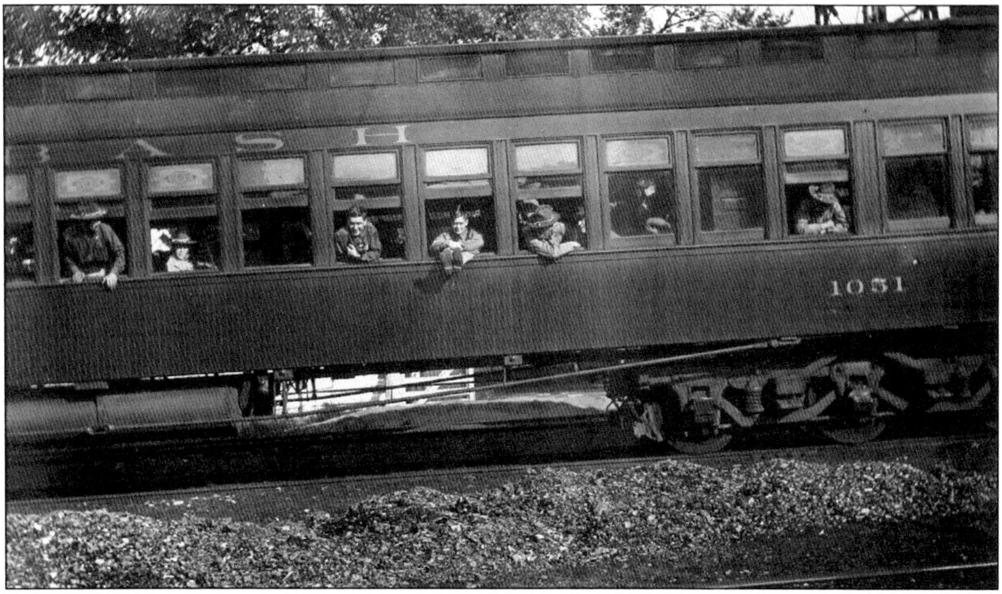

WABASH TROOP TRAIN. This vintage postcard, made in 1917, shows exuberant draftees heading off to a processing and induction center. Great masses of troops and war materiel were moved by troop trains, anticipating the even larger volumes of World War II. (Courtesy Pat Riley.)

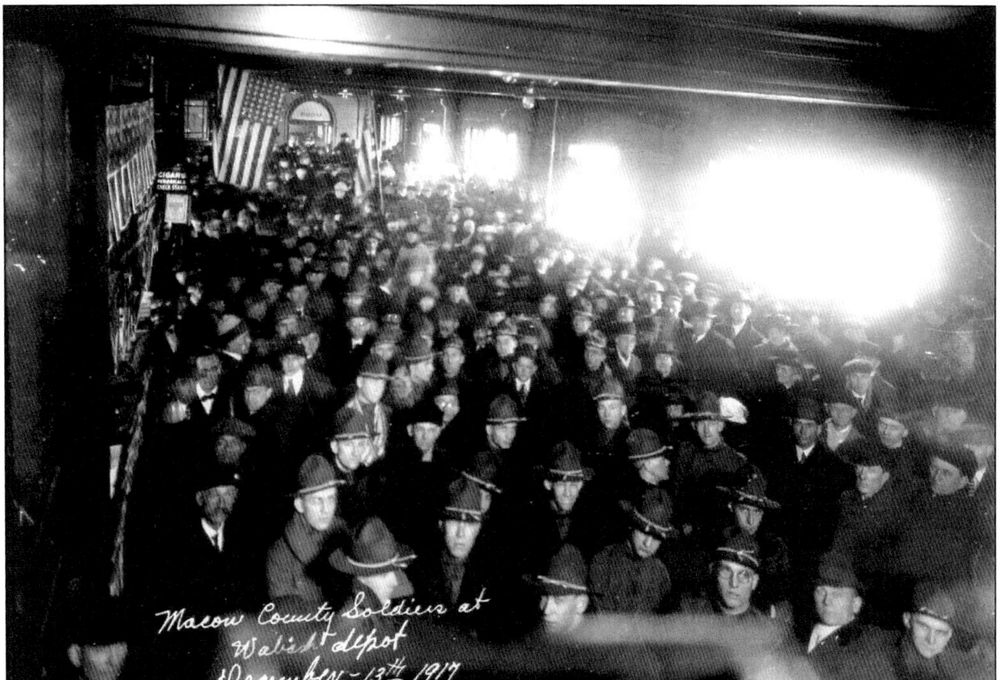

INSIDE THE WABASH DEPOT. On December 13, 1917, these Macon County soldiers, huddled inside the dark paneled lobby of the Wabash Train Station in Decatur, are awaiting transport that would ultimately take them to France. At this point in time, the war would not end before 10 more bloody months of combat had occurred. (Courtesy Decatur Public Library.)

ABOARD THE U.S.S. CONNECTICUT. Decatur did not have many of its sons in the U.S. Navy during World War I, but Thomas Daly served on the U.S.S. *Connecticut* as a fireman. He is shown here leaning on a naval gun, but the exact location and date of this photograph are unknown. (Courtesy Decatur Public Library.)

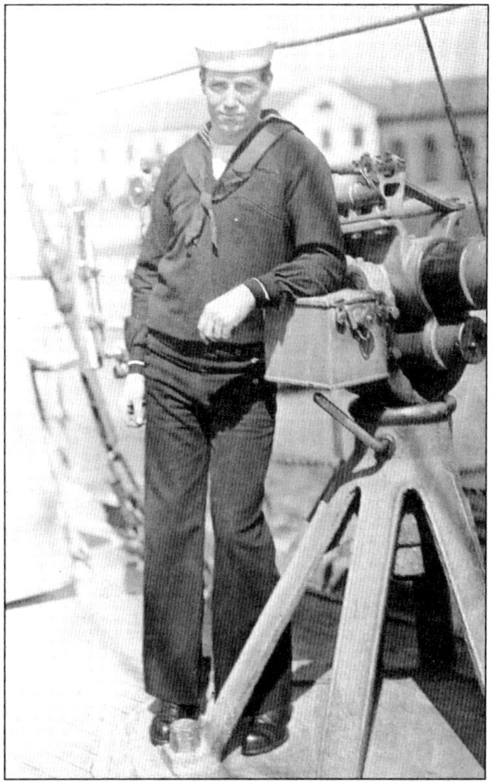

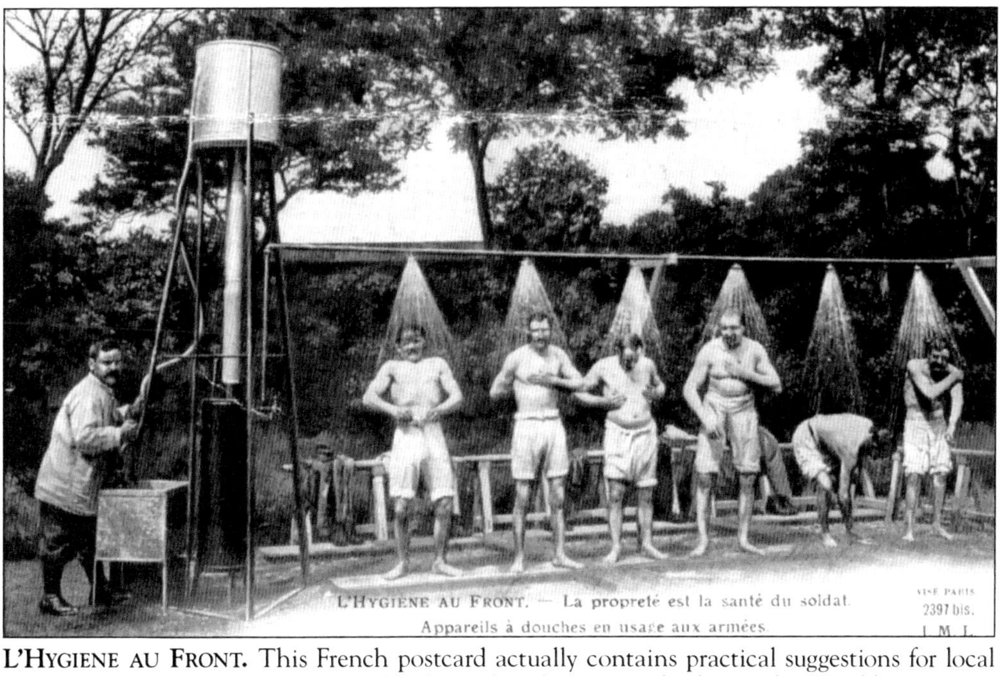

L'HYGIENE AU FRONT. This French postcard actually contains practical suggestions for local agencies to raise money for *douches chaudes*, or hot showers, at the front. The portable apparatus was designed for quick installation. Lice and other vermin were a constant torment for World War I soldiers, so the hot water was most welcome. (Courtesy Decatur Public Library.)

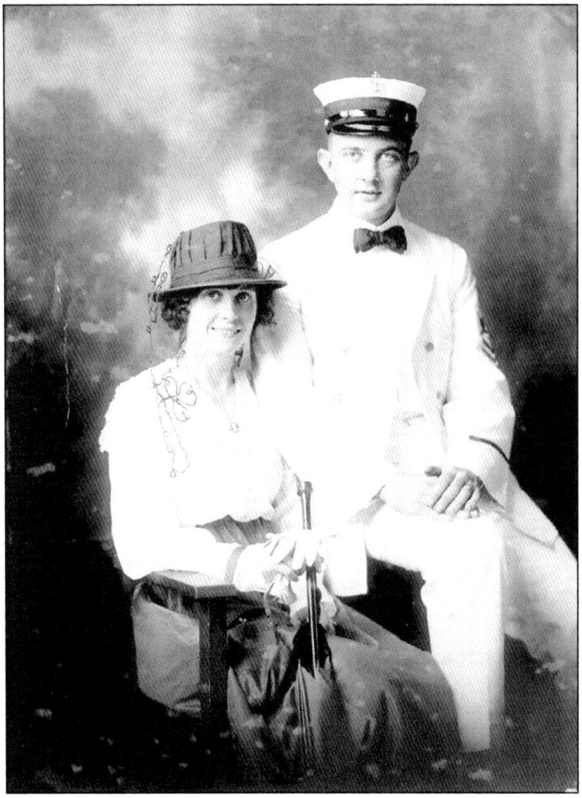

LT. H. C. MECHTOLDT AND WIFE. Lt. H. C. Mechtoldt and his wife posed for this formal portrait in the C. L. Wasson Studios in late 1918. At that time, he had been in the Navy for seven years and had served in World War I. Lieutenant Mechtoldt was buried in Arlington National Cemetery after his death on February 26, 1938. (Courtesy Decatur Public Library.)

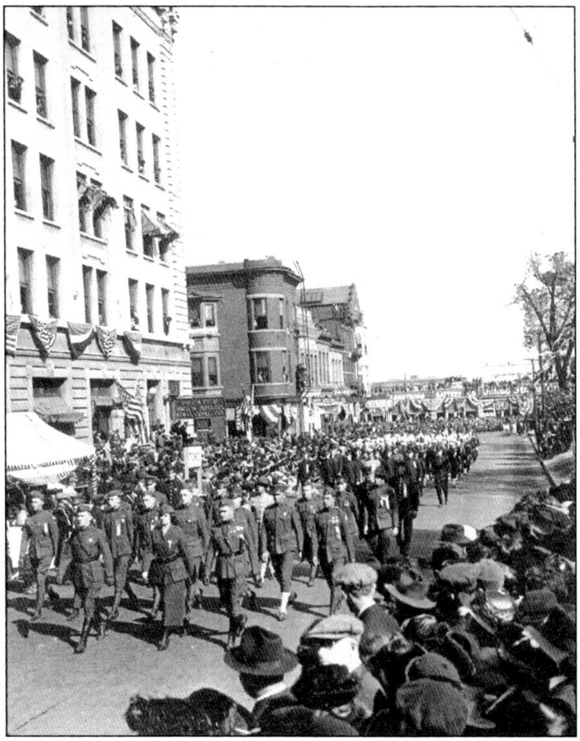

POST-WAR VICTORY PARADE. Probably taking place in May 1919, this victory parade is unique in that it shows African-American and Caucasian troops marching together in the same unit. There is also a woman in uniform, who was probably a nurse, doctor, or medic. They are all marching in front of the Decatur Brick Manufacturing Company at 222 North Park Street. (Courtesy Decatur Public Library.)

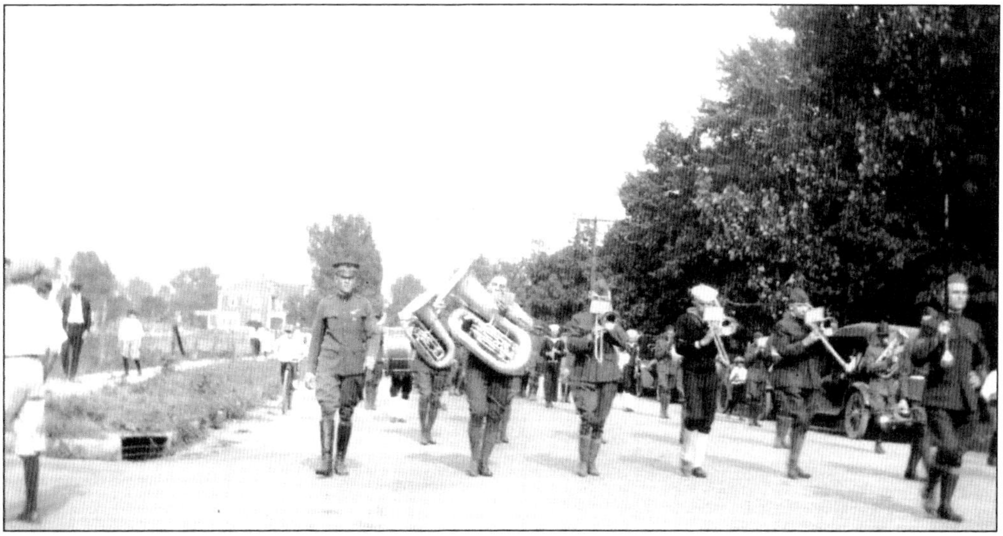

FUNERAL PROCESSION, PART ONE. Sgt. Castle Williams, the first soldier from Decatur to be killed, is still honored by the local American Legion post. Williams was buried on July 25, 1919, in the largest military funeral ever held in Decatur. Hundreds of people participated, and over 600 cars were used in the procession, which began with this military band. (Courtesy Decatur Public Library.)

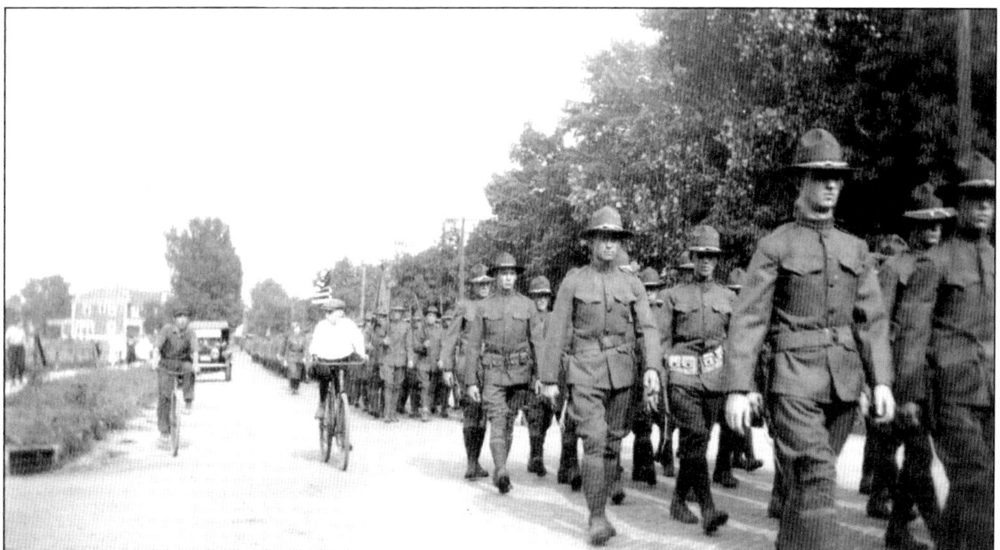

FUNERAL PROCESSION, PART TWO. These marching doughboys are honoring their fallen comrade as two young boys ride by on bicycles. A black police car in the background follows at a discreet distance. (Courtesy Decatur Public Library.)

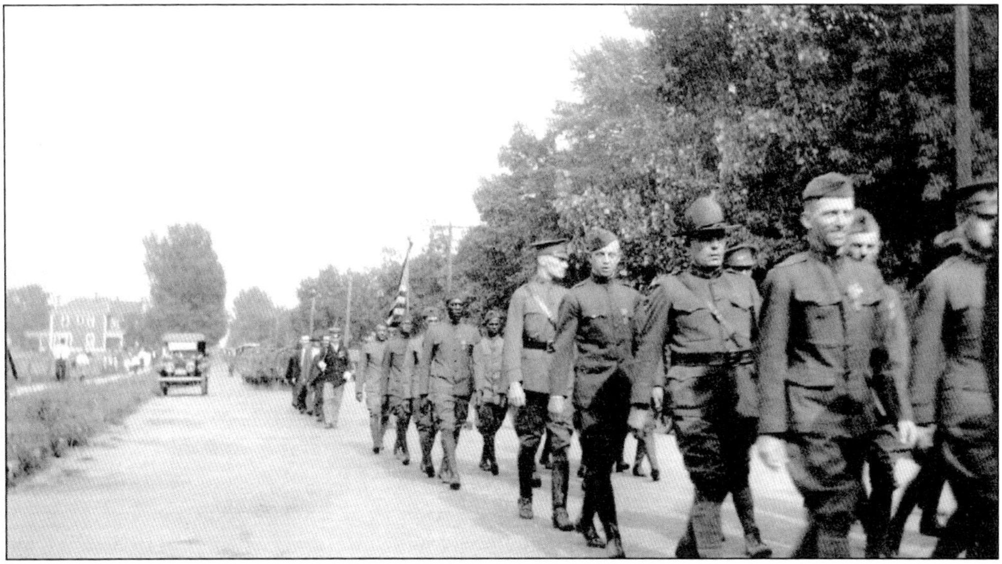

Funeral Procession, Part Three. These soldiers are near the very end of the military part of the funeral procession. A separate group of African-American soldiers are marching immediately in front of the furled flag. (Courtesy Decatur Public Library.)

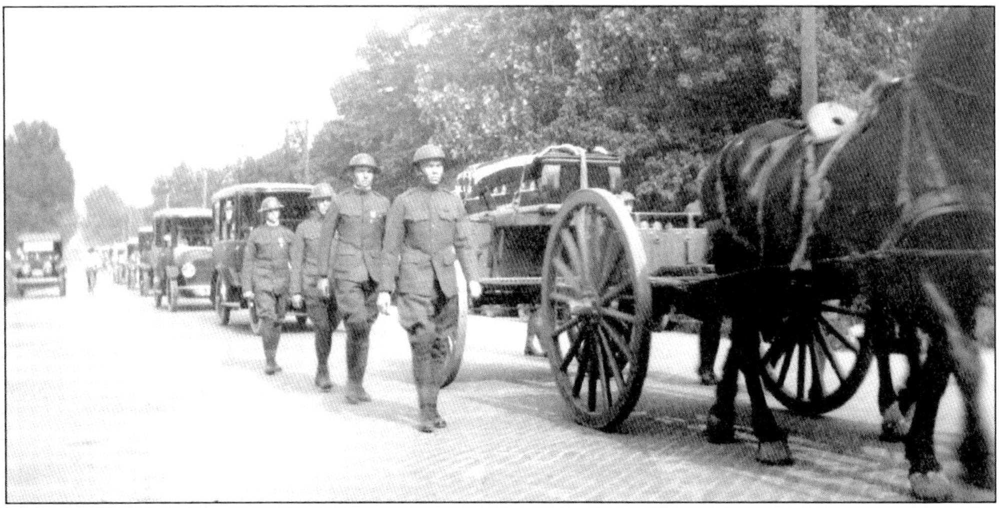

Funeral Procession, Part Four. Sgt. Castle Williams's caisson is being drawn by the traditional riderless horse. Hundreds of cars followed the casket. The grand funeral of Sergeant Williams marked an emotional closing point for the citizens of Decatur, the end of the war, the end of the decade, and the end of an era. (Courtesy Decatur Public Library.)

Three

WORLD WAR II 1941–1945

World War II has been called the defining moment of the entire 20th-century. If one considers the famous names and places associated with that long war, the statement seems eminently true: Roosevelt, Truman, Eisenhower, Patton, MacArthur, Churchill, Montgomery, Hitler, Stalin, Pearl Harbor, Stalingrad, Normandy (D-Day), Hiroshima, and Nagasaki. World War II introduced atomic power, jet aircraft, radar, sonar, and genocide on a mass scale, especially in the concentration camps of Germany and Poland. World War II was the crowning achievement of American industrial might, as factories churned out endless copies of M-1 Rifles, Jeeps, B-17 Bombers, P-51 Mustangs, aircraft carriers, and Victory ships. At one time or another, Americans saw action in almost every time zone, in places like the Aleutian Islands, Tunisia, Burma, Belgium, Italy, Germany, Guadalcanal, the Philippines, and Okinawa. American culture in the form of big band jazz, jitterbug dancing, Hershey bars, Doublemint gum, and Coca-Cola were introduced all over the world. Decatur servicemen, and women, were contributing partners in this truly global undertaking. Many served in the states in various supporting roles. Some fought in North Africa or flew bombers over Italy and Germany. Perhaps the largest group fought in the Pacific, on ships and in places like Luzon in the Philippines.

On the home front, loyal citizens repeated many of the actions taken by their predecessors during World War I. They stinted on butter, coffee, sugar, and meat. They collected heaps of newspapers (used in cartridge shells), scrap iron, and rubber. They tooled around the city on nearly bald and unsafe tires. They scrounged for rationed gasoline, they bought more war bonds, and planted more victory gardens, but there were far fewer parades. The war became so complex that, even in spite of radio and newspaper coverage, it was not always easy to understand what was actually going on. Jewish concentration camps, for example, were not revealed until the end of the war in Europe (May 1945), and, of course, the Manhattan Project (or construction of the atom bomb) was kept tightly under wraps until after Hiroshima and Nagasaki (August 1945).

The government itself was better organized, so the military did not need as many people to make bandages or sew hospital gowns. However, there was a great need for nurses, clerks, weather forecasters, accountants, engine mechanics, and hundreds of other less-than-glamorous occupations. It is estimated that 16 support personnel were needed to keep one soldier equipped in the field. Most of the Army, Navy, and Air Force were serving on the bases and in ports, not on the front lines. Millions of tons of food and supplies had to be organized and transported all over the globe as quickly as possible. The amount of work that Americans performed between 1941 and 1945—at home and in the field—was simply staggering.

Decatur's old 130th Regiment, with historical roots in the Civil War and World War I, saw action in New Guinea in March 1944. Decatur troops, however, served in a variety of regiments and branches as part of the new global service. Women in the Navy were called Women Accepted for Volunteer Emergency Service or WAVES, those in the Army, the Women's Army Corps or WACS, and those in the Coast Guard, SPARS, after the Coast Guard motto *Semper Paratus*, or "always prepared." Women in Decatur worked at the Remington Rand plant in nearby Illiopolis, making ordnance for the U.S. Army. At the same time, the Caterpillar Victory Engine Plant was making tank engines in Decatur. Even the Houdaille-Hershey Plant secretly made parts for the atom bomb. Burks pumps and Mueller valves helped submarines to dive and resurface. Decatur was such a model for wartime involvement that, in 1943, the War Department made a film in Decatur, *Jalopies on Parade,* showing how to recycle old cars and trucks for military use. Decatur also produced two generals during this war: Edwin Randle and John McDavid. Italian-American Vito Bertoldo won the Congressional Medal of Honor for singular bravery in Hatten, France. When the Japanese finally surrendered on August 14, 1945, confetti rained down on the crowds in downtown Decatur, and people literally danced in the streets. The citizens celebrated their common victory, for everyone was a winner.

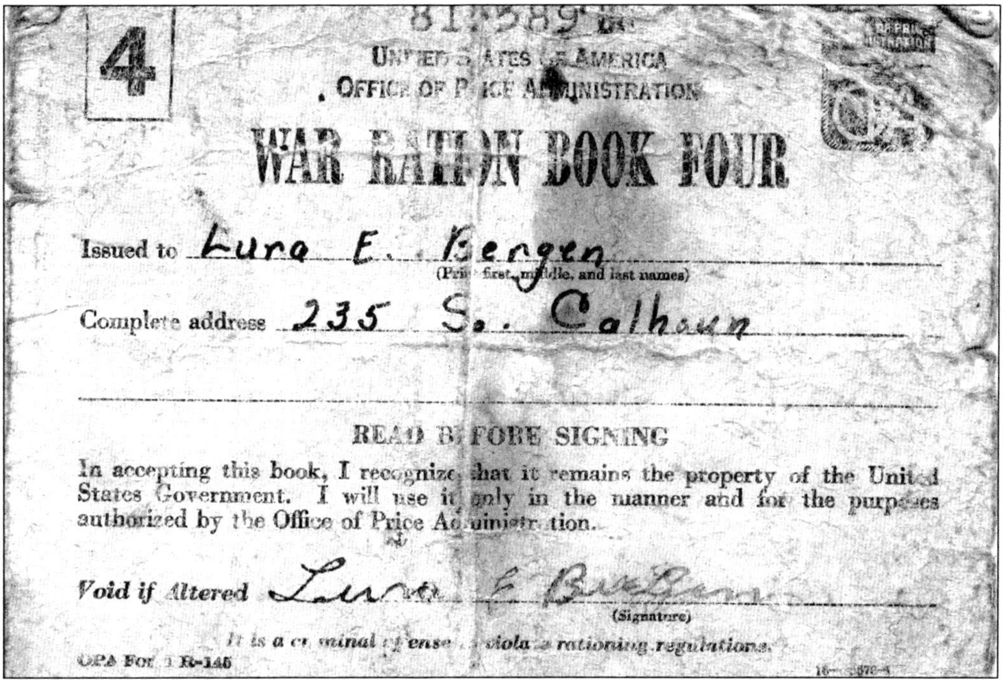

FOOD RATION BOOK. Issued by the Office of Price Administration, food ration books had to be presented when consumers were buying items in short supply like sugar, butter, coffee, or meat. The tattered state of this particular book confirms that it was obviously well used by its owner. (Courtesy Peggy Bergen.)

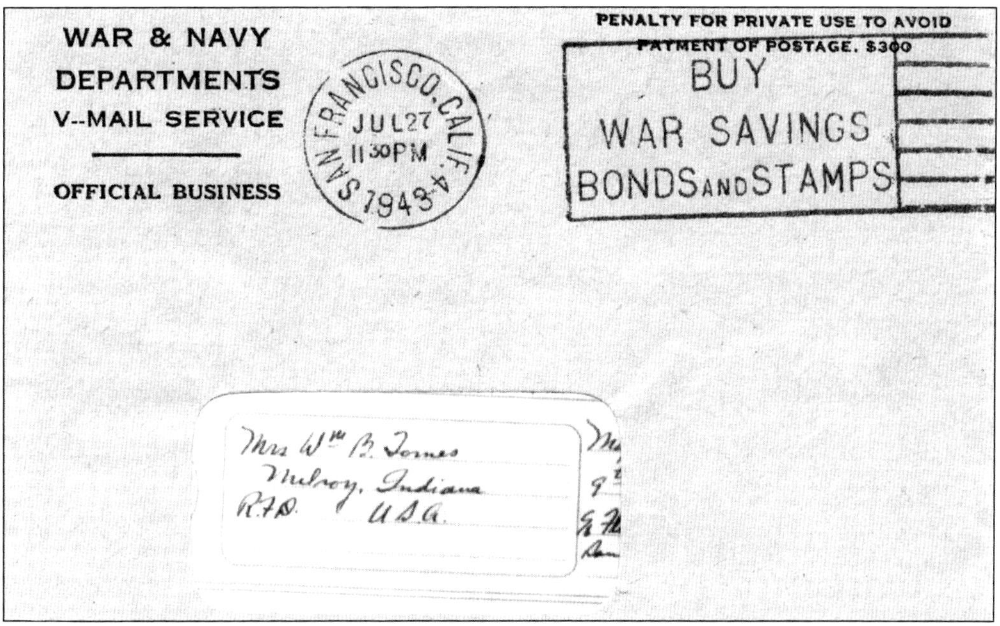

V-MAIL LETTER. Another icon from World War II is the famous V-mail or victory letter, a compact form of communication used especially by the service personnel in the Pacific. Like all military mail, V-letters were censored. After the war, American poet Karl Shapiro published a book of colloquial poetry entitled *V-Letters.* (Courtesy Peggy Bergen.)

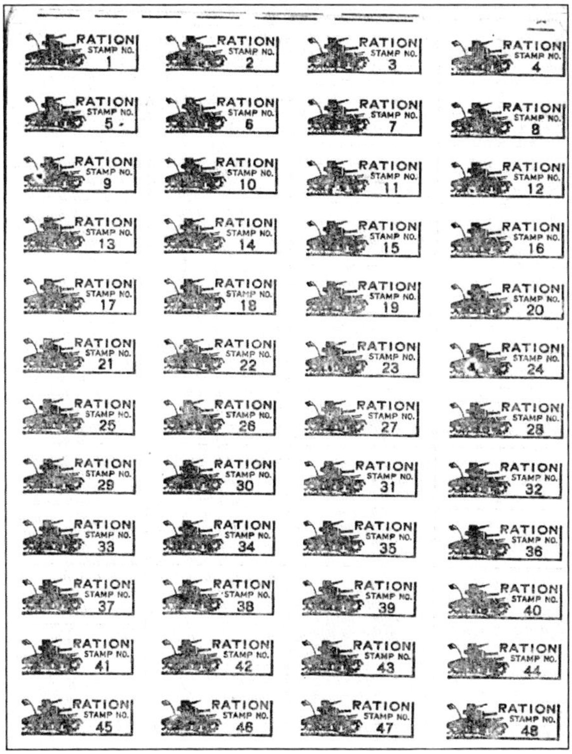

RATION STAMPS. These little stamps, issued by the Office of Price Administration, were to be used in conjunction with the Food Ration Book. These particular stamps, with the little tank symbol, probably date to the end of the war when supply began to catch up with demand. (Courtesy Peggy Bergen.)

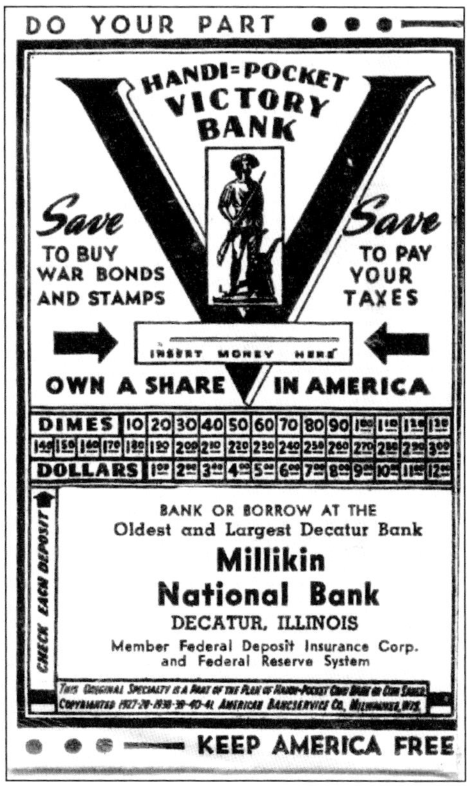

V-BANK ENVELOPE. The "Handi-Pocket Victory Bank" envelope was distributed by the Millikin National Bank as a catalyst for the purchase of war bonds and war stamps. As in World War I, war bonds became a critical part of the financing. Many people who later bought "EE" Savings Bonds had developed the habit during World War II. (Courtesy Decatur Public Library.)

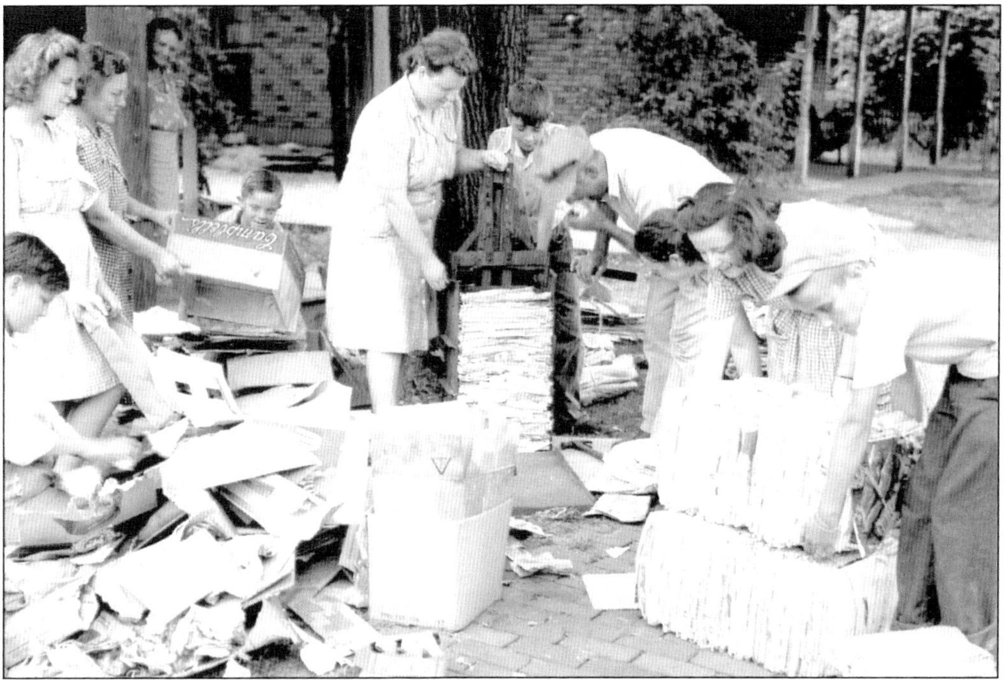

NEIGHBORHOOD PAPER DRIVE. Moms and kids gather on a warm summer day in 1944 to bundle newspapers they had collected for the war effort. As in World War I, Decaturites showed ingenuity and perseverance in their collection strategies, as in the re-use of the Campbell's Soup carton. (Courtesy Dayle Cochran Irwin.)

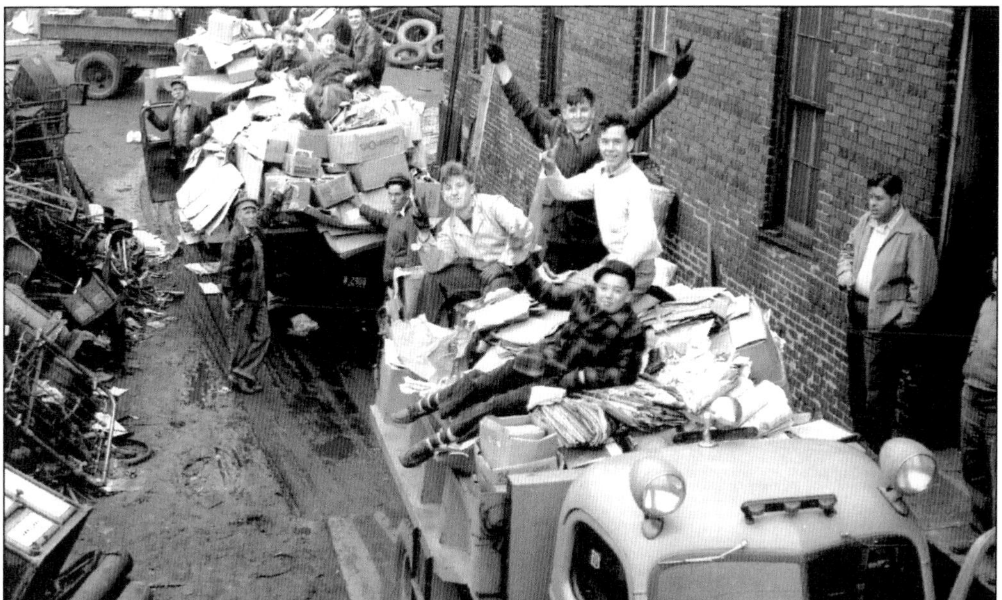

FLASHING THE V-SIGN. These high-school and junior-high students are exuberantly flashing V-signs as they loll atop four separate truckloads of paper and cardboard collected in a 1944 paper drive. They are proudly celebrating their undeniable success. (Courtesy Dayle Cochran Irwin.)

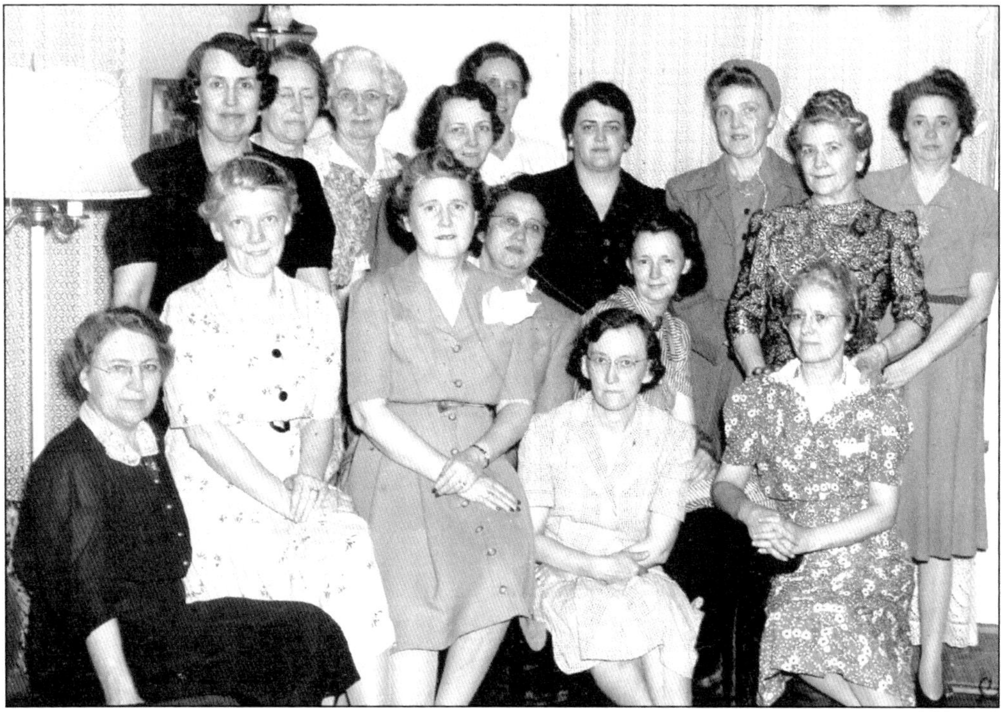

LADIES AUXILIARY. This group of Decatur women, probably photographed in 1942, was composed of wives or mothers of servicemen and servicewomen, as well as the wives of veterans. Their mission as the American Legion Ladies Auxiliary was to help the families of those serving in the war. (Courtesy Decatur Public Library.)

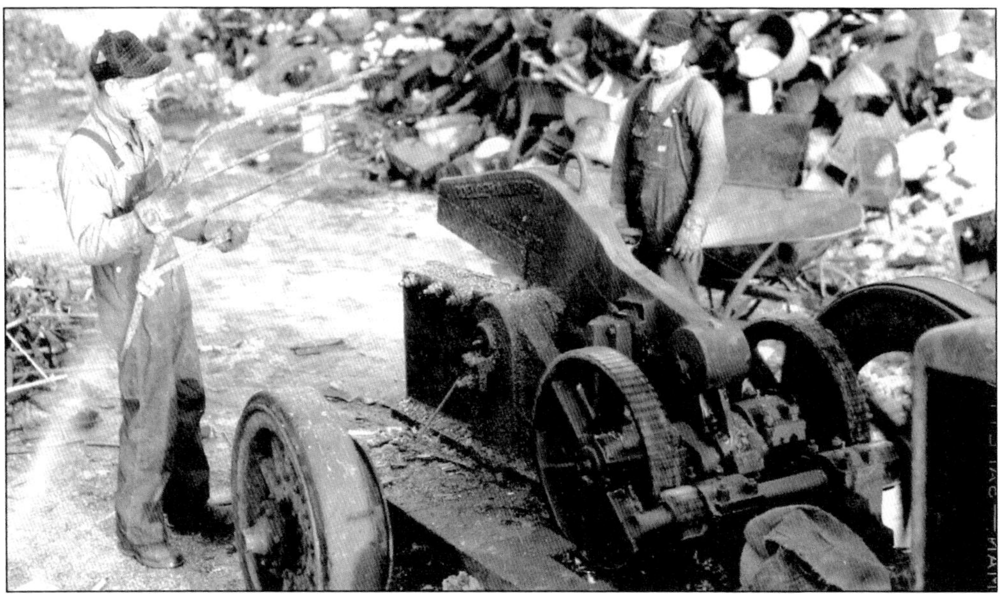

PROCESSING SCRAP IRON. These two workers are processing various pieces of scrap iron as part of the war effort in the winter of 1942. The pile of junk in the background gives some idea of their working inventory. Scrap metal was very quickly turned into Jeeps, tanks, canteens, bayonets, and other wartime necessities. (Courtesy Dayle Cochran Irwin.)

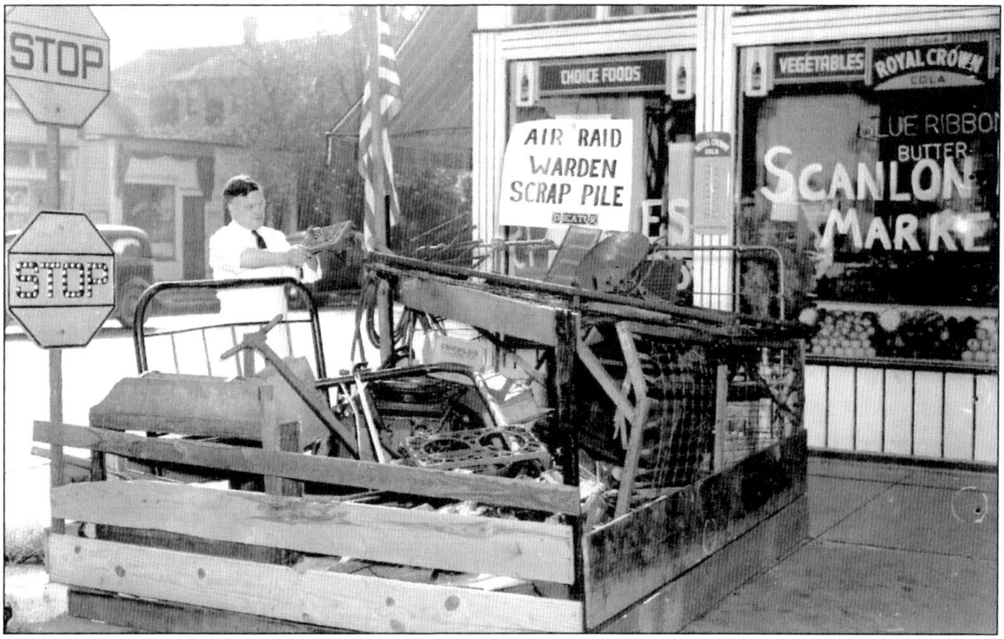

SCANLON'S FOOD MARKET. Bedsprings were turned into bullets because of neighborhood scrap collection heaps like this one in front of Scanlon's Food Market, located at 1273 North Edward Street. Typical of 1940s culture are the advertisements for Royal Crown Cola and Blue Ribbon Butter. (Courtesy Dayle Cochran Irwin.)

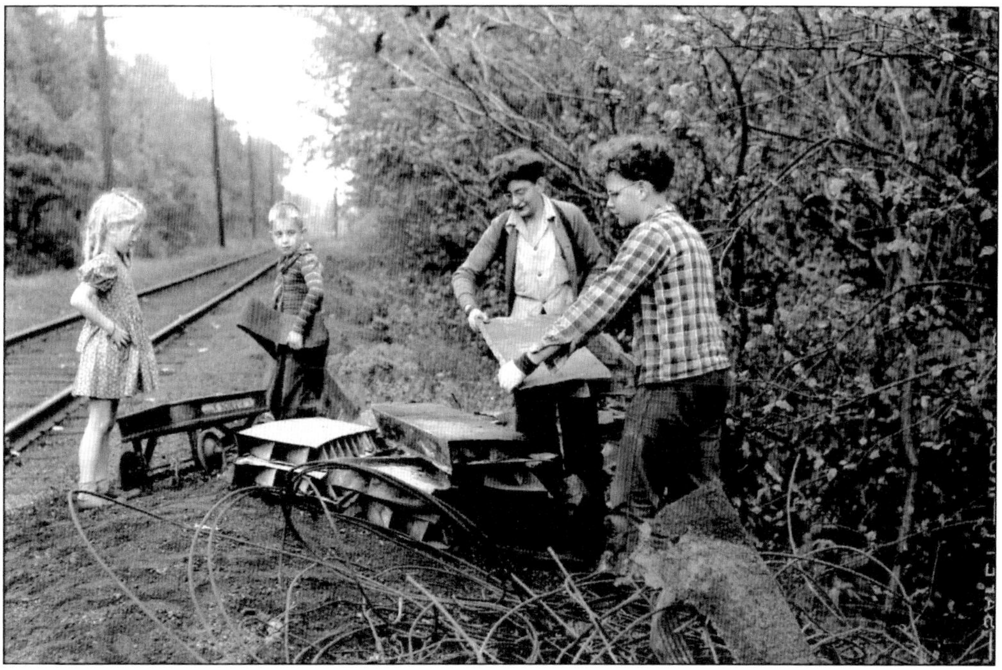

KIDS COLLECTING SCRAP METAL. This picture of children collecting scrap metal by the railroad tracks is one of the most poignant images from the World War II photographic archives of Decatur. The scrap collecting effort involved the whole human spectrum, from preschoolers to grandparents. Everyone participated. (Courtesy Dayle Cochran Irwin.)

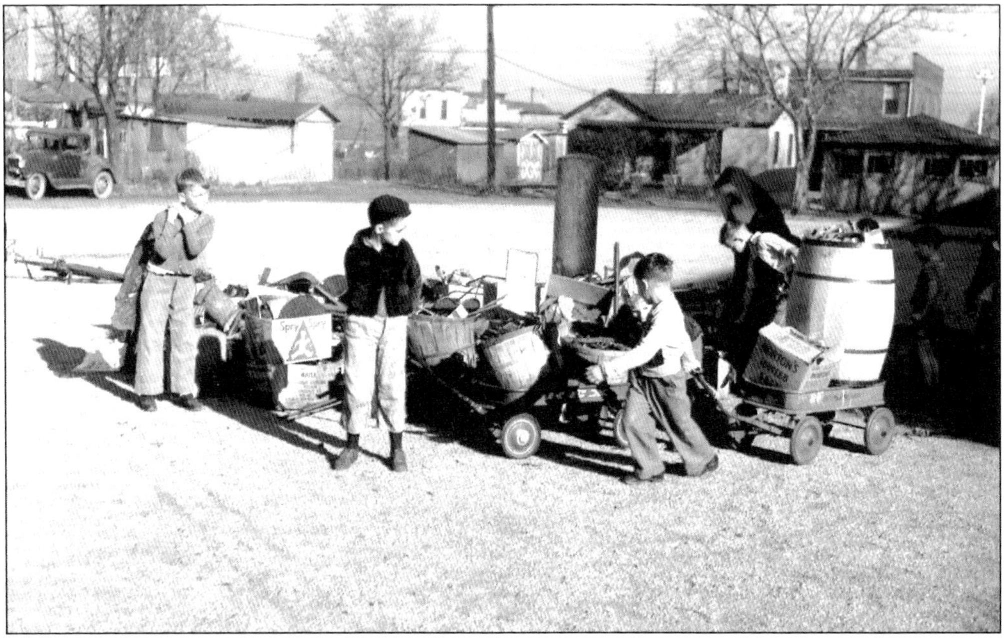

A NUN AND HER STUDENTS. In another touching documentary photograph, a self-effacing nun shepherds her little wards as they pull wagons and haul bags of scrap metal. The Spry shortening box holds other treasures to be transported later. In the background, an old Chevrolet Roadster is parked at the edge of the graveled lot. (Courtesy Dayle Cochran Irwin.)

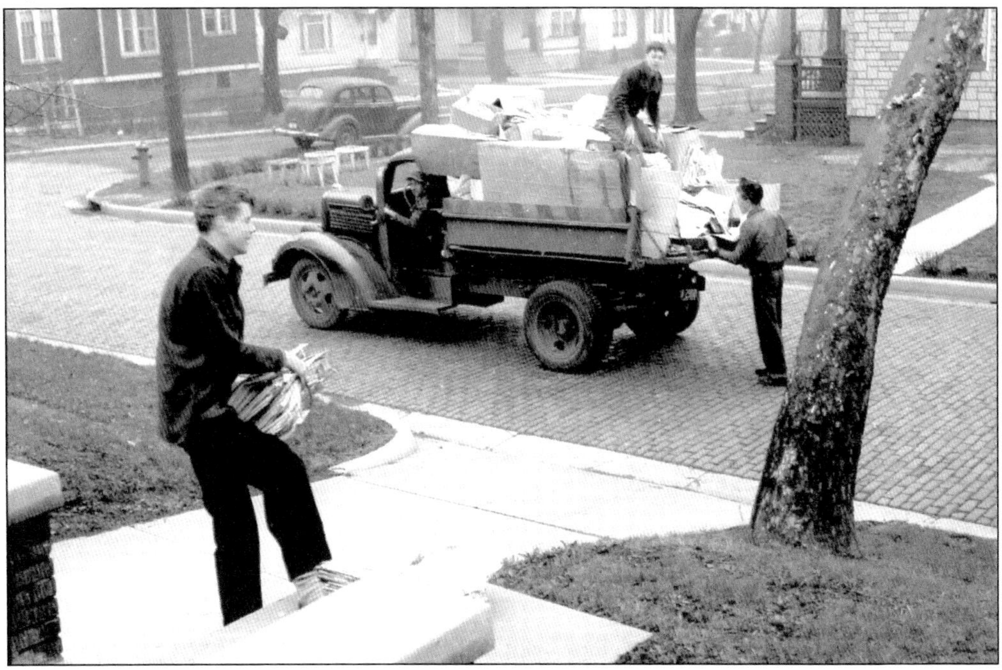

DOOR-TO-DOOR COLLECTIONS. These young men are busily going from door to door, collecting bundles of newspapers for a city-wide newspaper drive in 1942. Judging from the load in their truck, they have been very successful in their effort on a brisk spring day in 1942. Some of these young men probably fought overseas before the war's end. (Courtesy Dayle Cochran Irwin.)

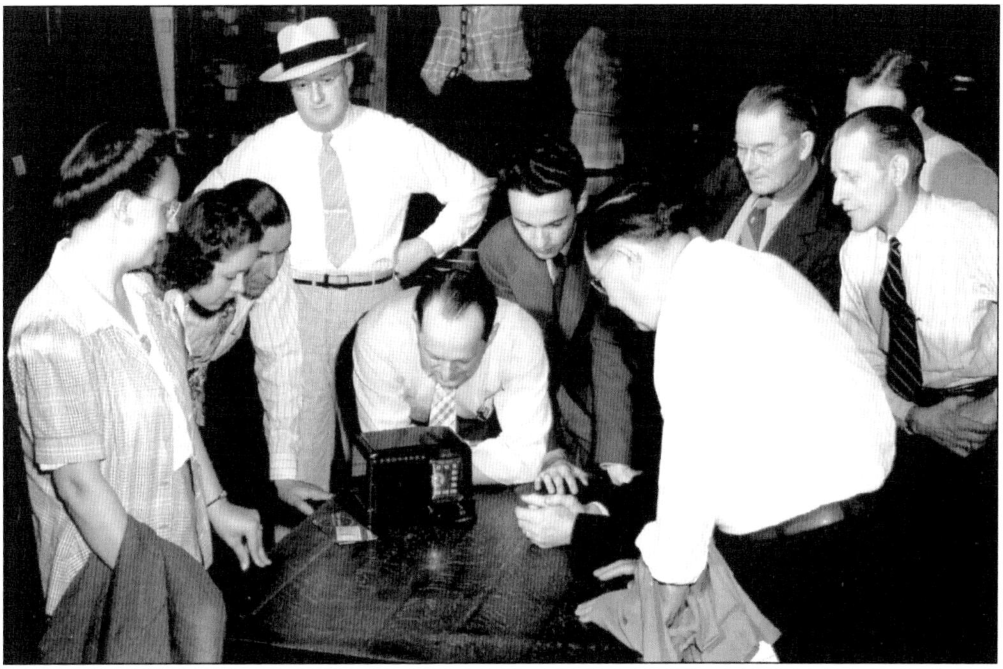

LISTENING TO THE RADIO. These Decatur citizens are gathered around a small radio just after D-Day (June 6, 1944), eagerly soaking up news on the massive invasion of the Normandy coast. The 1940s were the golden age of radio, with comedians like George Burns and Gracie Allen, as well as world-class newsmen like Edward R. Murrow, who reported from London. (Courtesy Dayle Cochran Irwin.)

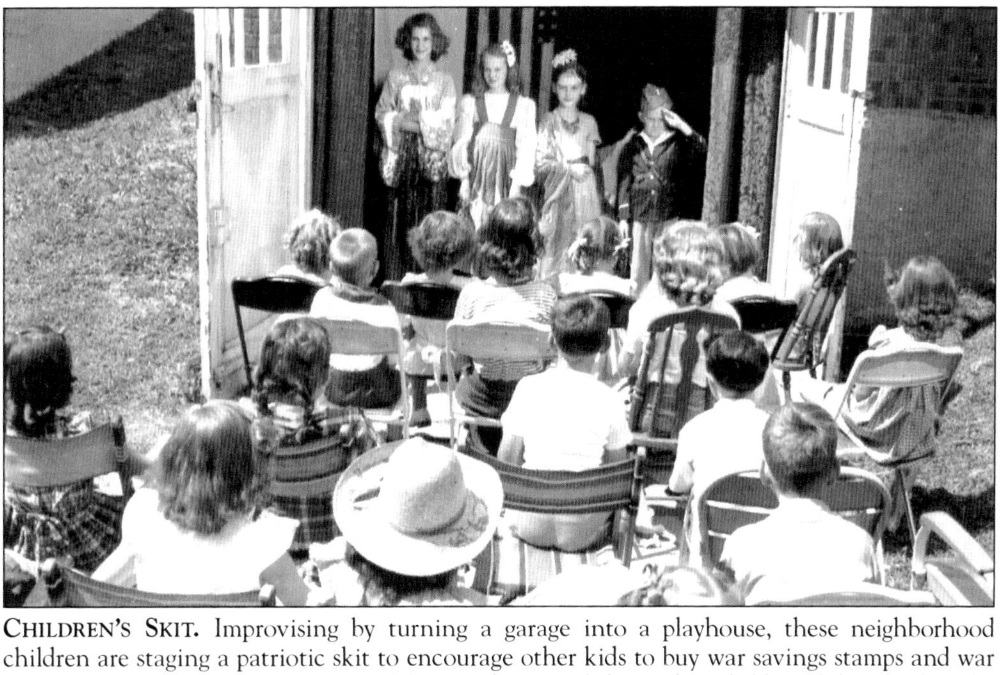

CHILDREN'S SKIT. Improvising by turning a garage into a playhouse, these neighborhood children are staging a patriotic skit to encourage other kids to buy war savings stamps and war bonds. They were apparently successful since the record shows that children did, indeed, make such purchases, possibly from their little allowances. (Courtesy Dayle Cochran Irwin.)

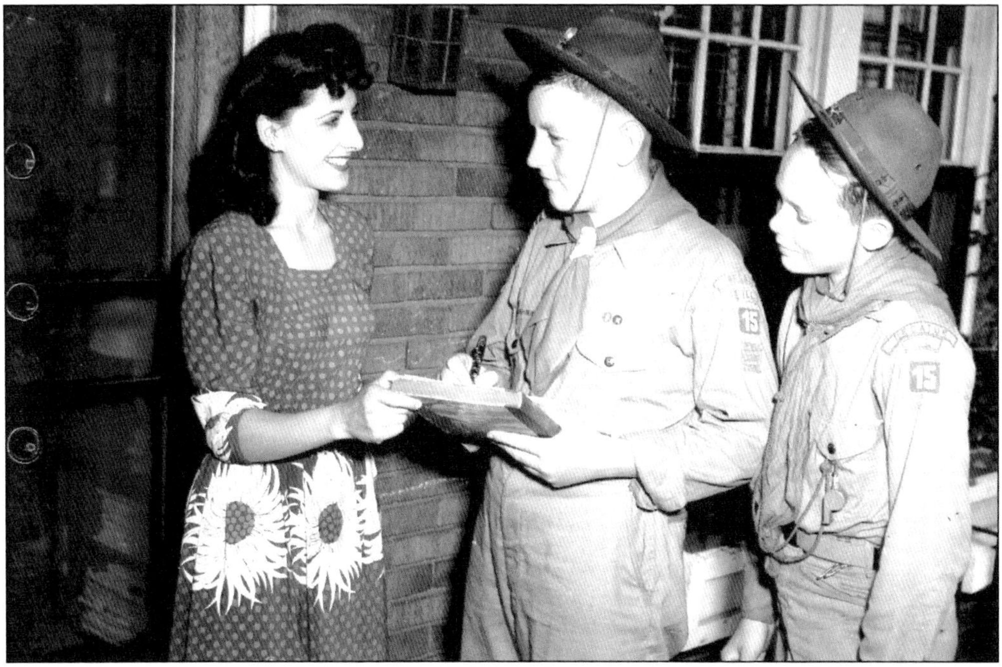

BOY SCOUTS SELLING BONDS. These Boy Scouts, presumably working for another merit badge, are selling war bonds to a Decatur housewife with large sunflower designs on her dress. Every organization tried to find a way to join in the war effort. This photograph was taken in 1944. (Courtesy Dayle Cochran Irwin.)

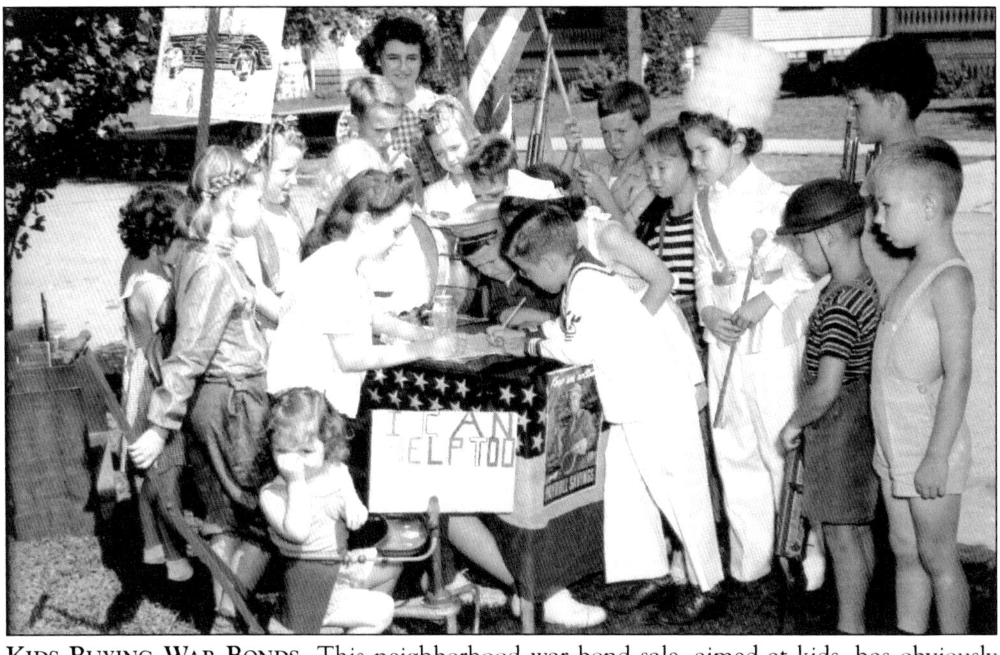

KIDS BUYING WAR BONDS. This neighborhood war bond sale, aimed at kids, has obviously drawn quite a motley crowd, including a drum majorette, a boy soldier with World War I-style helmet, a flag bearer, and a boy in a sailor suit, who is actually the customer signing up for a bond. (Courtesy Dayle Cochran Irwin.)

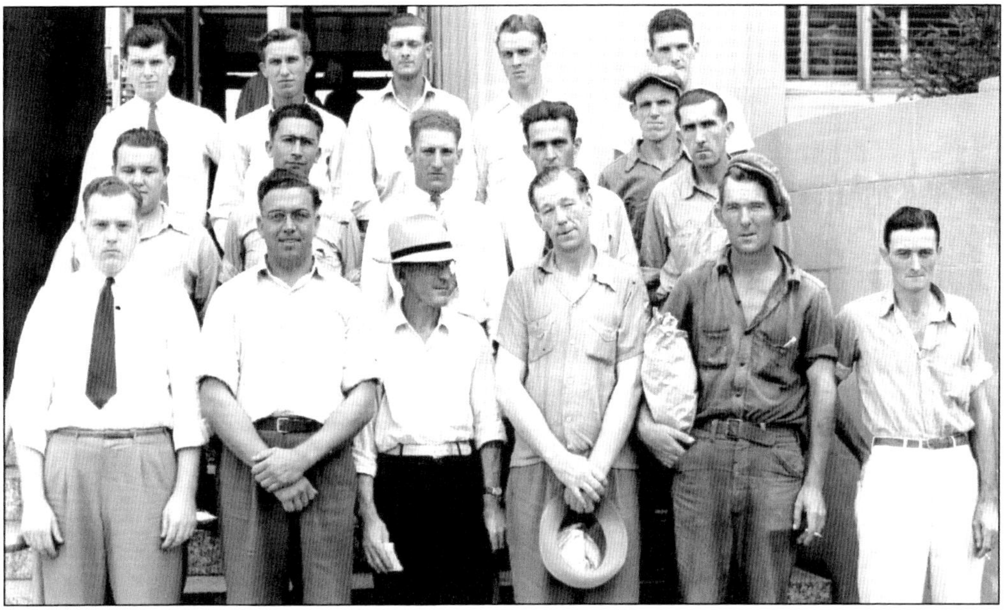

MACON COUNTY DRAFTEES, AUGUST 1942. This group of draftees represents a true cross-section of the community, including laborers like the man in the front row holding the paper bag to businessmen like the fellows with ties and pressed shirts. Decatur sent some 6,000 draftees into the war. Over 10 million Americans served in the war, and about 309,000 gave their lives. (Courtesy Decatur Public Library.)

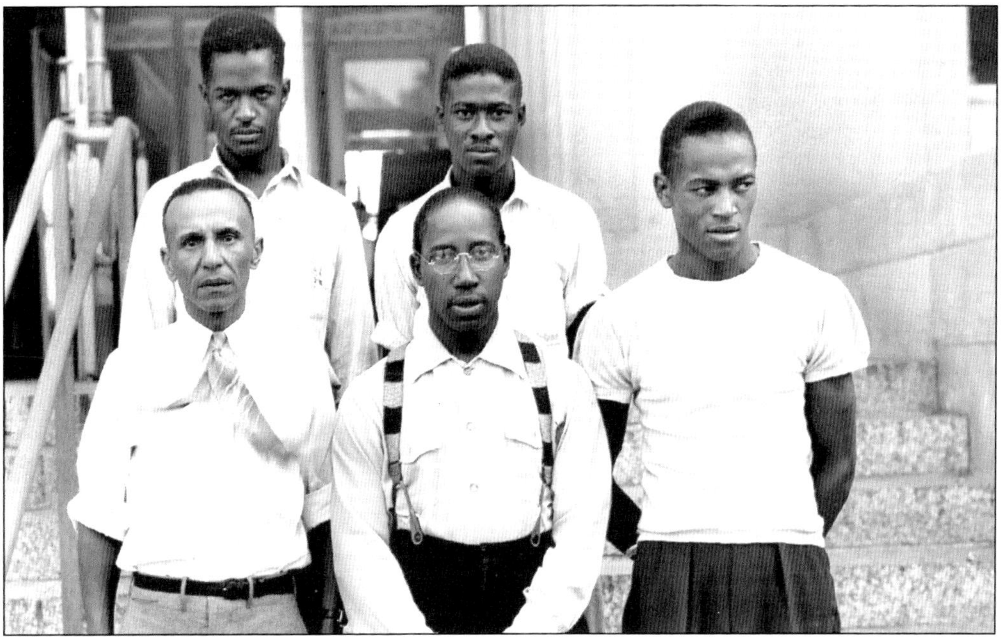

AFRICAN-AMERICAN DRAFTEES, SEPTEMBER 1942. Later in the war, draftees were not grouped or photographed by race as in this September 16, 1942 photograph. From left to right the men are as follows: (first row) Major Holliday, Quenton Fort, and Robert Jones; (second row) Joseph Hunt, and Grady Hinton. The men were then sent to Peoria for further processing. (Courtesy Decatur Public Library.)

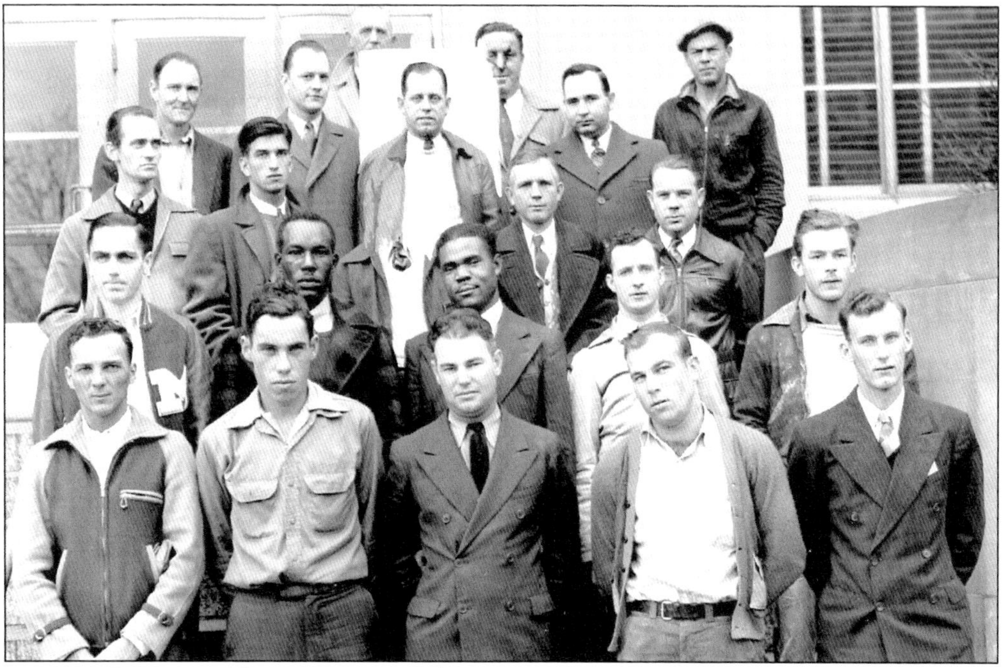

DECATUR DRAFTEES, NOVEMBER 1942. A heterogeneous group—in terms of race and class—stood outside the Draft Board on a mild November 7, 1942, 11 months after the war had begun. Note the man on the left side wearing the Millikin University letter jacket. These men were then sent on to Peoria for additional processing. (Courtesy Decatur Public Library.)

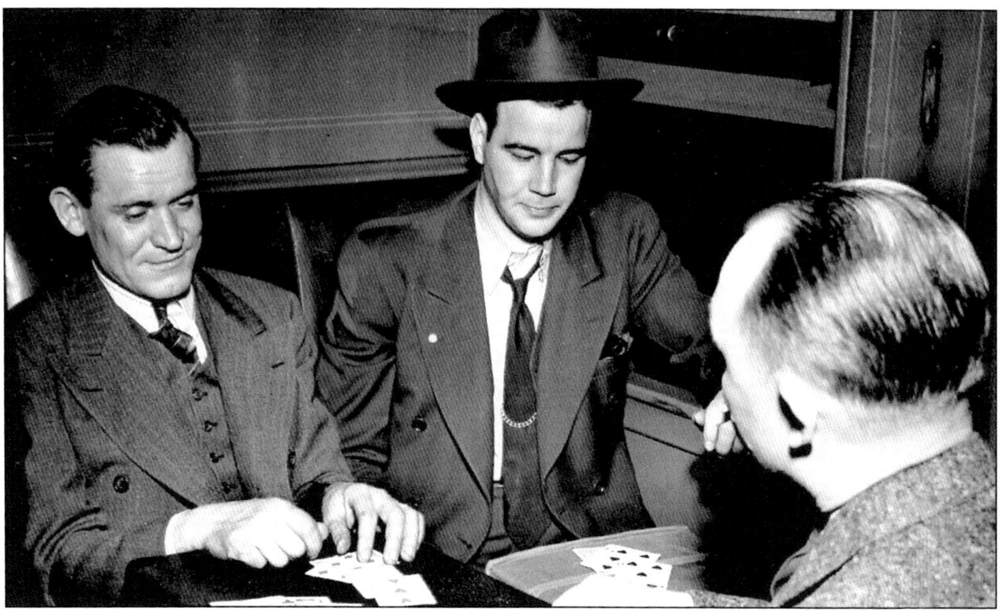

PREWAR DRAFTEES PLAYING CARDS. The draft or Compulsory Military Training Act actually began before President Roosevelt's formal declaration of the war on December 8, 1941. This March 21, 1941 photograph shows three draftees enjoying a little game of cards as the Illinois Central Railroad speeds them towards Chicago and more processing. (Courtesy Decatur Public Library.)

ZOOT SUIT. On March 21, 1941, this young man, attired in a snappy zoot suit and hat, peers out of the train window, deeply absorbed in thought. This group of prewar draftees was heading for Chicago, and the conductor seems to have been surprised by the cameraman. For the next four years trains would be swamped with soldiers. (Courtesy Decatur Public Library.)

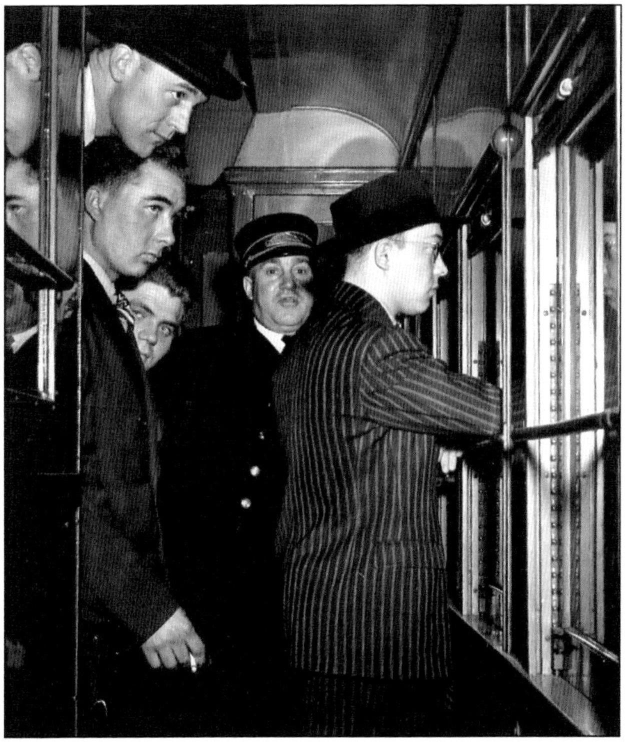

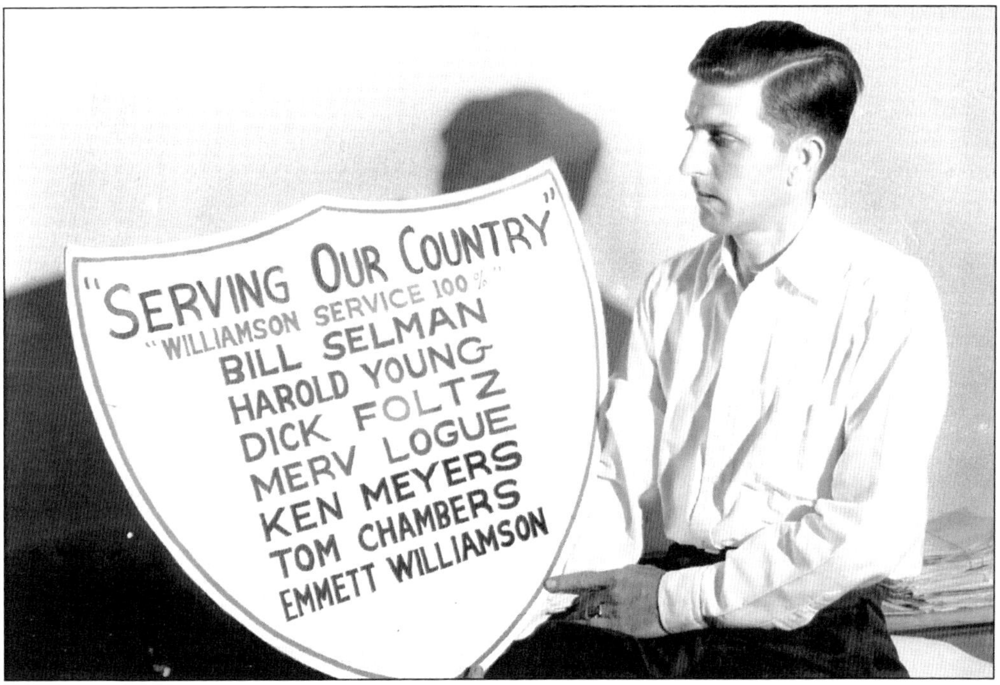

A SHIELD OF SERVICE. On June 7, 1942, Emmett Williamson, who had been the owner of a profitable service station, decided to follow the lead of his six former employees, and volunteer for service in the Army. The shield symbolizes the strong service ethic of Williamson and his crew and that of the whole wartime community. (Courtesy Decatur Public Library.)

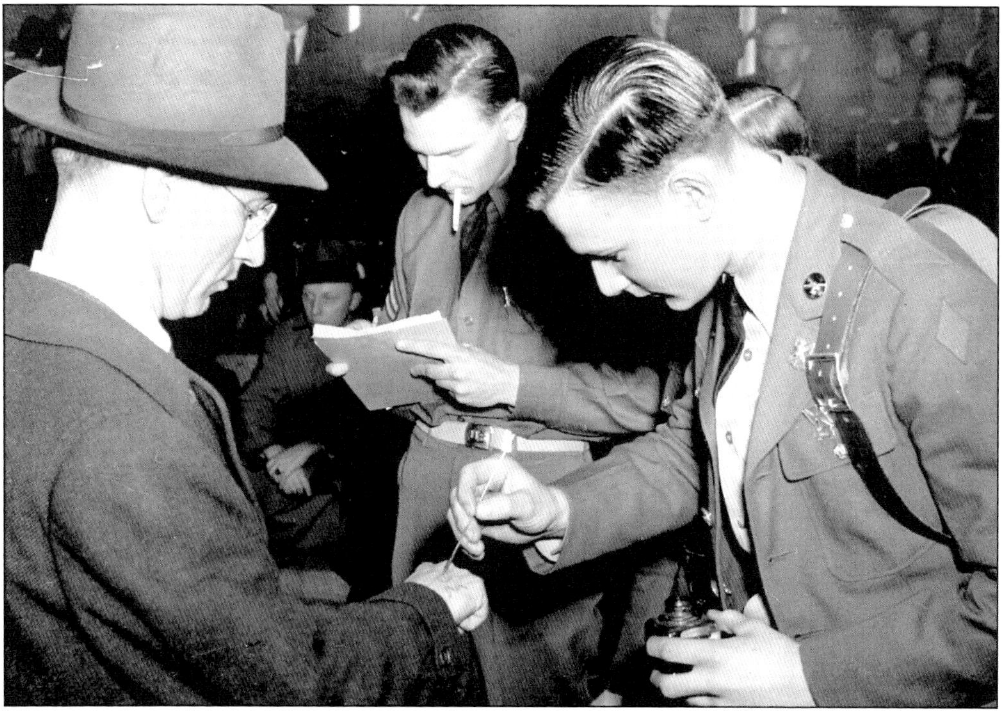

GETTING INKED. Millikin University violin instructor Raymond Earl Duffey (left) has his hand inked with a number by Pvt. Allen M. Hill (right) at the Chicago Armory as part of a prewar induction. Duffey and 107 other men from Decatur were sent to Chicago as part of the Compulsory Military Training Act on March 21, 1941. (Courtesy Decatur Public Library.)

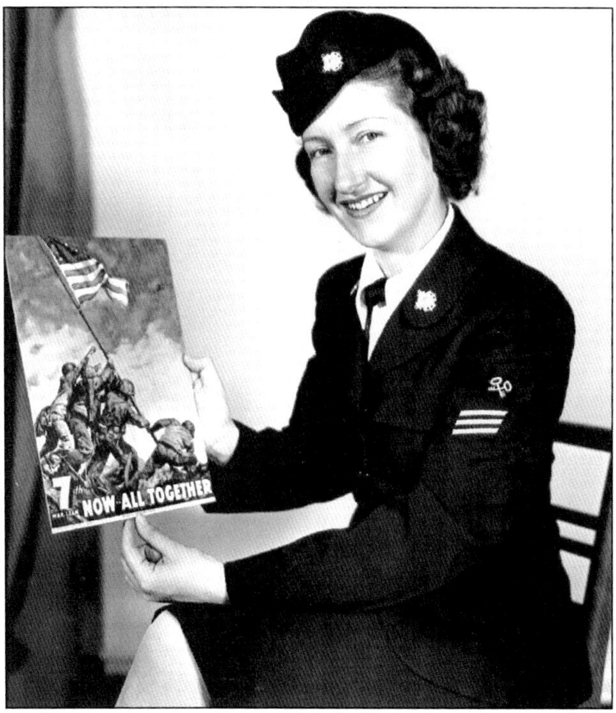

ESTHER MAUDE DELONG. Seaman First Class Esther Maude DeLong, a SPAR in the Coast Guard, poses next to a poster for the seventh war loan or bond campaign. "Now all together," reads the slogan. DeLong's desk job freed one more male soldier for field duty. Her brother, Burke DeLong, was fighting in Okinawa when this photograph was taken at Manhattan Beach, New York, June 18, 1945. (Courtesy Decatur Public Library.)

ENSIGN ANN HARP. Ann Harp had served as an instructor in ships and aircraft at the Navy's WAVE school. When this photograph was taken on April 27, 1944, she was the senior officer for procurement at Jacksonville, Florida. She previously had been an English teacher in Decatur. (Courtesy Decatur Public Library.)

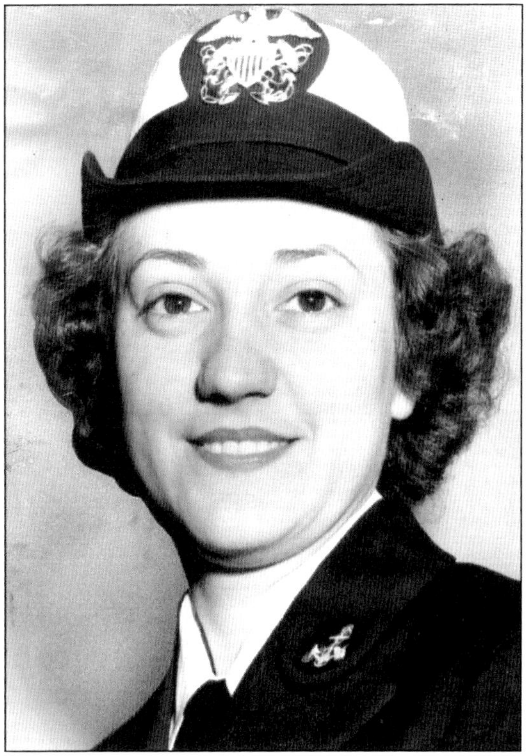

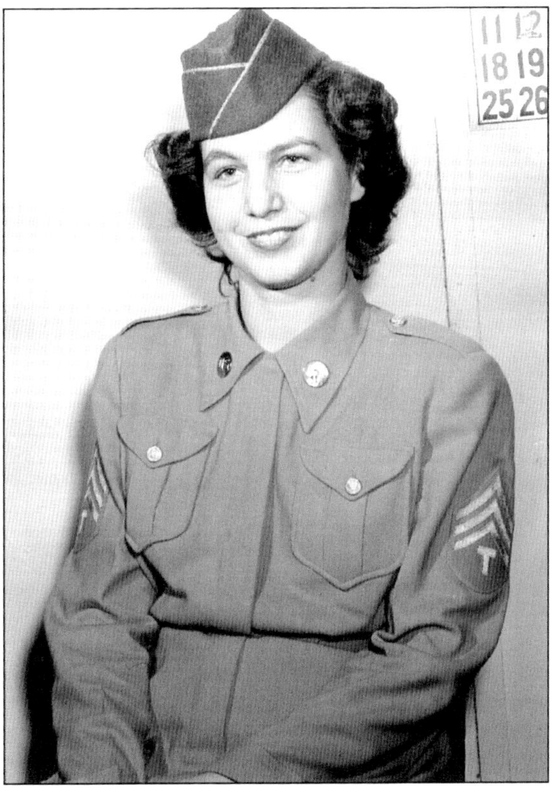

ARMY PHARMACIST. Technical Sgt. Margaret Hoffman serves at the General Hospital in Denver, Colorado, where she is a pharmacy technician. Previously a druggist at St. Mary's Hospital in Decatur, Sergeant Hoffman had been in the Army for 28 months when this photograph was taken on February 18, 1945. (Courtesy Decatur Public Library.)

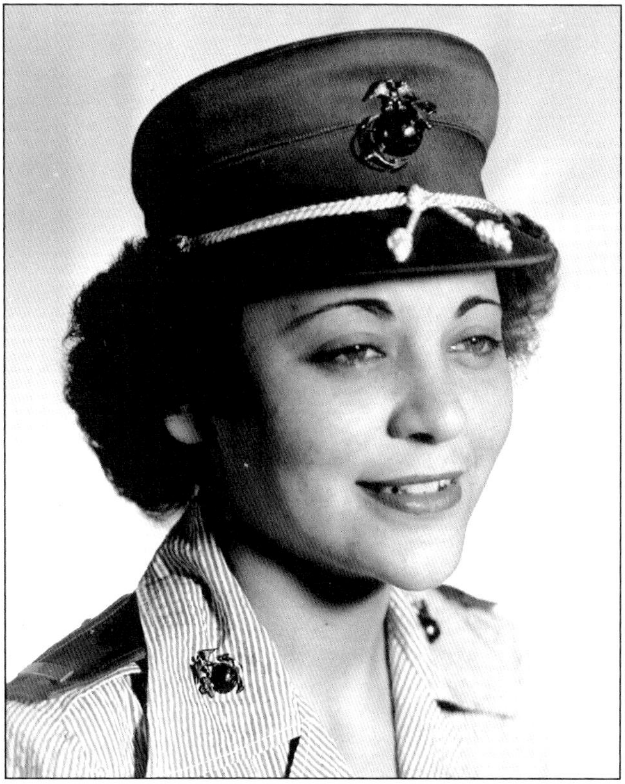

MARINE CORPS SECOND LIEUTENANT. Estelle R. Cohn had just completed officer training when this photograph, dated July 27, 1945, was shot. She was en route to the Marine base at Quantico, Virginia, for her next assignment. Only a few short weeks of war remained. (Courtesy Decatur Public Library.)

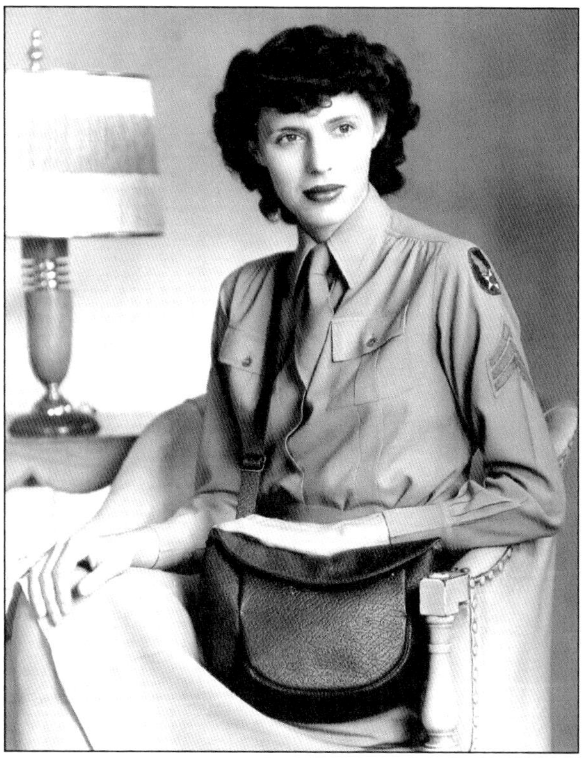

SGT. ANN WEILEPP. Sgt. Ann Weilepp was assigned to Army Air Force communications at an air base in New Mexico. Her husband, Capt. James Weilepp of Decatur, was also stationed at the same base. She is shown in a perfectly pressed uniform in this photograph of June 3, 1945. (Courtesy Decatur Public Library.)

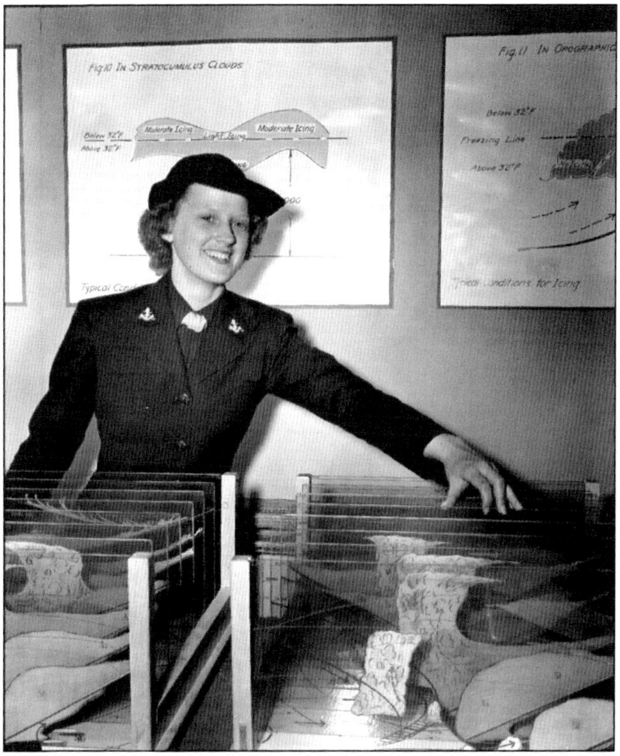

WAVE IN THE CLOUDS. Seaman Norma Jean Walton studies visual aids of cloud formations at Hunter College in New York as part of her WAVE boot camp training in air studies. She attended high school in Decatur and worked at Staley Manufacturing Company before enlisting in the Navy. (Courtesy Decatur Public Library.)

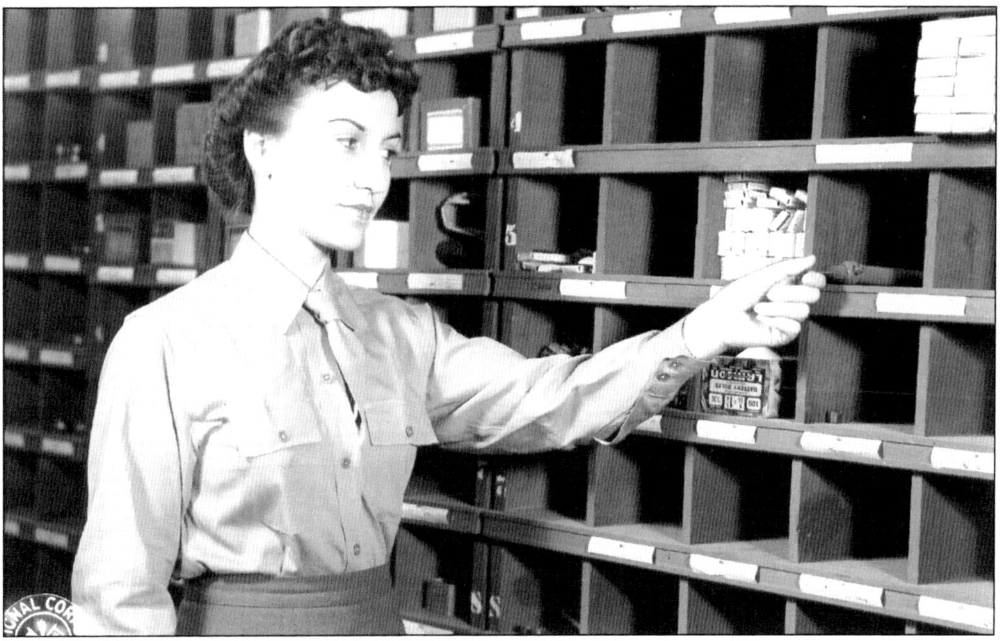

STOCK RECORD CLERK. In this February 28, 1944, photograph, Pfc. Elizabeth Pressley Urbanowicz checks inventory in the ordnance supply warehouse at Fort Brady, Michigan. She married Sgt. M. Urbanowicz at the post chapel. The couple was then given a three-day honeymoon pass before the new groom was transferred to a camp near the Mexican border. (Courtesy Decatur Public Library.)

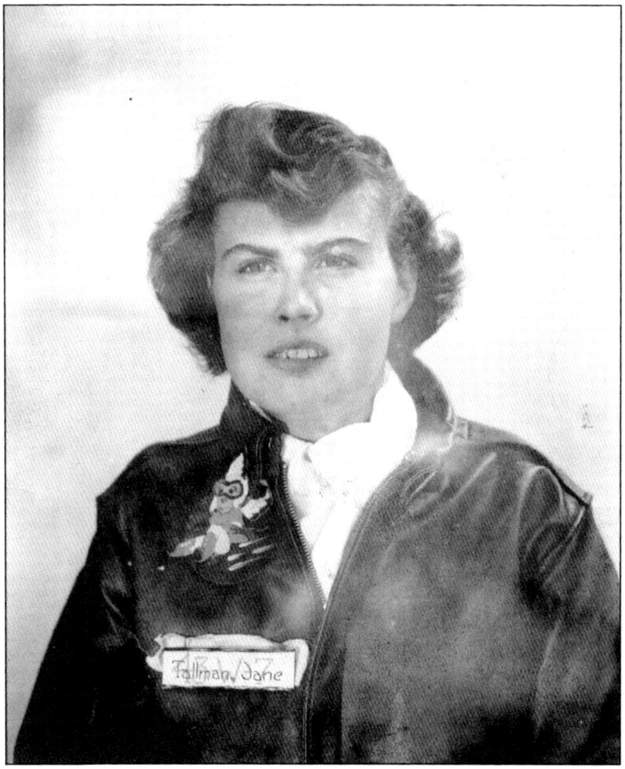

WASP—WOMEN'S AIR FORCE SERVICE PILOT. Taken November 17, 1943, this photograph shows Jane Tallman just after she completed her pilot's training in Sweetwater, Texas. Service pilots flew new bombers from the aircraft plants to the Air Force fields, freeing up combat pilots who were needed in Europe and the Pacific. (Courtesy Decatur Public Library.)

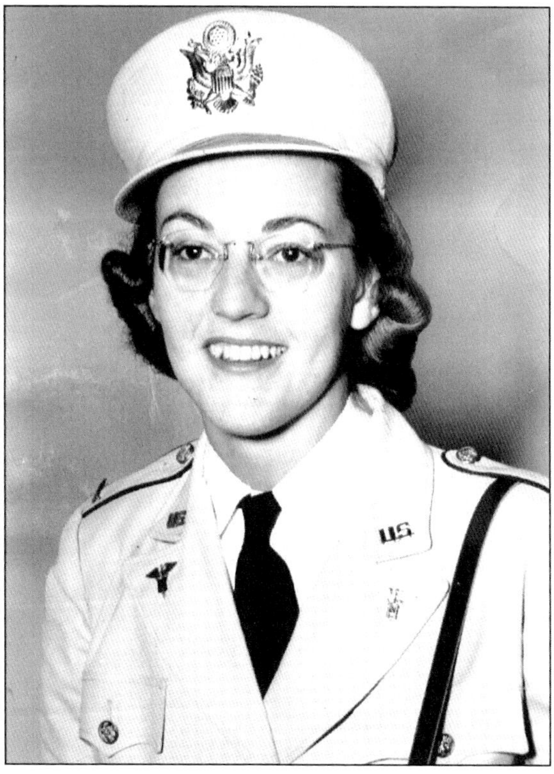

SECOND LT. BARBARA HUSTON. When this photograph was made on August 1, 1943, 2nd Lt. Barbara Huston was in Decatur visiting her father, E. V. Huston. The day after she left, her brother, John, arrived from basic training in Norman, Oklahoma. Although it is partially hidden by her cap, Lieutenant Huston sports a wavy coiffure typical of the period. (Courtesy Decatur Public Library.)

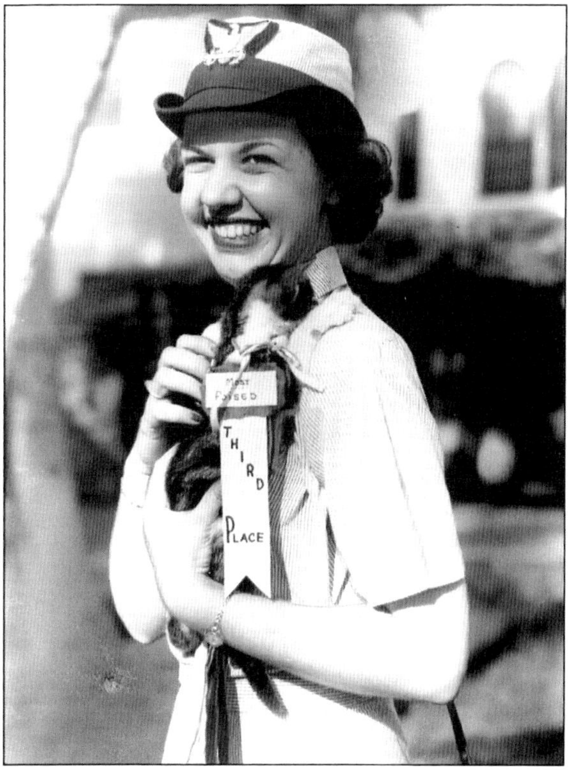

ENSIGN RUTH SUTHERLAND AND "BOOTIE." Bootie was named after the new SPARS in the Coast Guard, also called "booties." She had just won third place in a pet show at the Coast Guard training station in Palm Beach, Florida. Such activities might seem frivolous, but they helped to boost morale during the hectic days of the war. This photograph was taken on October 18, 1944. (Courtesy Decatur Public Library.)

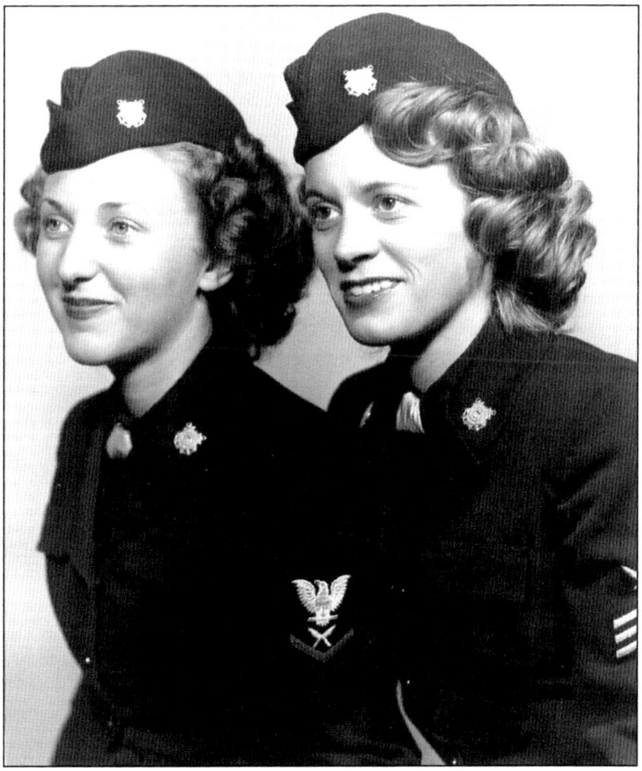

A PAIR OF SPARS. Ruth Scheiter (left), yeoman third class, and Jayne Peel (right), seaman first class, strike a pose in this portrait made on February 19, 1945. The women were old friends and attended Decatur High School together, graduating in the class of 1941. Both had attended college for a few years before enlisting, Peel at Illinois State Normal College and Schieter at Millikin University. (Courtesy Decatur Public Library.)

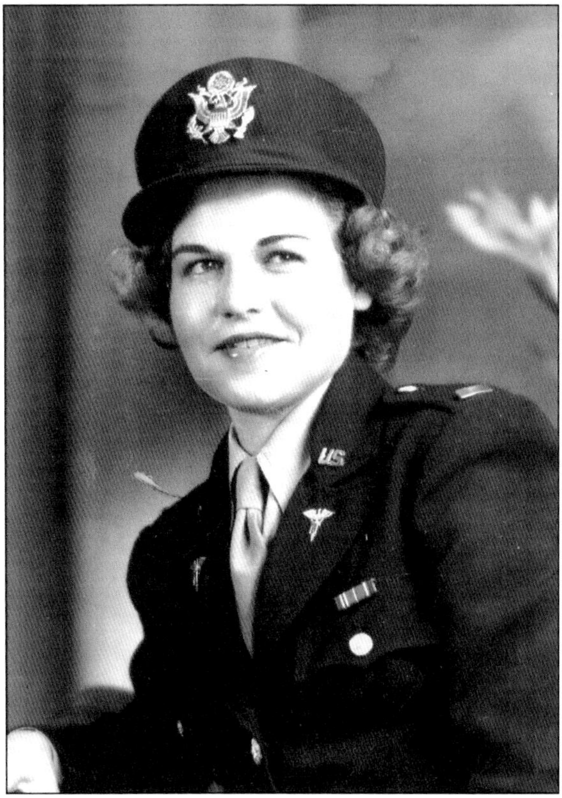

SECOND LT. ENID SCHAUB. Stationed in Oran, Algeria, 2nd Lt. Enid Schaub was serving with the medical staff at the Army hospital. She was in charge of central supply, keeping track of such crucial items as sterile materials, surgical instruments, and trays. "Things are different here in the States," she quietly observed. This photograph was taken on April 1, 1944. (Courtesy Decatur Public Library.)

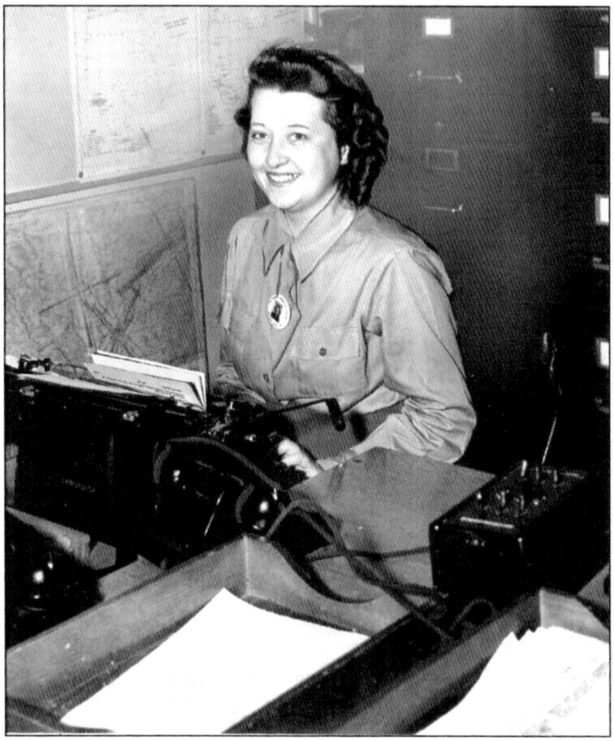

WAC CLERK IN SAN FRANCISCO. Rosemary Moore, shown at the typewriter in this August 27, 1943, photograph, had just finished five months of service in the Women's Army Corps, including basic training at Fort Oglethorpe, Georgia and additional training at Conway, Arkansas. Note the identification badge pinned to her khaki tie. (Courtesy Decatur Public Library.)

RED CROSS RECREATION WORKER. This photograph of Betty South was taken outside of London in the spring of 1944, just before D-Day. Accompanied by three other Decatur women, South was in England serving as a Red Cross Recreation Worker. Her unique uniform rarely appears in photographs of the period. (Courtesy Decatur Public Library.)

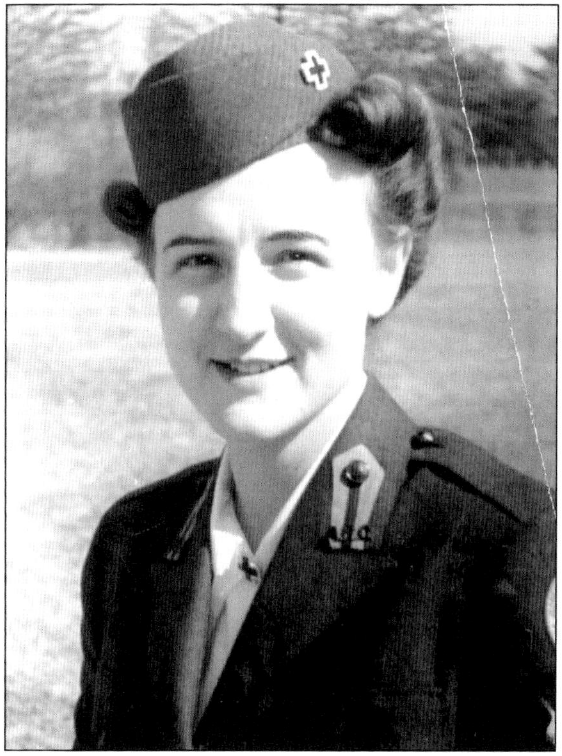

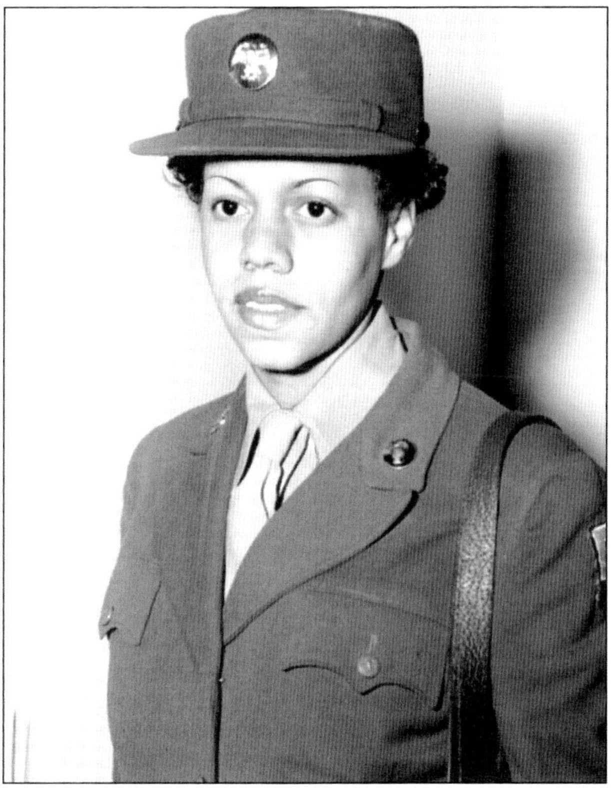

PVT. GERTRUDE HUNT. Pvt. Gertrude Hunt served as a WAC on Staten Island, New York. Her husband, Pvt. Laban Hunt, was stationed in California, and her brother, Pvt. Julius Mason, was serving at Camp Beauregard, Louisiana. The photograph was taken October 17, 1943, while she was in Decatur on furlough. (Courtesy Decatur Public Library.)

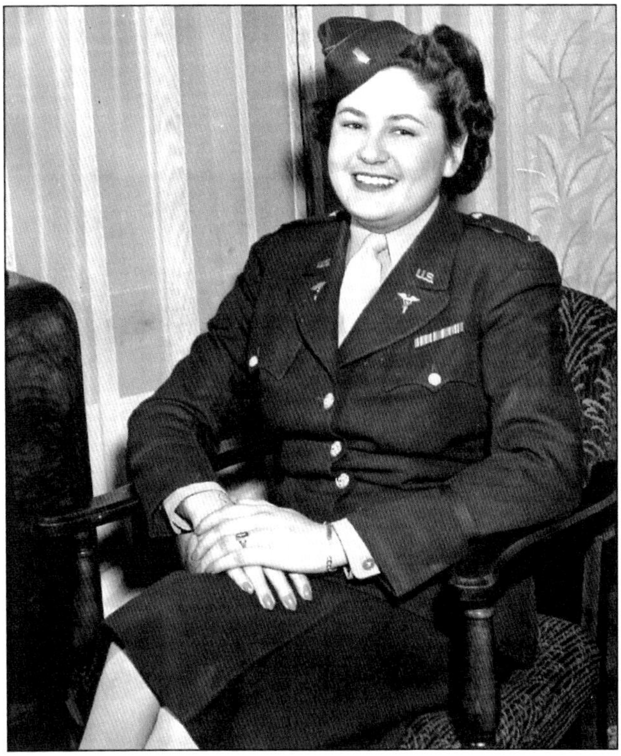

Lt. Velera Matson. Lt. Velera Matson was visiting Decatur in February 1944, after four months of intensive service as a nurse in North Africa. She returned home on a ship filled with many wounded American soldiers. "We were glad to be getting home," she confided. (Courtesy Decatur Public Library.)

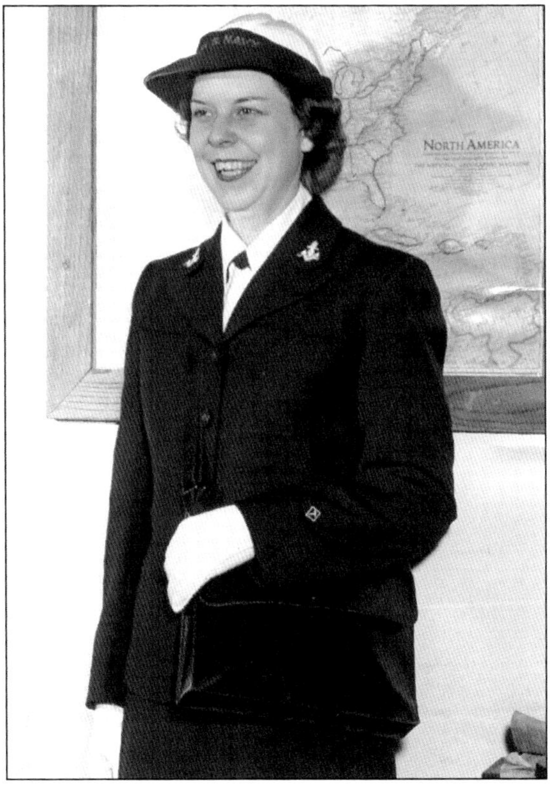

"Link" Telephone Operator. Seaman First Class Lois Daniels, who was serving in Pensacola, Florida, was visiting her mother in Decatur when this photograph was snapped on October 29, 1944. Her job was to train Navy men. Before the war, Louis worked in the classified advertising department of the *Herald-Review* newspaper. (Courtesy Decatur Public Library.)

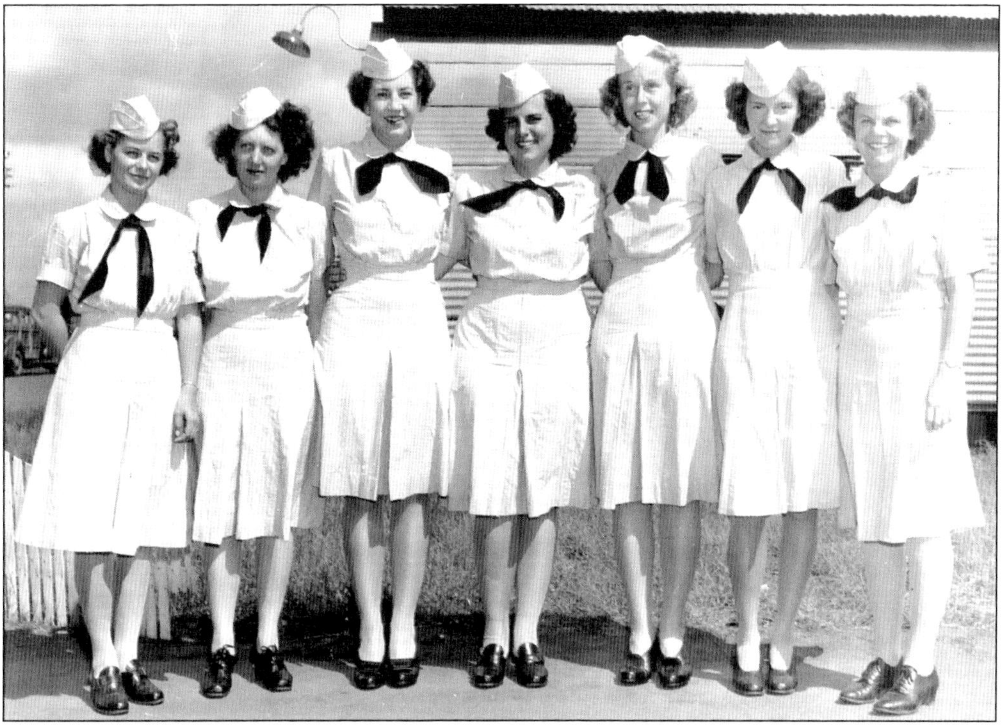

Yeoman Third Class Cora Jane Wasson. Yeoman Cora Jane Wasson is standing in the very center of this line of seven WAVES on a naval base in Hawaii. Wasson, a former Millikin student, completed basic training at Hunter College and preflight training in Iowa City, Iowa. The photograph was taken June 30, 1945, about six weeks before the end of the war. (Courtesy Decatur Public Library.)

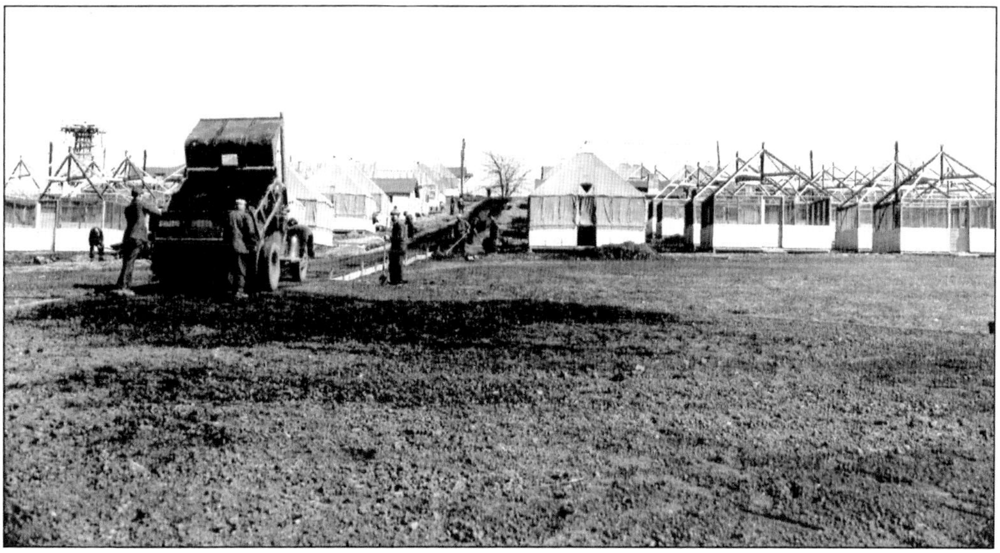

Army Tent Camp on Lake Decatur. In April 1942, the U.S. Army created a rest and recreation area for troops near Lake Decatur. Among other activities, the Army sponsored dances, card games, dinners, and group singing. In this shot, a dump truck is spreading fill dirt along a roadway between the tents. (Courtesy Decatur Public Library.)

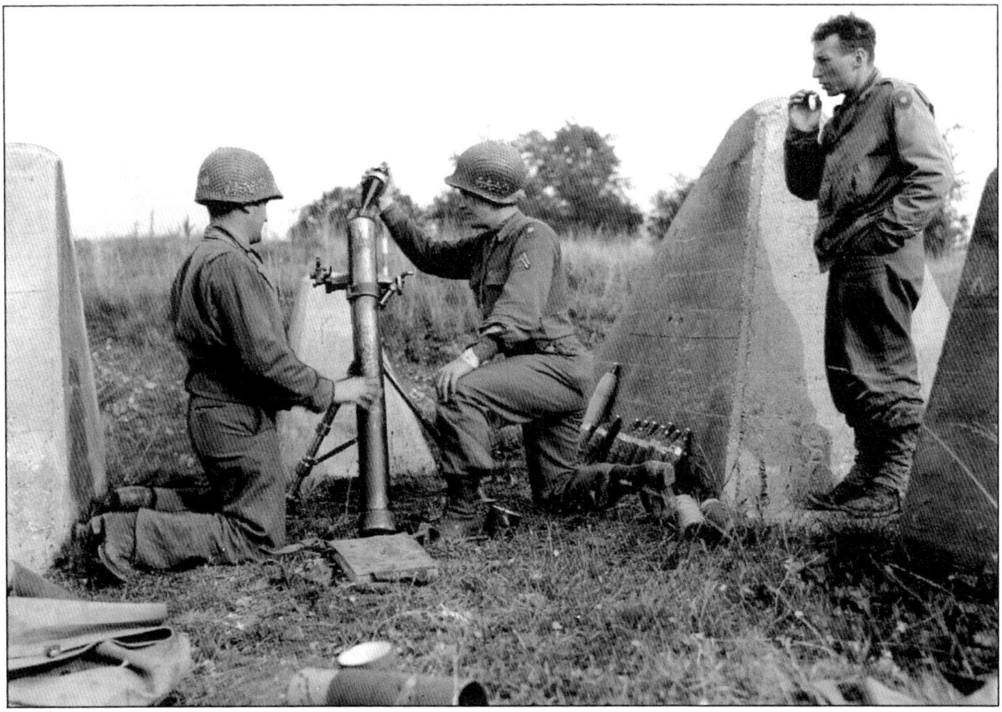

ON THE SIEGFRIED LINE. Cpl. Kenneth Ferguson, kneeling on the right, feeds a shell into an 81 millimeter mortar which has been set up in the midst of the concrete "dragon's teeth" that form the Siegfried Line near Lammersdorf, Germany. This photograph was taken December 19, 1944. (Courtesy Decatur Public Library.)

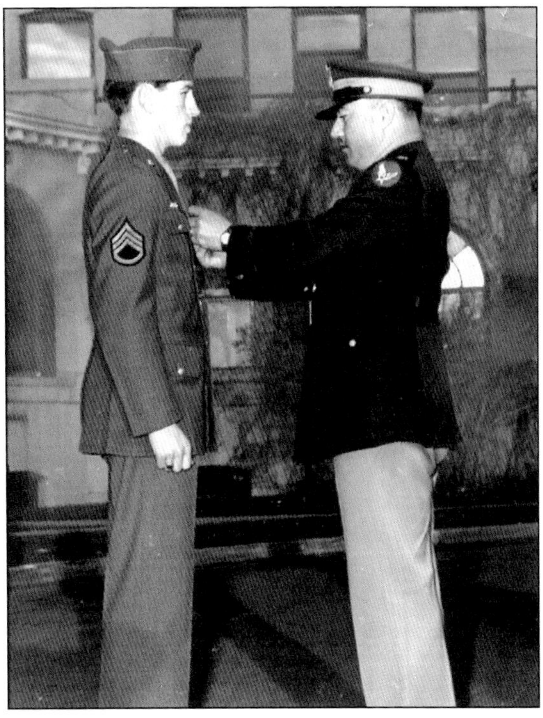

DISTINGUISHED FLYING CROSS. S.Sgt. Melburn L. Cox is shown here receiving the Distinguished Flying Cross (DFC) from Col. R. P. Todd on December 18, 1944. S.Sgt. Cox was trained as a ball turret gunner and flew 30 missions over Europe. He was already decorated with the Air Medal and three Oak Leaf clusters. (Courtesy Decatur Public Library.)

CPL. GEORGE EATON JR. Cpl. George Eaton Jr. was photographed during a three-week furlough on May 25, 1945, shortly after Germany surrendered. Corporal Eaton had served in Egypt, North Africa, Sicily, Italy, England, France, and Germany. Although he had won many decorations, he wore only a few because he didn't want to "look like a German officer." (Courtesy Decatur Public Library.)

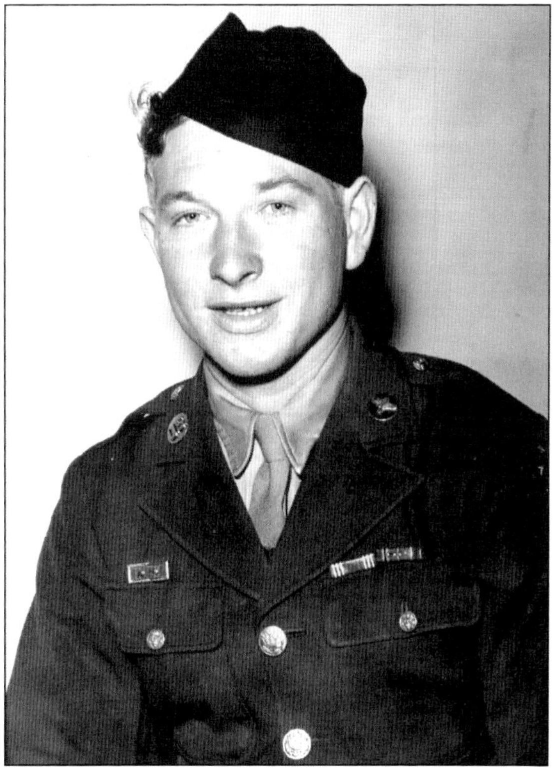

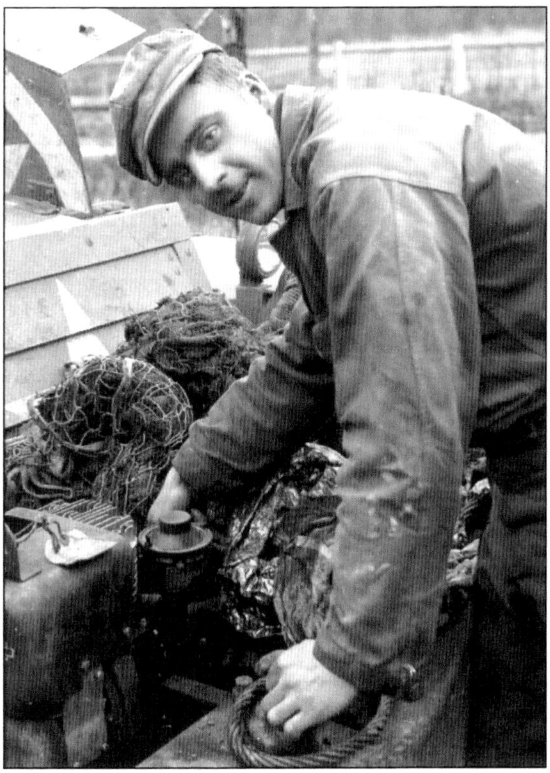

REPAIRING A GENERATOR. On May 5, 1945, Donald Tipsword, Technician Fourth Grade, is shown repairing a power generator somewhere in Germany around the time of the surrender. Tipsword had been in the Army for three years; previously he was employed as a mechanic at Laswell's Garage in Decatur. (Courtesy Decatur Public Library.)

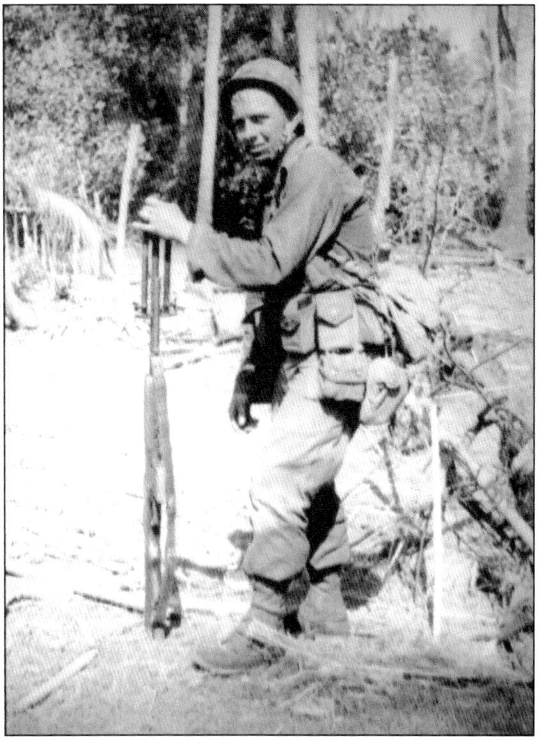

FIGHTING IN LUZON, PHILIPPINE ISLANDS. Pfc. John L. Shribner, infantry automatic rifleman, is shown taking a break during the Luzon campaign in this January 29, 1945, photograph. Service in the Pacific was especially onerous because the Japanese Imperial Army and the physical environments were both implacable foes. (Courtesy Decatur Public Library.)

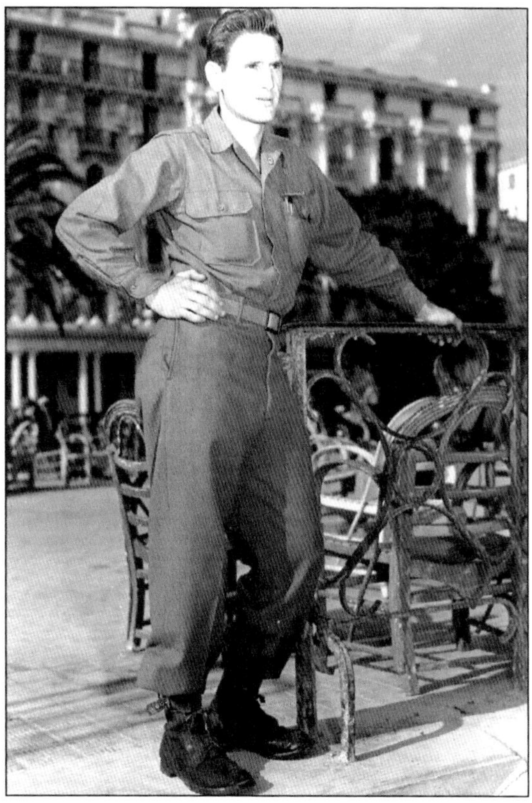

ON THE RIVIERA. Pfc. Loren Lauter is shown striking a pose on the French Riviera during the last days of the war in Europe. Private First Class Lauter was visiting the U.S. Army Riviera Recreational Area, located on the Mediterranean coast in Nice, France. Not every soldier was as lucky as Lauter, and he seems to be savoring the moment. (Courtesy Decatur Public Library.)

Pvt. Charles Cook Jr. Pvt. Charles Cook Jr. appears young enough to still be in high school, and he probably joined the Army shortly after graduation, like millions of other American men and women. He served as an artilleryman. This photograph was taken on February 26, 1944. (Courtesy Decatur Public Library.)

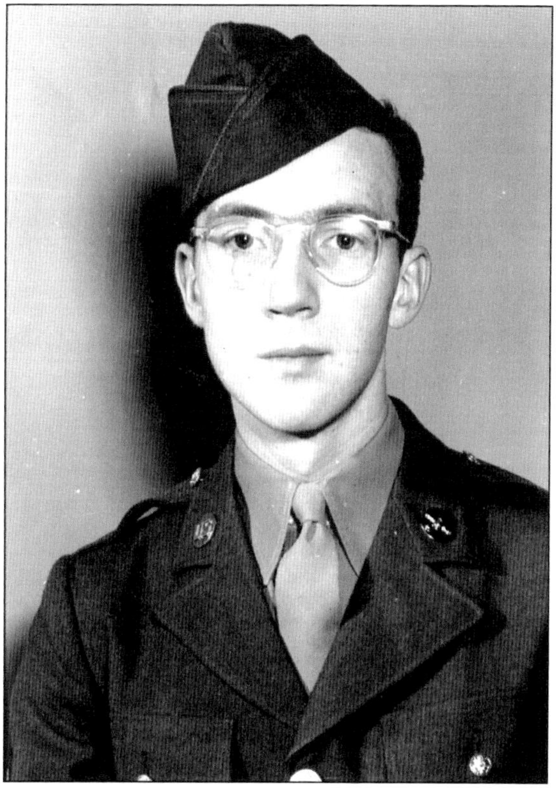

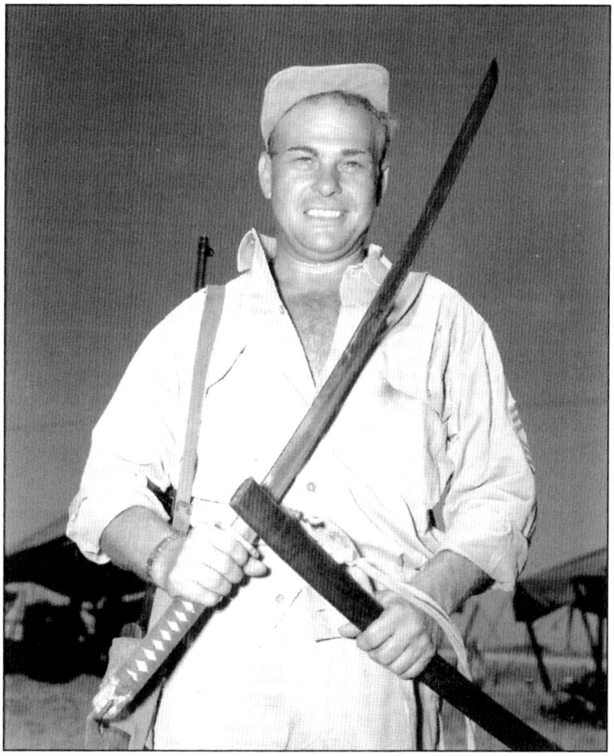

Captured Samurai Sword. M.Sgt. Charles R. Kinney helped to kill 12 Japanese in a single raid where, presumably, this sword was taken as a trophy. This particular raid took place in a rice paddy in the Philippines. Master Sergeant Kinney had also served in New Guinea. He was a crack shot with a carbine. This photograph was taken on June 10, 1945. (Courtesy Decatur Public Library.)

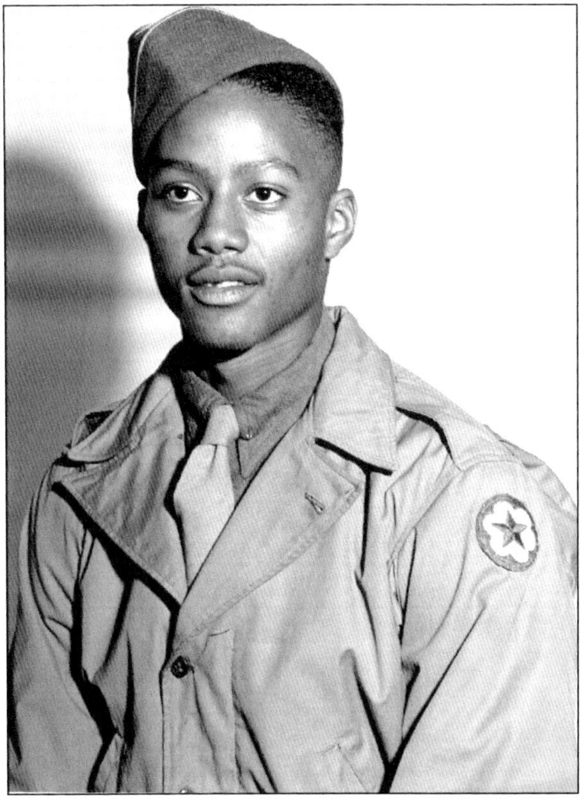

PVT. ROY WILLIAMS. Roy Williams was an outstanding athlete during the 1942–1943 high school season; he excelled in basketball and football. After graduating from Decatur High School, he immediately joined the Army and was assigned to the Transportation Corps in New Orleans. This photograph was taken on October 29, 1943 during a 12 day furlough. (Courtesy Decatur Public Library.)

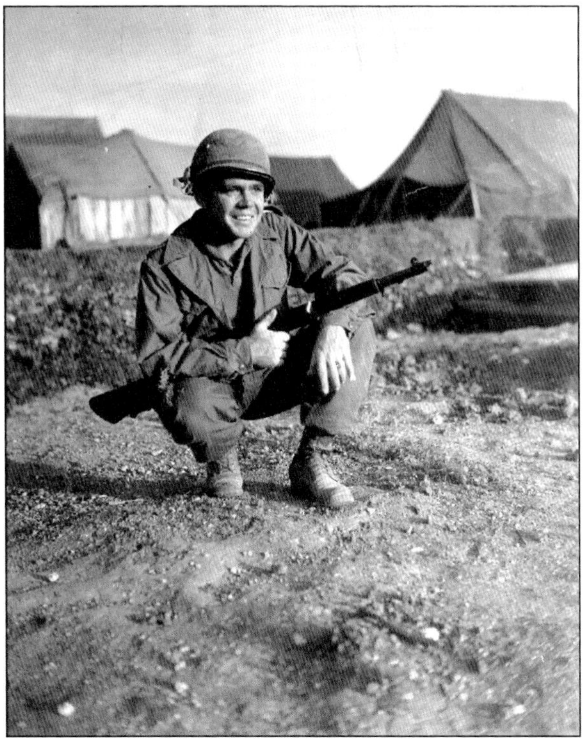

PFC. LEO GRANT ON OKINAWA. Private First Class Grant served with the combat engineers on Leyte and Okinawa, where he was involved with the construction and repair of roads and bridges. Before the war, he was employed at A. E. Staley Manufacturing Company. The photograph was taken in June 1944. (Courtesy Decatur Public Library.)

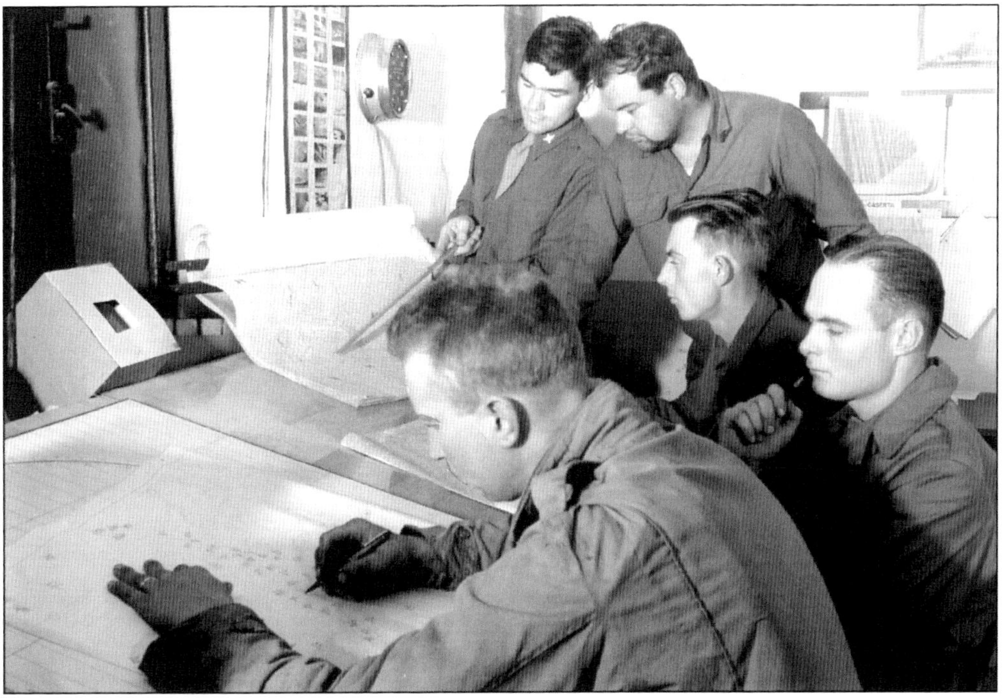

WEATHER FORECASTING IN ITALY. Instructing members of a B-17 Flying Fortress crew crowd around at a base in Italy in April 1944. Seen here is 2nd Lt. Paul Green (left, rear, holding the pointer). Lieutenant Green completed his aviation meteorology cadet training at Grand Rapids, Michigan. (Courtesy Decatur Public Library.)

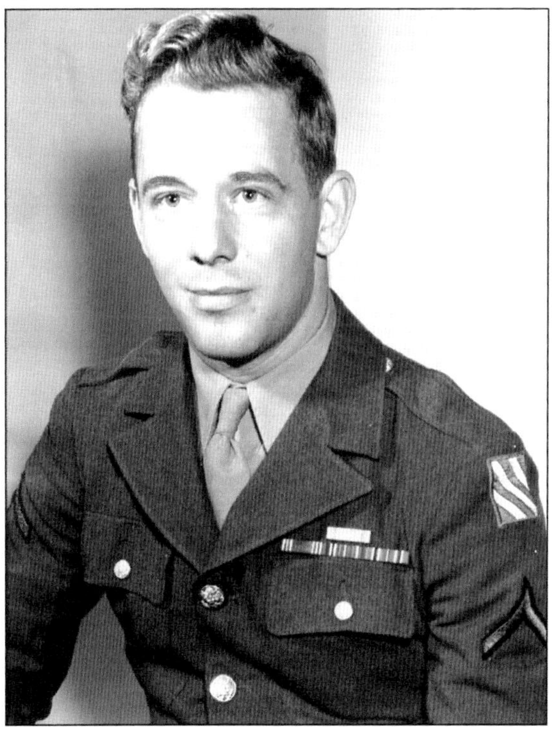

PFC. WILLIAM A. GATES. Private First Class Gates was proud to have served with "Old Blood and Guts" Gen. George Patton in North Africa and Sicily. His favorite experiences were the live United Service Organizations (USO) shows featuring popular stars like Carole Landis, Martha Raye, Al Jolson, and Adolph Menjou. He is shown in this April 18, 1944, photograph. (Courtesy Decatur Public Library.)

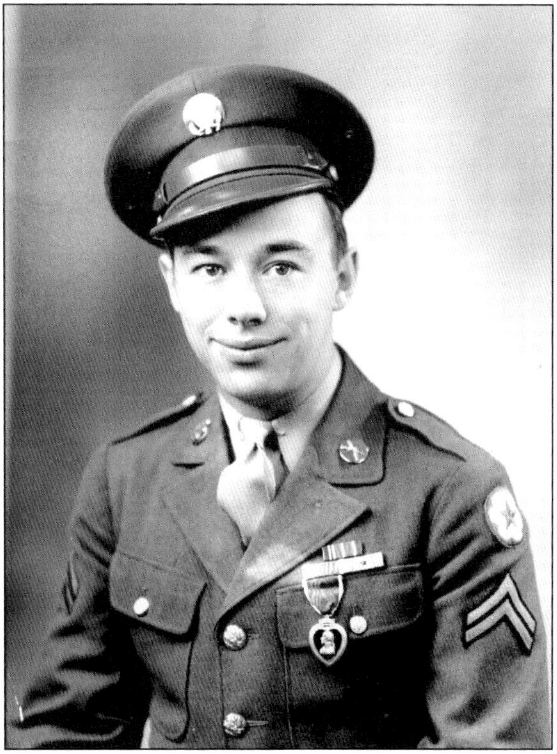

Recipient of Purple Heart. Cpl. Dale Miller smiles proudly in this photograph taken on February 12, 1943, after his recuperation at the Walter Reed Hospital in Washington, D.C. Miller was wounded during the invasion of North Africa. (Courtesy Decatur Public Library.)

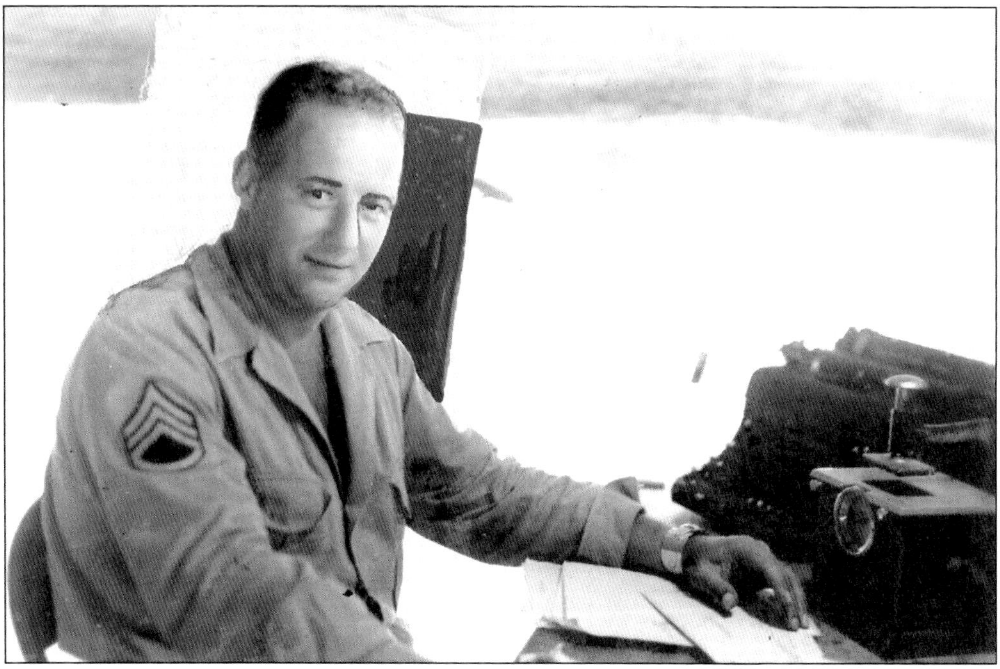

S.Sgt. Henry Musselman. This photograph was taken on August 18, 1944, somewhere in the South Pacific Area about one year before the end of the war with Japan. S.Sgt. Henry Musselman served as a chief message clerk for an entire company. Before the war, he worked for Standard Oil Company of Indiana. (Courtesy Decatur Public Library.)

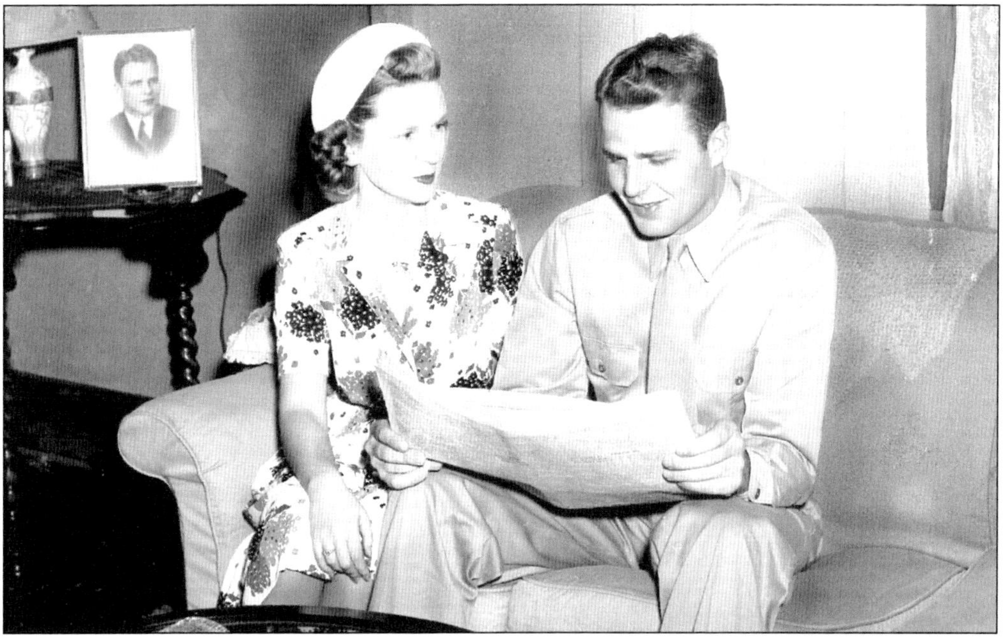

JACK AND CAROLYN COUGHLIN. Cpl. Jack Coughlin is seen visiting with his wife, Carolyn, in this June 24, 1942 photograph. Sailing from England as part of a convoy, his ship was torpedoed by a German submarine 60 miles off the New England coast. In spite of this mishap, Corporal Coughlin made it home safely. He was en route to officer's training school at Camp Davis, North Carolina. (Courtesy Decatur Public Library.)

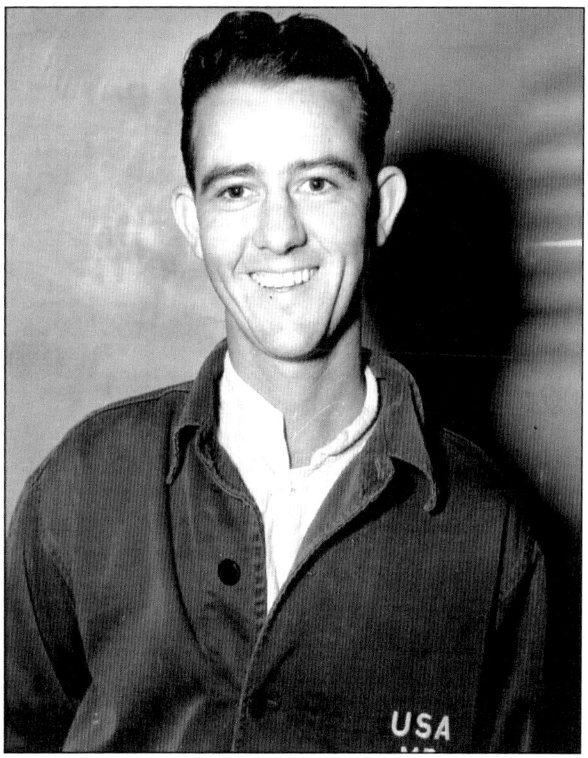

BUSHMASTER. Pfc. Melvin Mize of Decatur is pictured here in this May 4, 1945 image from Letterman General Hospital, San Francisco, where he was recovering from wounds received in fighting on Luzon. Mize was a member of the famed 158th Regiment, the "Bushmasters." (Courtesy Decatur Public Library.)

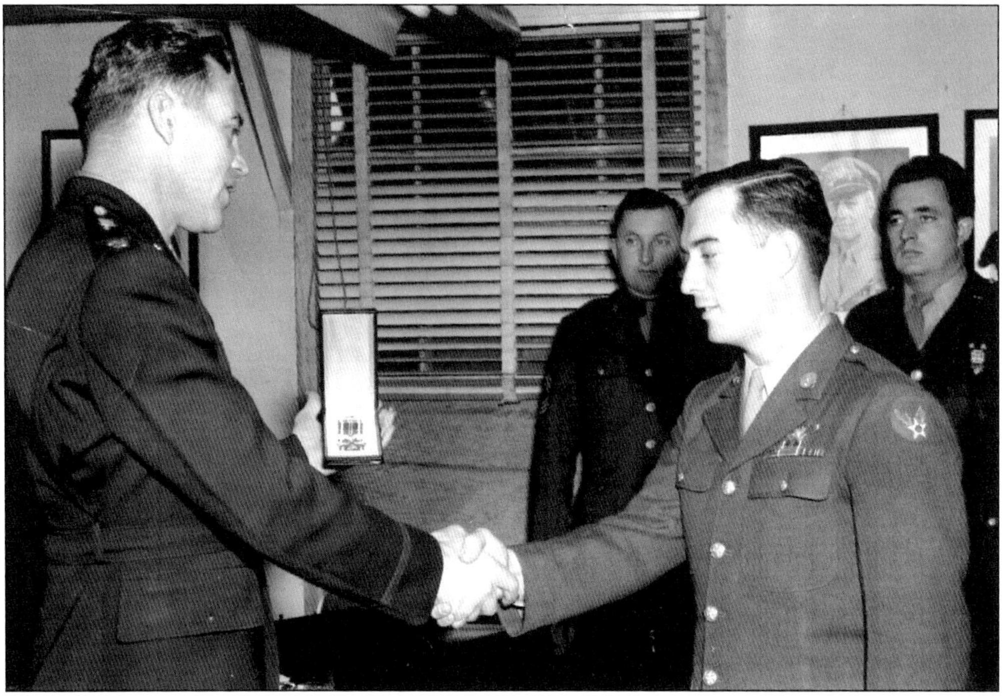

WAIST GUNNER RECEIVES DFC. Sgt. Samuel Conroy receives the Distinguished Flying Cross in Blytheville, Arkansas on December 20, 1944 for "extraordinary achievement" while flying 25 missions in a B-17 Flying Fortress bomber over "enemy occupied Europe." (Courtesy Decatur Public Library.)

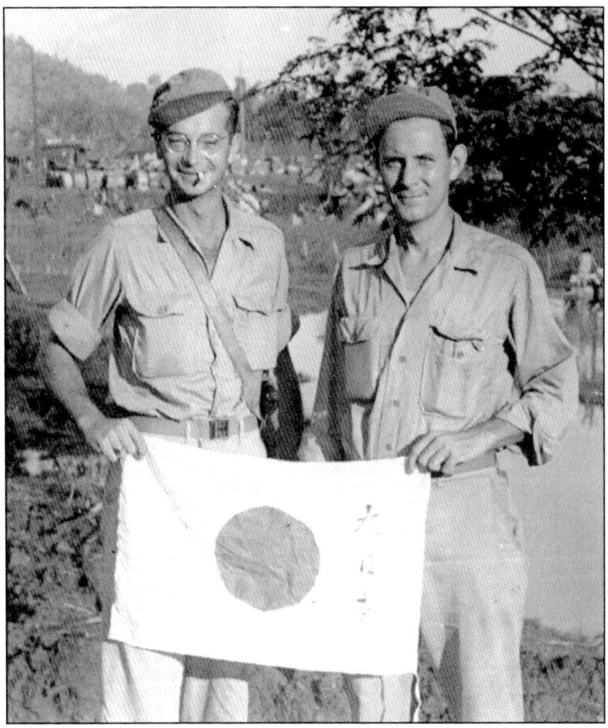

JAPANESE BATTLE FLAG. On January 18, 1945, Cpl. Wade Garner (left) and Cpl. Robert Meadows (right) proudly exhibit a captured Japanese battle flag. Given the tenacity and ferocity of the Japanese Imperial Army, this flag was a very special keepsake. (Courtesy Decatur Public Library.)

MEDICAL DISCHARGE. Pfc. Ralph Duddleston was given a medical discharge for wounds he incurred during the Tunisian campaign. Duddleston was on duty for 18 months in North Africa and the Middle East. About returning stateside, he said, "You feel so tickled to be home." This photograph is dated January 30, 1944. (Courtesy Decatur Public Library.)

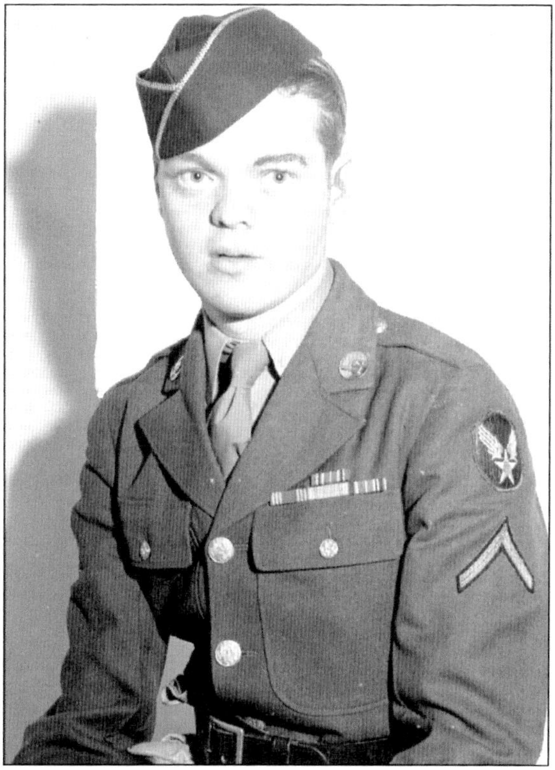

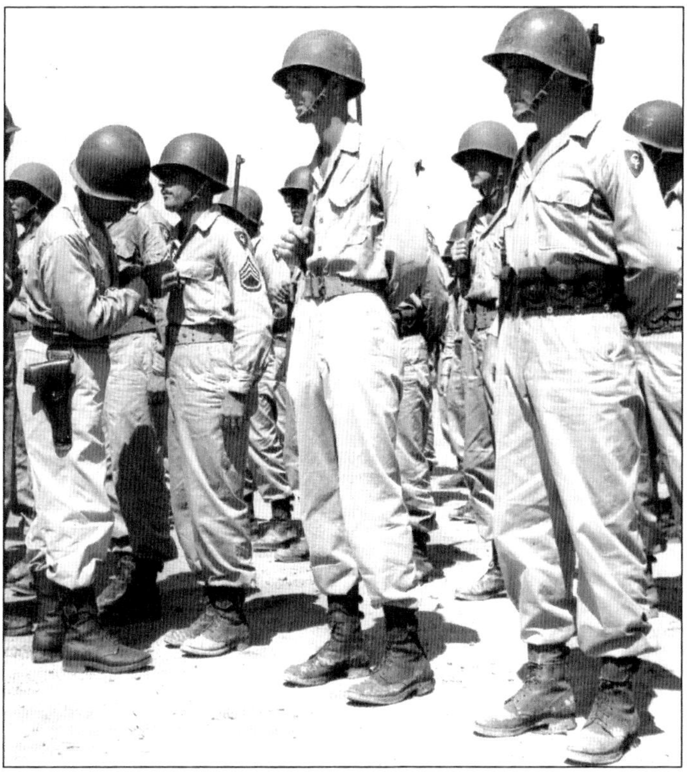

DECORATED ON LUZON. S.Sgt. Richard Jostes received the Bronze Star on September 22, 1945—after the war had ended—from Maj. Gen. William Chase. Luzon was a "hot spot" for Decatur soldiers; many saw action there. Jostes was a member of the 38th Division, 149th Infantry Regiment. (Courtesy Decatur Public Library.)

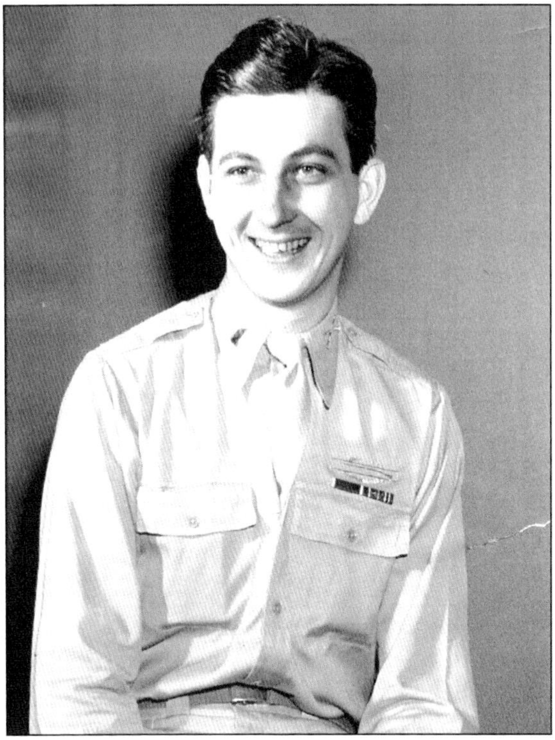

MILLION-DOLLAR WOUND. Lt. Orville Harlan received a grenade wound to the foot in the Hurtgen Forest in Germany. The only evidence is a slight incision in his foot, requiring him to sit and wait for the healing to occur. Harlan was put in a litter and flown home on a C-57 aircraft. This photograph was taken April 30, 1945. (Courtesy Decatur Public Library.)

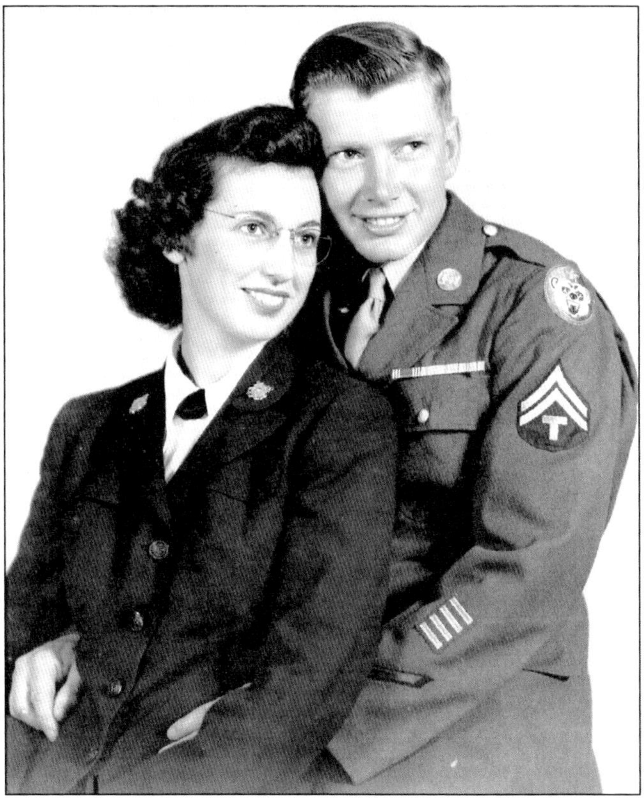

INTER-SERVICE MARRIAGE. Figuratively, the Coast Guard married the Army when Yeoman Evelyn Lorene Friis married Cpl. Darrell C. Dash in a parsonage outside Decatur. Corporal Dash had just returned from 30 months of service in the Aleutian Islands. The happy couple is all smiles in this August 29, 1944, wedding portrait. (Courtesy Decatur Public Library.)

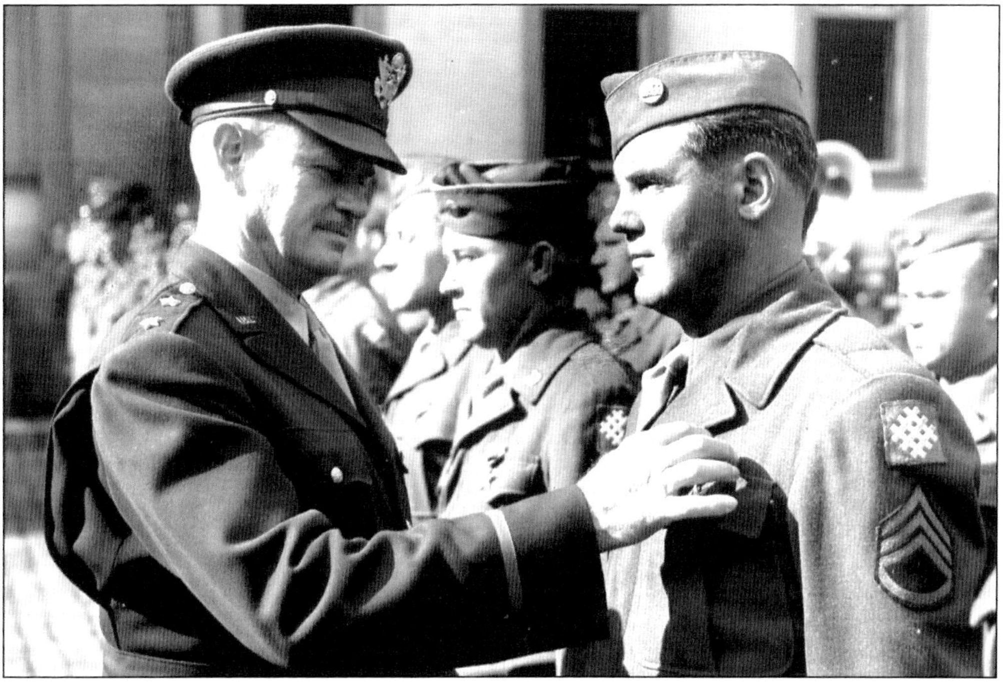

S.Sgt. Foustine Endrizzi. Maj. Gen. Davis Barr is seen here pinning a Bronze Star medal for meritorious achievement on S.Sgt. Foustine Endrizzi late in June of 1945, after Germany surrendered. He served with an antiaircraft artillery battalion during the Allied march into Germany. Endrizzi's family still resides in Decatur. (Courtesy Decatur Public Library.)

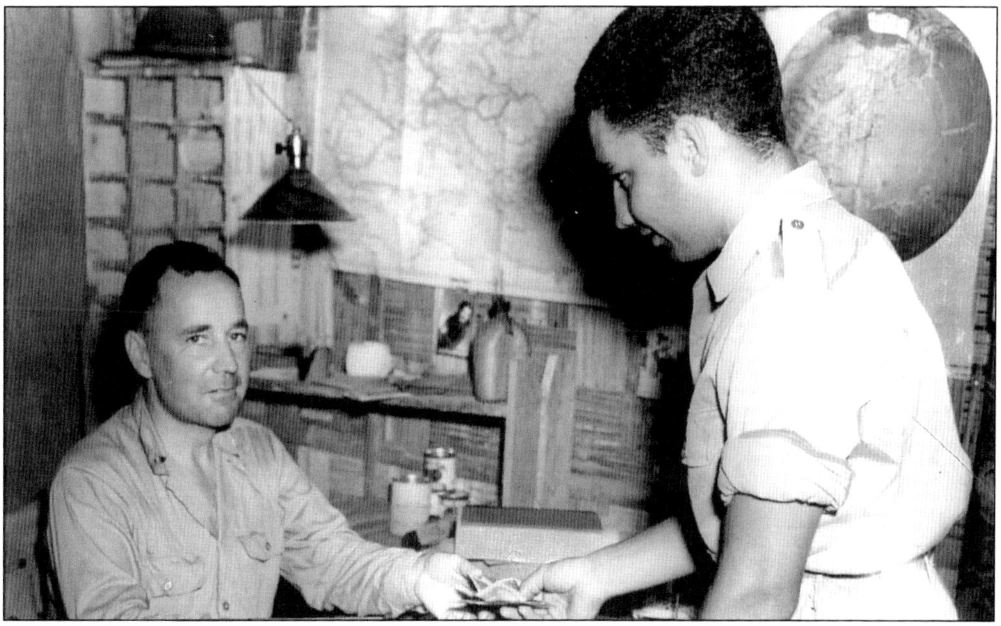

Father and Son. Lt. Howard E. Wrench is pictured cashing a check for his son, Cpl. Howard T. Wrench. They encountered each other in Assam, India in July 1944. Lieutenant Wrench was a former teacher at Centennial Junior High; he serves here as a personnel officer with an engineering unit on the Ledo road between China and India. (Courtesy Decatur Public Library.)

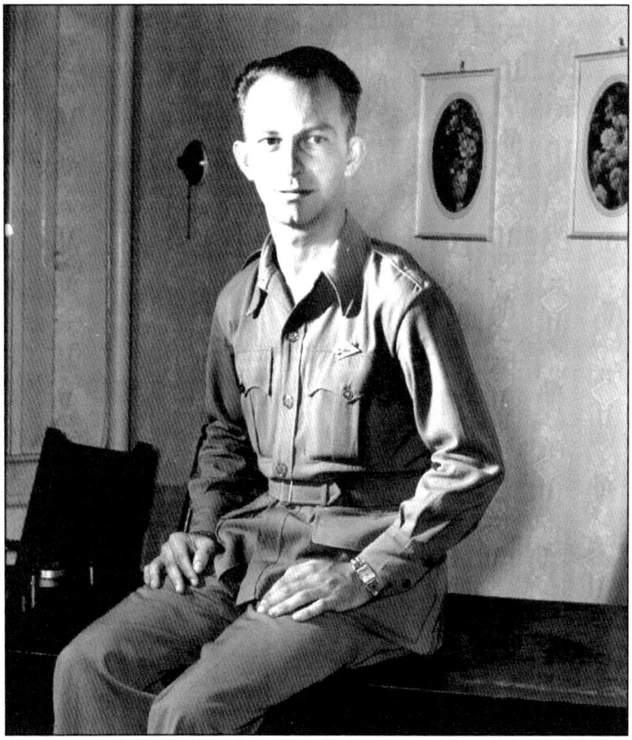

FLYING TIGER. John Young decided to serve with the Flying Tigers, a volunteer air squadron in China comprising 250 men, in July 1941. Young was with the Tigers until July 1943, when he decided to transfer to the Army Air Corps. He said American planes shot "full of holes" could still fly home. (Courtesy Decatur Public Library.)

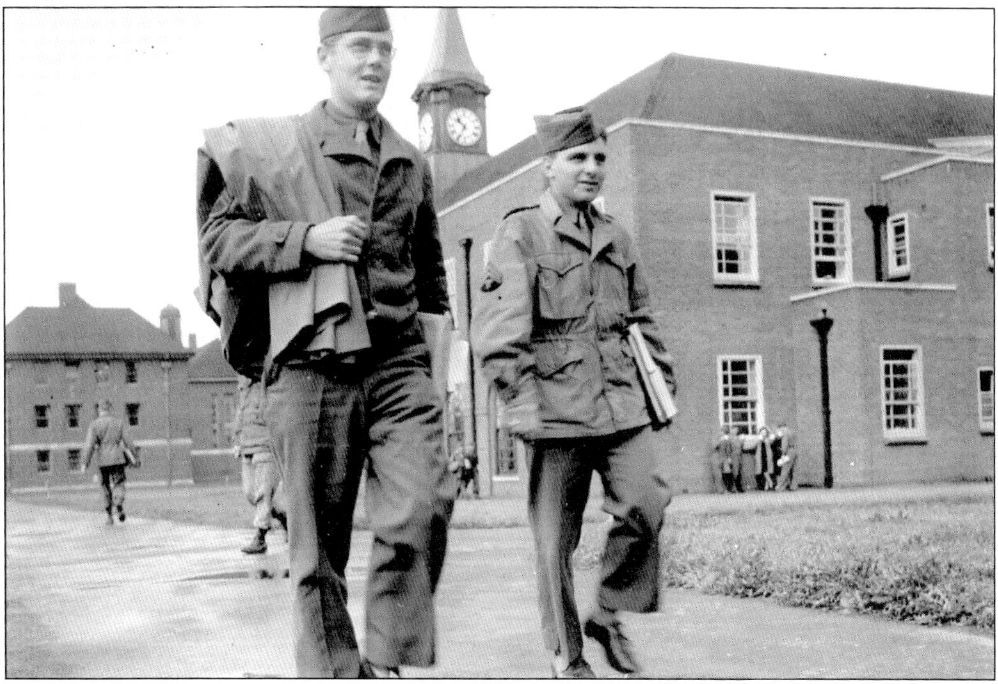

CAMPUS OF THE NEW UNIVERSITY CENTER. On August 25, 1945, S.Sgt. John G. Wayne (left) talks over courses with a friend as they walk on the university campus of a facility run by the U.S. Army Signal Corps in Shrivenham, England. It seems like typical English weather, wet and gloomy. At this point the war was over. (Courtesy Decatur Public Library.)

ELEANORE THE BABOON. Sgt. Edward S. Weeks served a 33-month tour of duty in the country of Iran, and in the process he acquired ownership of Eleanore, a seven-month-old baboon. She had a complete wardrobe, including a red dress made by a Polish woman. This photograph was taken on July 20, 1945. (Courtesy Decatur Public Library.)

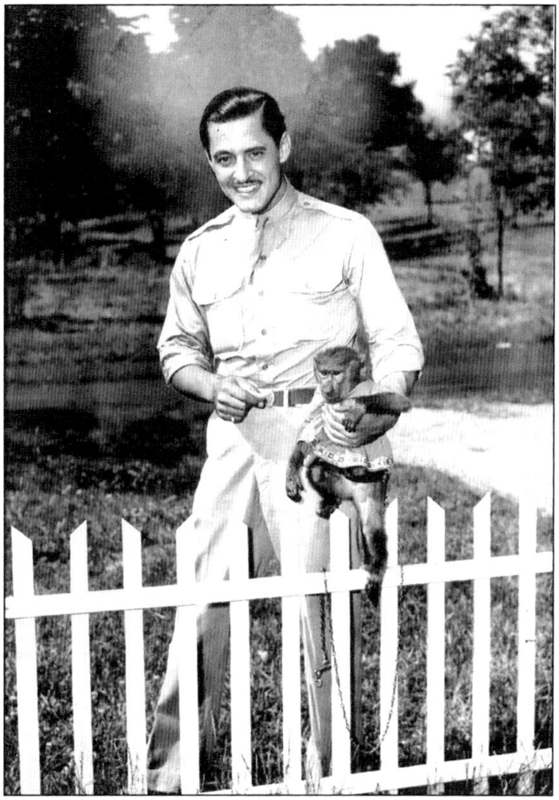

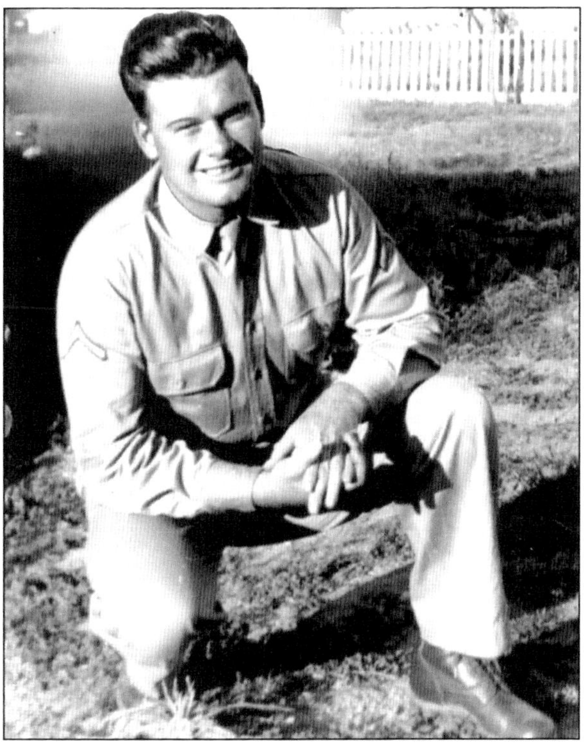

SGT. HERBERT VAN HOOSER. Sgt. Herbert Van Hooser, part of a railway engineers battalion, was killed in action in North Africa. His brother, Paul Van Hooser, was stationed at Camp Toccoa, Georgia. This photograph, dated July 16, 1943, was taken when Sergeant Van Hooser still held the rank of private first class. (Courtesy Decatur Public Library.)

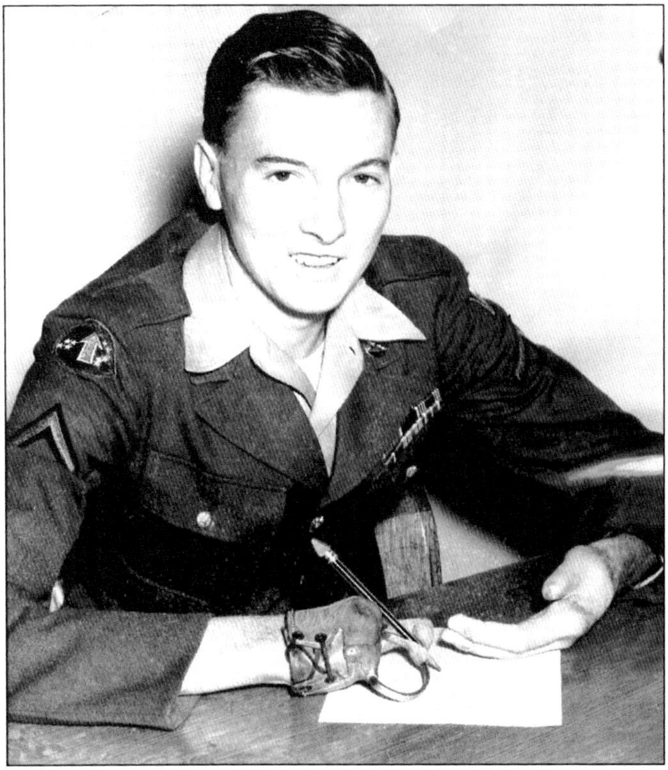

Hero of Luzon Island. Pfc. Edgar E. Nicholls lost six fingers when he tried to save his buddies by covering a Japanese explosive with his helmet. Nicholls has also written a book about the Persian Gulf War called *Heroes in our Midst*, and he has been the prime mover behind a drive to erect a World War II memorial in Decatur. This photograph was taken November 16, 1945. (Courtesy Decatur Public Library.)

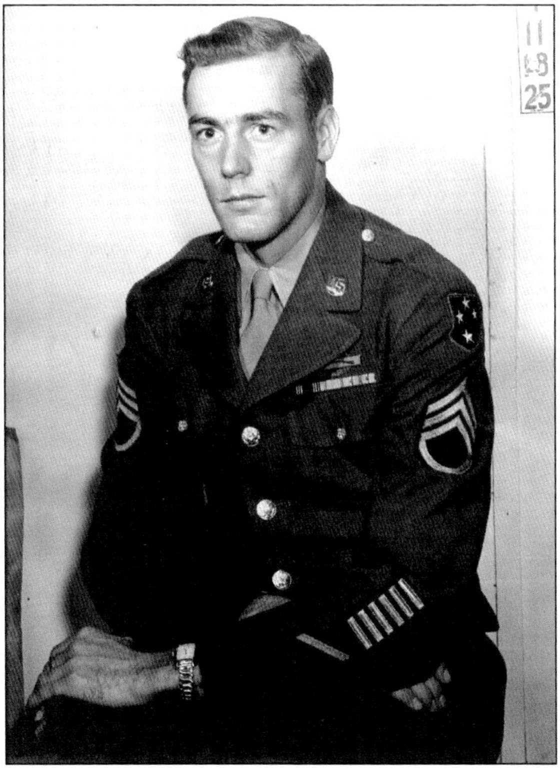

S.Sgt. Earl Smith. Although every soldier fighting on the front lines dreams of a surprise furlough, it actually happened to S.Sgt. Earl Smith while in his tent in the Philippine Islands. He was ordered to report to the commanding officer. Thinking he had done something wrong, Smith was delighted to hear the words, "You're going home." The photograph was taken on April 3, 1945. (Courtesy Decatur Public Library.)

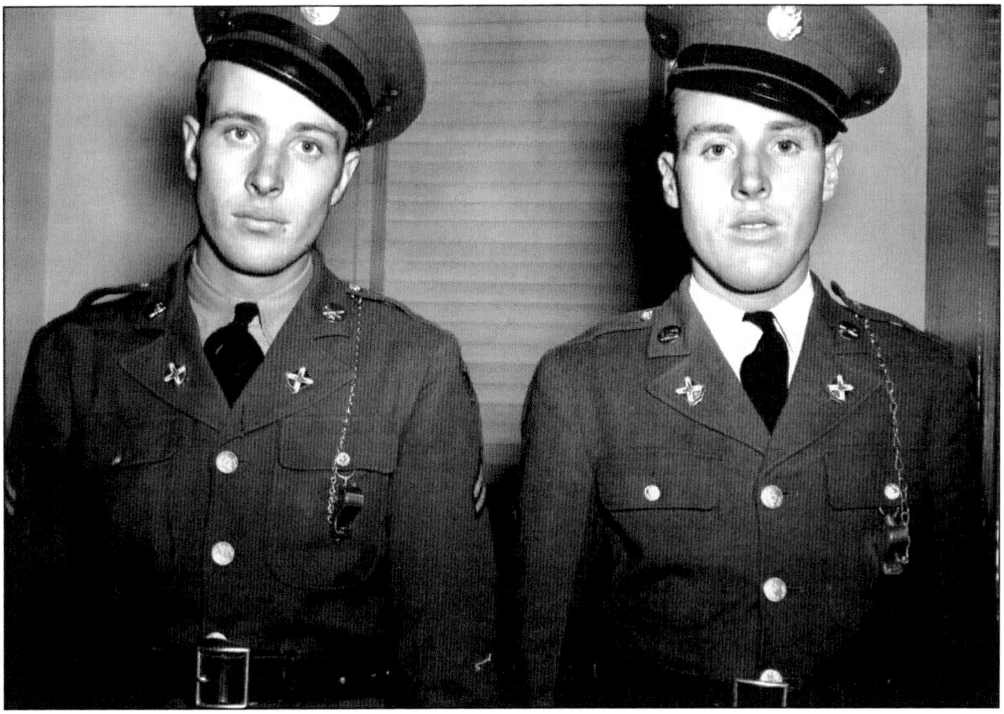

BROTHERS IN ARMS. The Stewart brothers, James (left) and Steve (right), both enlisted in the Army on the same day, July 3, 1941, about five months before the war began. They were both serving in the same company at Fort Bragg, North Carolina. James was 20 and Steve was 21 years old when this photograph was taken on January 14, 1942. (Courtesy Decatur Public Library.)

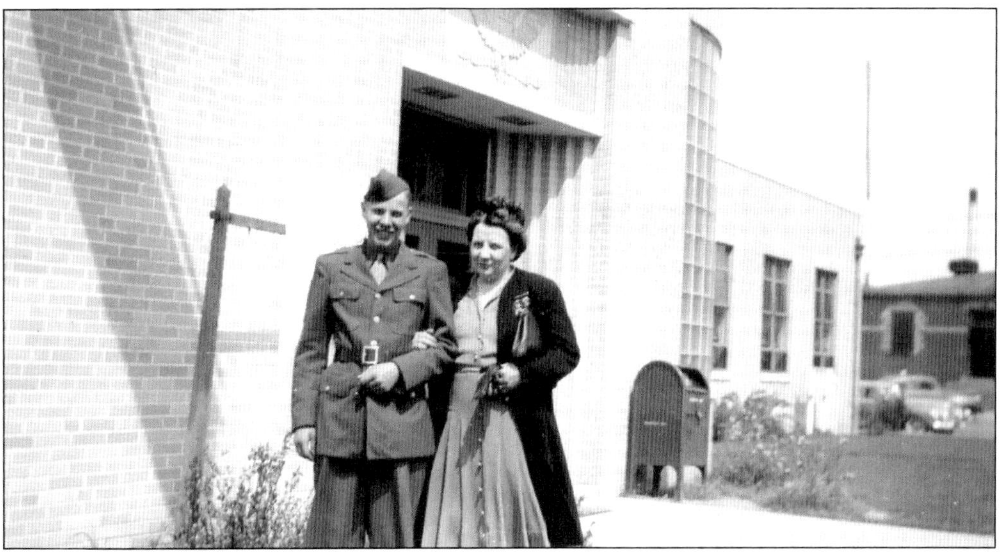

POSING WITH MOM. Pvt. Jack Graves had been a Millikin student when he signed up for the Army Reserves in 1942. After his basic training at Fort McClellan, Arkansas, he was shipped directly to North Africa, then Italy, without any home leave. He is shown next to his mother in this late 1942 snapshot. (Courtesy Decatur Public Library.)

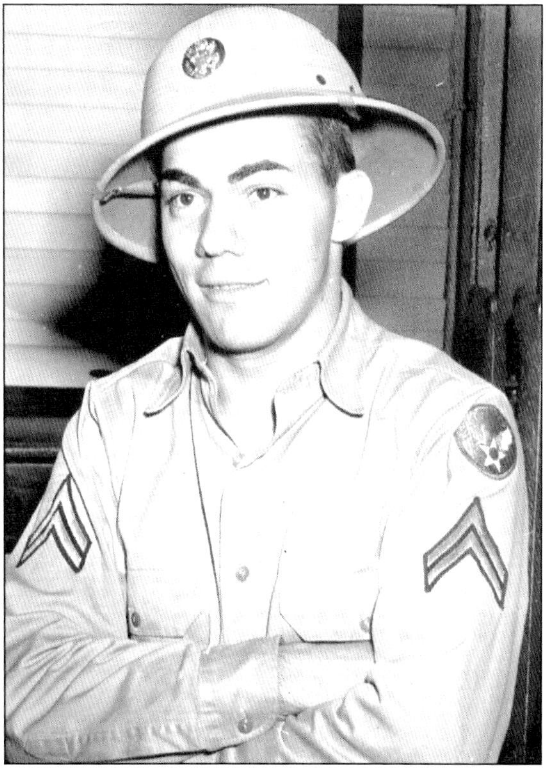

Cpl. W. E. Hanks. Nine months before the war began, W. E. Hanks signed up with the Decatur National Guard unit. He was sent to Harding Field, Baton Rouge, Louisiana, where he is shown posing in a pith helmet on July 10, 1942. Corporal Hanks had been recommended for officer training at Fort Benning, Georgia. (Courtesy Decatur Public Library.)

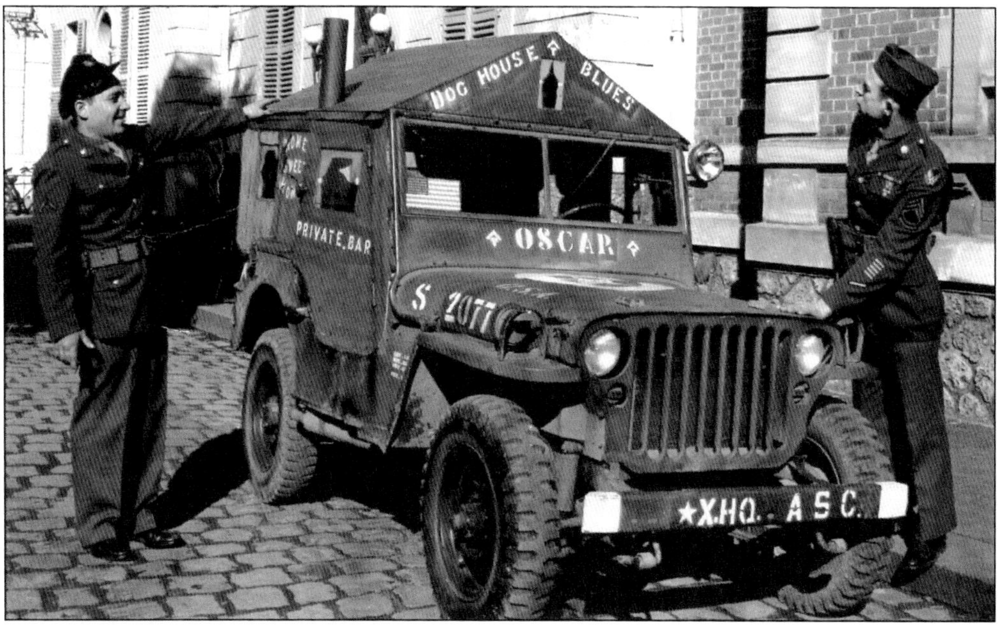

Improvisation in France. In the spirit of invention and creativity that defined Decatur's industrial life, Cpl. Lloyd Webb (left, still wearing his private first class stripe) personalized his Jeep to withstand the challenge of a French winter. Corporal Webb was in charge of a large garage; he had been employed by Caterpillar Military Engine Company before the war. (Courtesy Decatur Public Library.)

EDWARD P. IMBODEN. A member of the 609th Ordnance Battalion, Edward P. Imboden, had worked as a mechanic for International Harvester Farm Equipment Company before enlisting. He repaired and maintained tanks and trucks that were used in the D-Day invasion at Omaha Beach. He served from September 1942 to December 1945. (Courtesy Doug Imboden.)

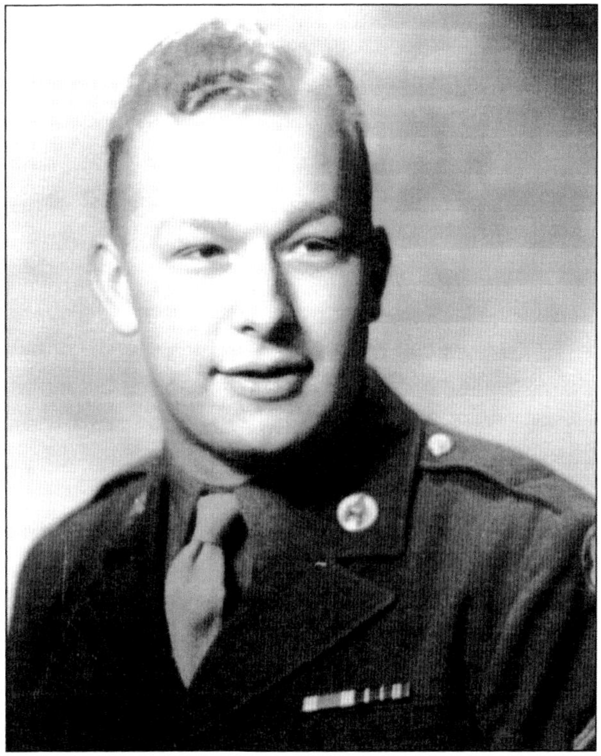

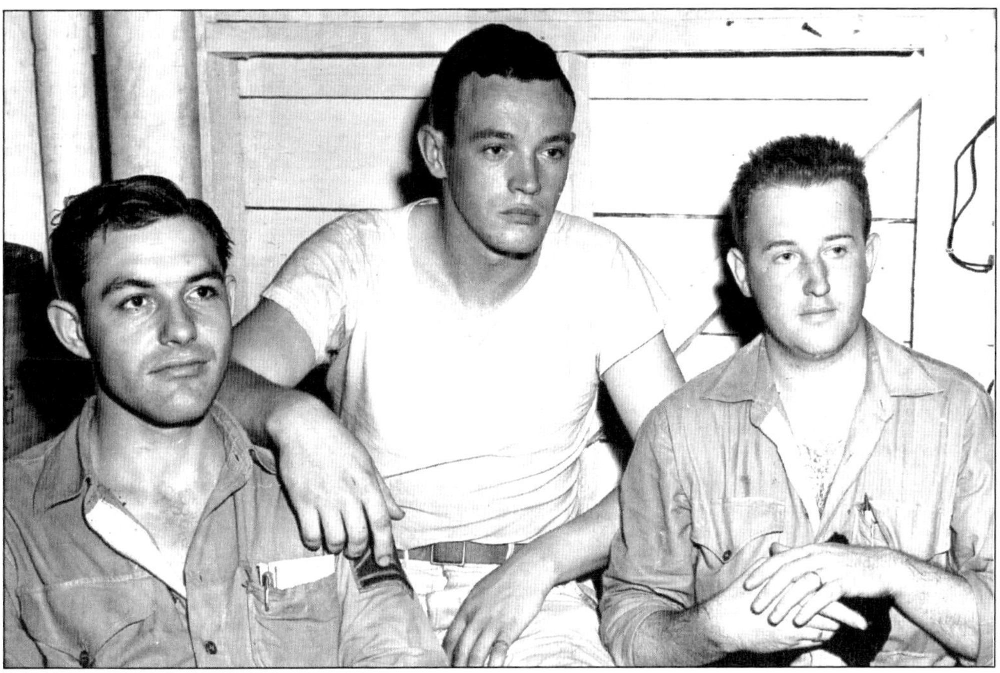

RESTING IN THE GALLEY. These three Marine messmen are catching their breath aboard ship somewhere in the Pacific in December 1942. They have just finished feeding a large contingent of Marines and are huddling with "Ink," the ship's mascot, as they plan the next day's menu. Holding Ink is Technical Sgt. Paul L. Davis of Decatur. (Courtesy Decatur Public Library.)

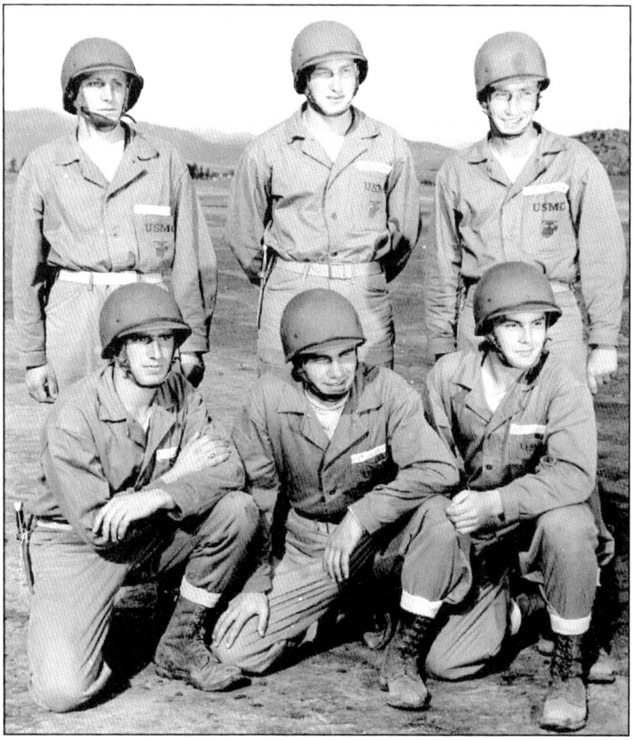

MARINE PARACHUTISTS. In this official Marine Corps photograph from March 1943, six parachutists have just completed their training at Camp Gillespie, California. All were promoted to the rank of private first class. The soldier in the back row on the far right is Thomas W. Crowdson of Decatur. (Courtesy Decatur Public Library.)

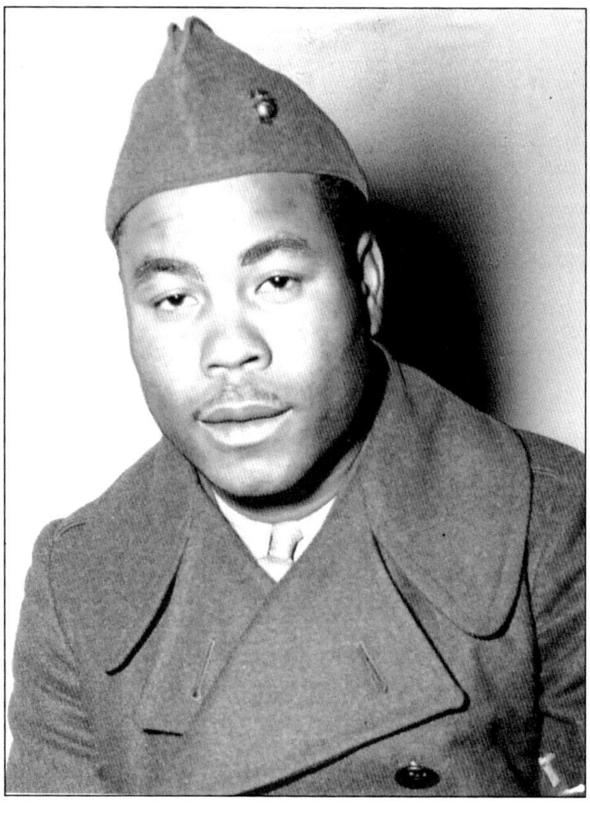

MARINE PVT. CHARLES JOHNSON JR. Pvt. Charles Johnson Jr. was en route to Camp Lejune, North Carolina, after this March 1944 photograph was taken. He had been on a four-day furlough visiting family in Decatur. Private Johnson's brother Clarence was serving in the Army, while his brother Robert served in the Navy. (Courtesy Decatur Public Library.)

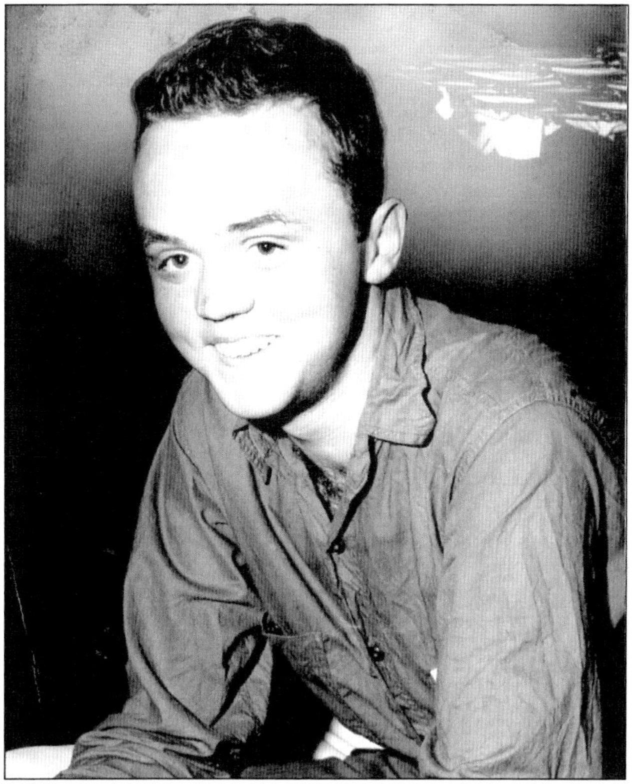

MARINE PFC. DONALD W. SULLIVAN. Pfc. Donald W. Sullivan was recuperating in a Navy hospital in Long Beach, California when this picture was snapped in July 1945. Private First Class Sullivan suffered severe burns when he dashed through flames and exploding ammunition to rescue a pilot from a crashed plane. Private First Class Sullivan served in Leyte, Guadalcanal, and Green Island. (Courtesy Decatur Public Library.)

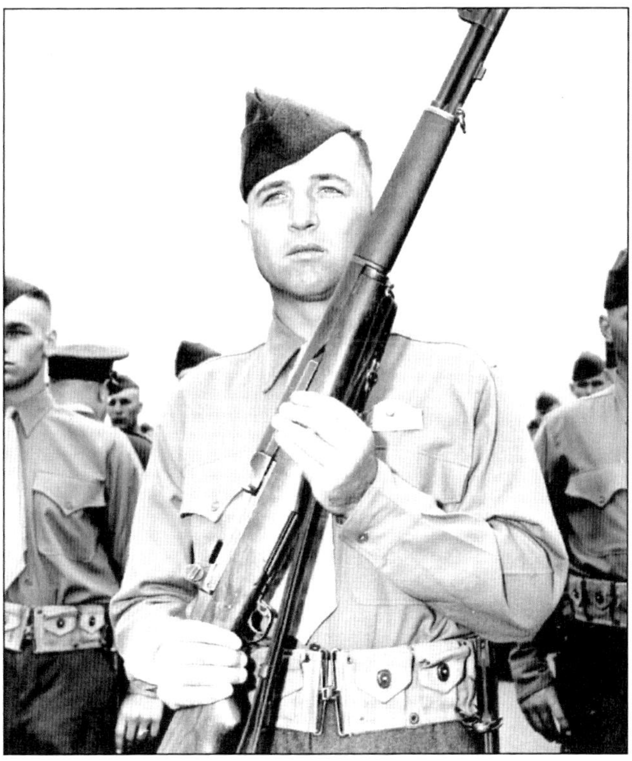

RECIPIENT OF HONOR BADGE. Demonstrating the rifle position known as "port arms," Marine Pvt. Merle Smith Nirider shows the kind of precision that earned him the honor badge pinned above his shirt pocket. He was a banker before the war. The photograph was taken in August 1943 at the Recruit Depot, Marine Corps Base, San Diego. (Courtesy Decatur Public Library.)

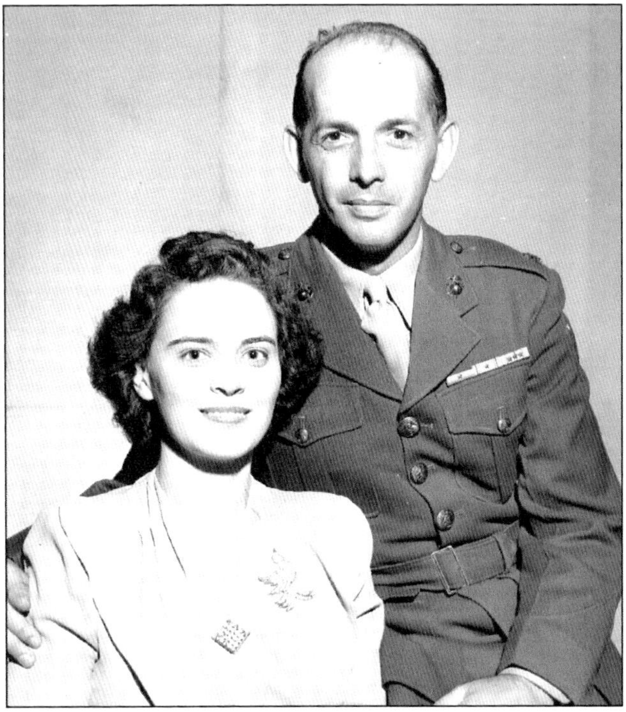

MARINE MAJ. RALPH MERRILL WISMER AND JEAN WISMER. Maj. Ralph Merrill Wismer returned to Decatur in April 1944 and was greeted by his 16-month-old daughter, Linda Jean, whom he had never seen. The major had just completed a two-year tour of overseas duty. He is shown with his wife Jean, seated in her parents' home. Jean and Linda Jean had traveled to Chicago to meet the major. (Courtesy Decatur Public Library.)

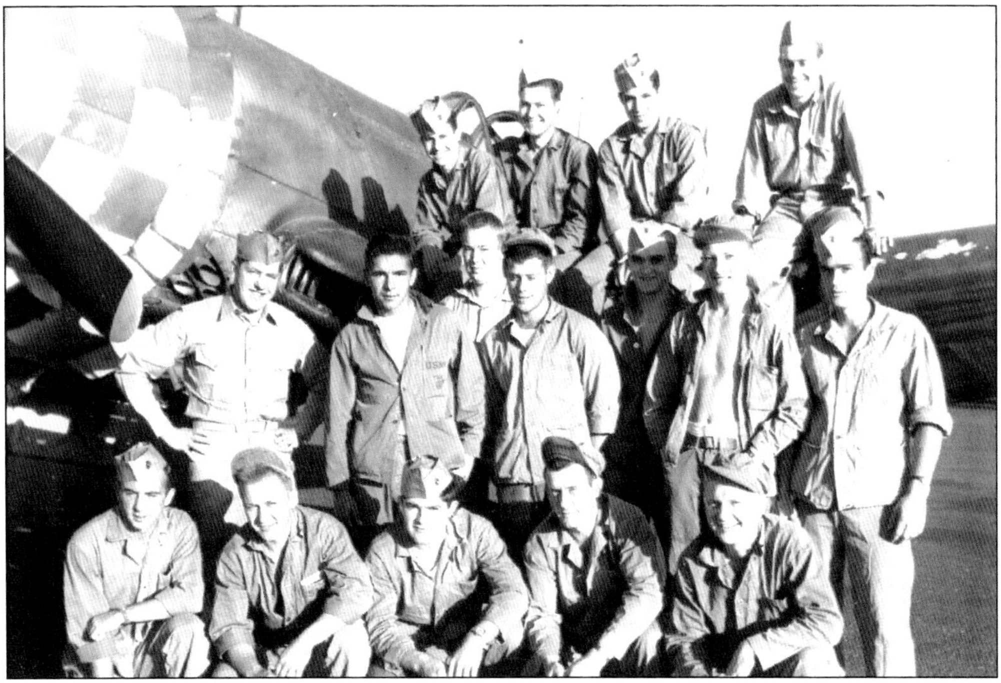

MARINE CHECKERBOARD SQUADRON. The Checkerboard Squadron was the first to fly the famous Corsair fighter, which is visible in the background. Their first wartime action was at Guadalcanal. Pfc. John A. Harding (kneeling, second from the right) lived at 438 West Wood Street in Decatur before the war. This photograph was taken in June 1944. (Courtesy Decatur Public Library.)

MISTAKENLY REPORTED DEAD. Marine Cpl. Arthur Fiedler, a veteran of seven Pacific battles, including Doolittle's raid on Tokyo in 1942, is smiling and very much alive in this March 1944 photograph. Corporal Fiedler, an antiaircraft gunner, had been unofficially reported dead for a year. He was photographed after convalescing at a Navy hospital in Santa Cruz, California. (Courtesy Decatur Public Library.)

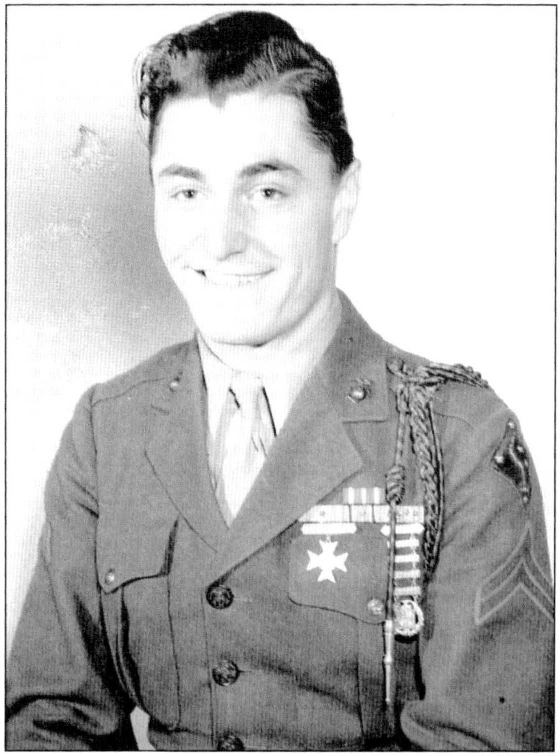

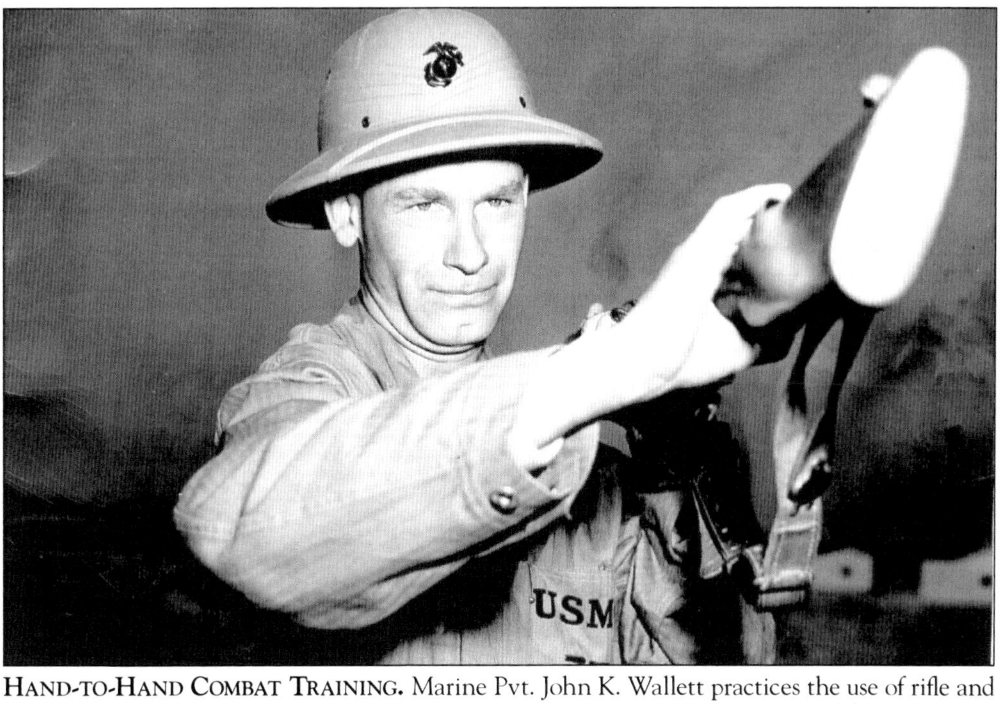

HAND-TO-HAND COMBAT TRAINING. Marine Pvt. John K. Wallett practices the use of rifle and bayonet in hand-to-hand combat at the Marine Corps Base in San Diego, California. Private Wallett left three children back in Decatur when he enlisted. Stress on family life is an inevitable part of war. This photograph was taken in February 1944. (Courtesy Decatur Public Library.)

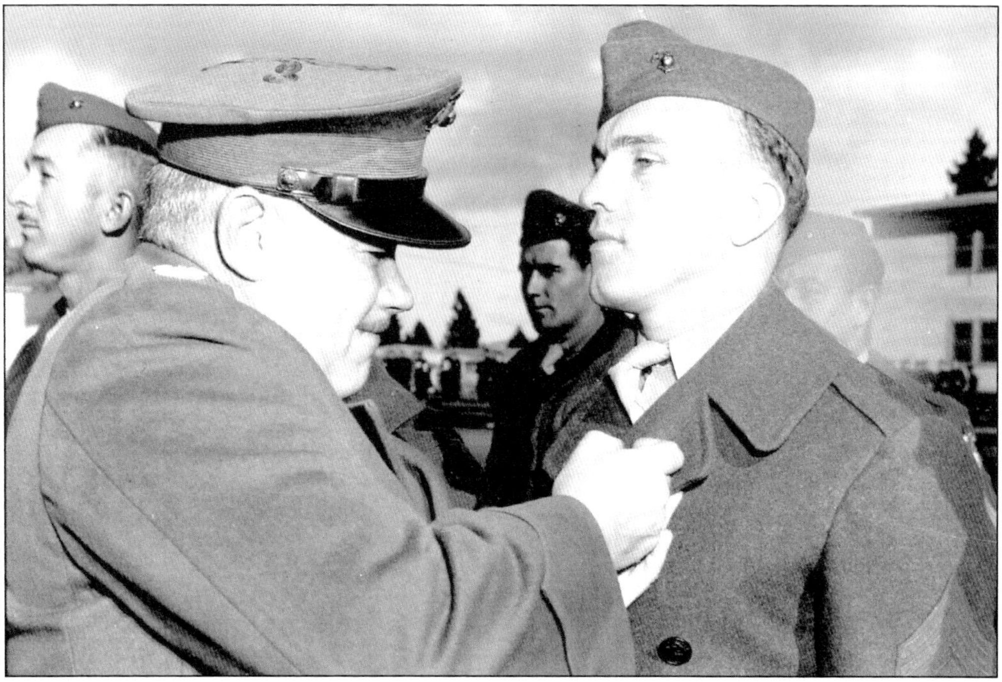

MARINE PLATOON SGT. JACOB PHILLIP ROBISON. Sgt. Jacob Phillip Robison was a veteran of three critical Pacific campaigns—Guadalcanal, Tarawa, and Saipan—when he was awarded the Bronze Star medal "for extraordinary courage and coolness under fire." Robison was wounded at Saipan, and spent 23 months in the Pacific before returning stateside. The photograph was taken in March of 1945. (Courtesy Decatur Public Library.)

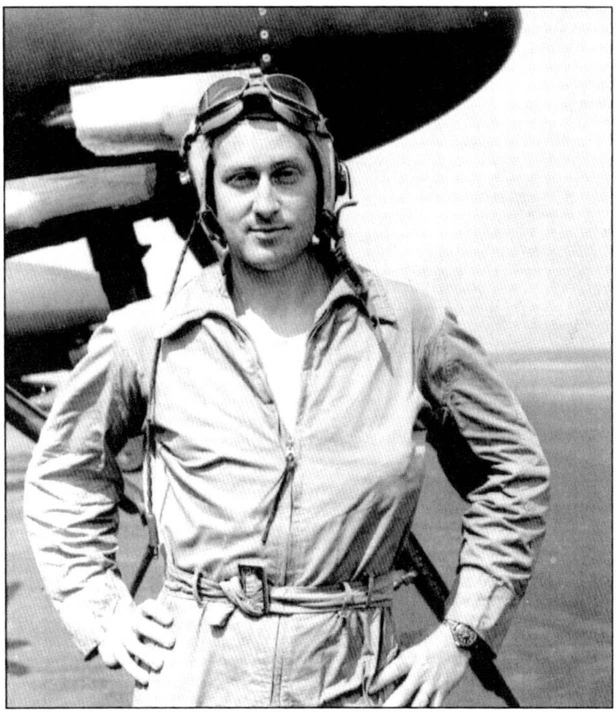

MARINE PILOT AT CHERRY POINT, NORTH CAROLINA. This official Marine Corps photograph was taken at Cherry Point, North Carolina, September 1945, at a time when the war was already over but many personnel were still in uniform. The picture shows Marine pilot Capt. Leroy T. Frey, son of Carolina Frey, 501½ South Crea Street, Decatur. (Courtesy Decatur Public Library.)

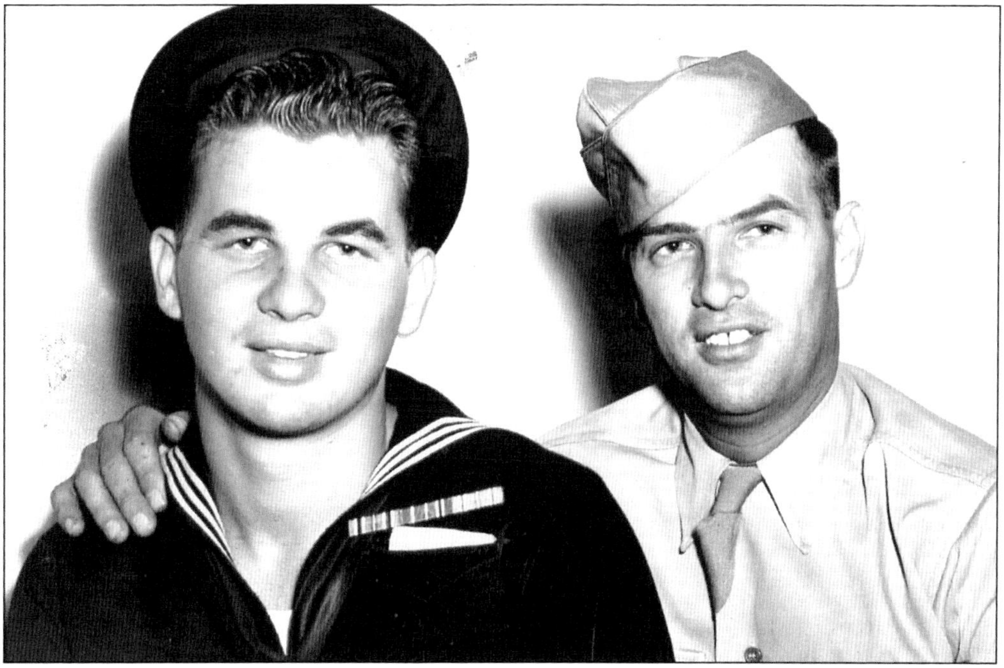

BROTHERS REUNITED. Navy Coxswain Earl W. Eschbaugh (left), and Army Sgt. Harold W. Harris (right), two brothers, were united in September 1944 as shown in this photograph. Neither brother knew the other was coming home to Decatur. Before the war, Earl worked at Taylor Dairy and Harold at A. E. Staley. A third brother, William Eschbaugh, was on a destroyer in the Pacific. (Courtesy Decatur Public Library.)

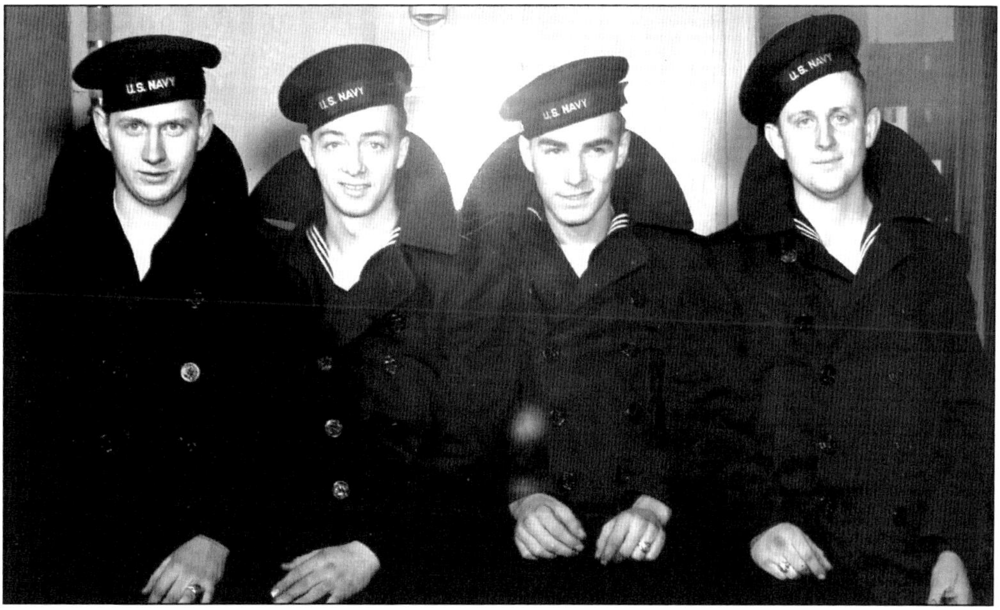

FOUR HIGH SCHOOL BUDDIES. This February 14, 1943, photograph shows, from left to right, Donald L. Warnick, Gerald E. Willis, Kenneth J. Mears, and Frederick Churchman. These former high school buddies remained together during basic training but were separating for careers as carpenters, gunners, and armed guards. (Courtesy Decatur Public Library.)

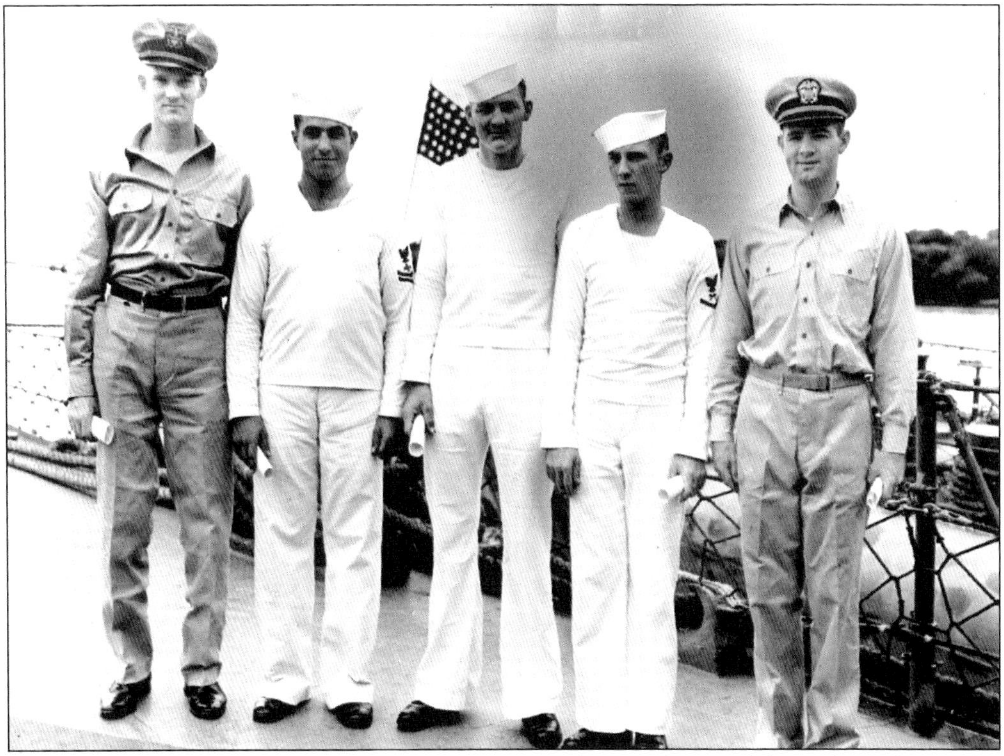

SEAMAN DALE C. ERWIN. Seaman Dale C. Erwin (pictured second from the right in this February 1943 photograph), along with the three other sailors, was honored aboard ship for outstanding military service in a fierce sea battle with Japanese naval forces off the Santa Cruz Islands. (Courtesy Decatur Public Library.)

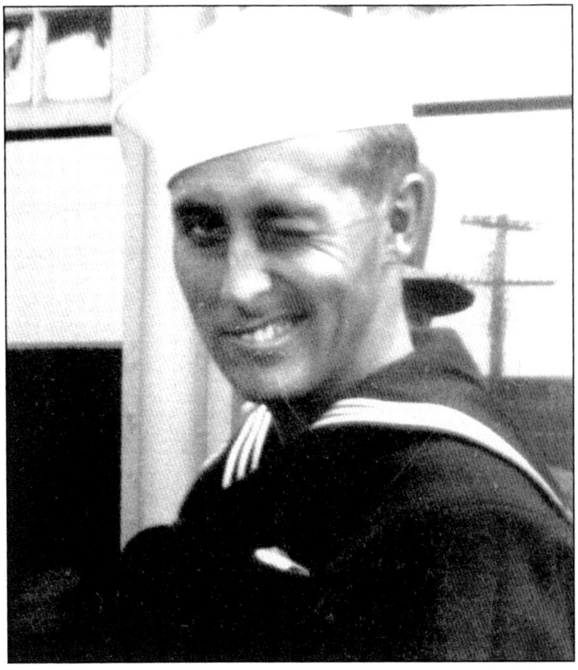

SEAMAN N. DALE COCHRAN. Seaman N. Dale Cochran was buried in Normandy. He participated in the D-Day operations and was killed in a torpedo attack on a Landing Ship-Tank (LST) ship, where he worked as an officers' cook. This photograph was taken in front of the Wabash Station in Decatur a few months before D-Day. Cochran was winking as a gesture of thanks for a box of cookies just presented to him. (Courtesy Dayle Cochran Irwin.)

SEAMAN VERNON GREEN AND "MIKE." In this postwar image, dated April 2, 1946, Seaman Vernon Green holds a Philippine Island monkey named "Mike," a pet he acquired in Tokyo from another sailor who said the winter weather did not agree with the animal. Mike was apparently fond of mayonnaise, beer, and whiskey, but not all at the same time. (Courtesy Decatur Public Library.)

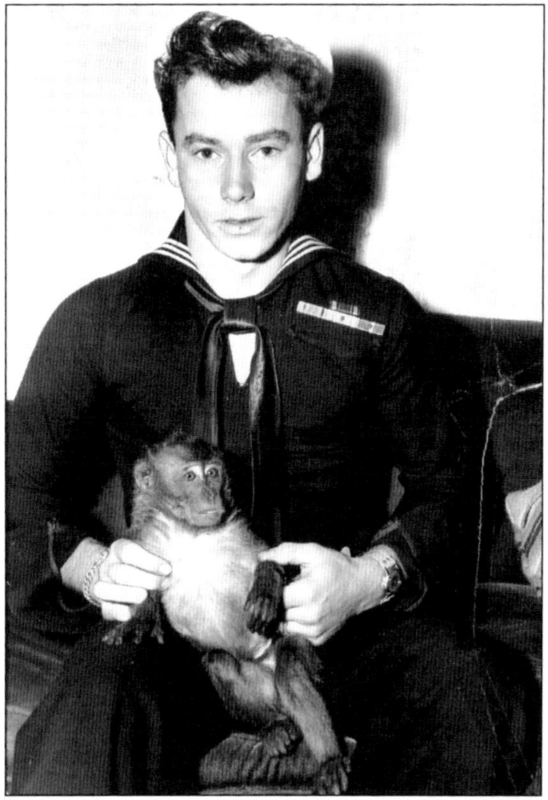

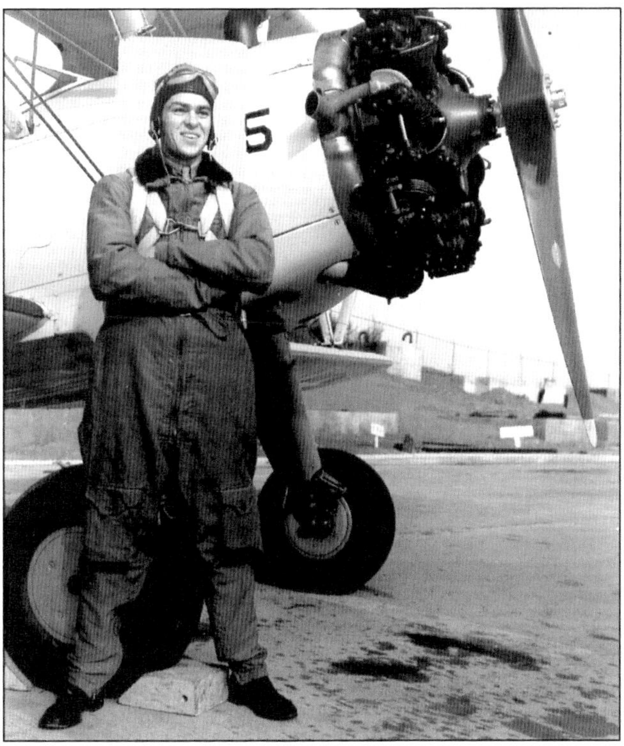

BOATSWAIN'S MATE FIRST CLASS. This official Navy photograph, taken in late 1942, shows Boatswain's Mate Paul E. Wilson at the U.S. Naval Reserve Aviation Base, Lambert Field, St. Louis, Missouri. Wilson was later assigned to duty in the Pacific. His brother, Oren Wilson, was stationed at Norfolk, Virginia. (Courtesy Decatur Public Library.)

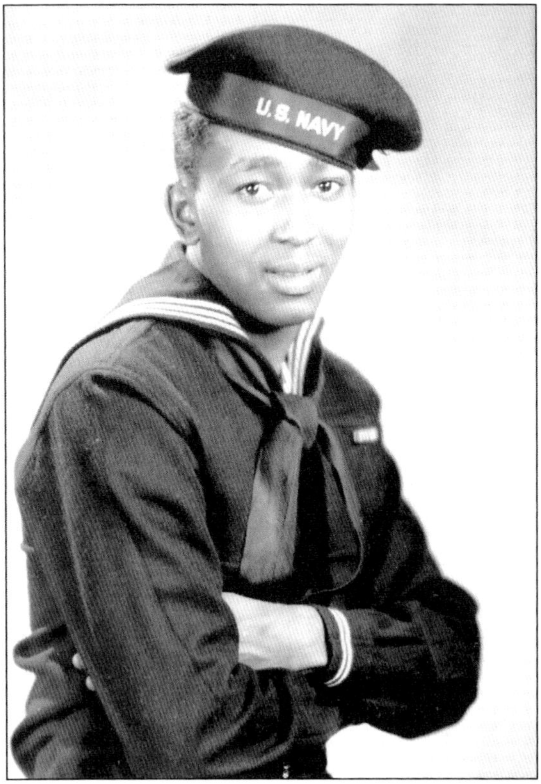

STEWARD MATE SECOND CLASS CHARLES T. CONLEY JR. Steward Charles T. Conley Jr. saw action in North Africa, and he was ultimately awarded two battle stars. This January 14, 1944, photograph was taken during a visit to Decatur. By that time, Conley had been reassigned to duties in New York City. (Courtesy Decatur Public Library.)

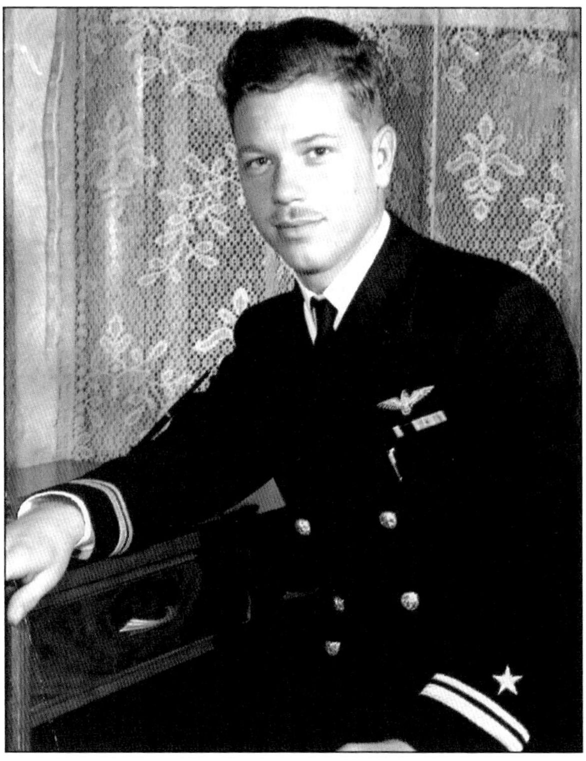

LT. R. E. RIES JR. As a naval aviator, Lt. R. E. Ries Jr. was involved in some of the most dangerous fighting in the Pacific theater of operations, including the Battle of Coral Sea and the Solomon Islands. For his meritorious service, he was awarded the Navy Cross and the Distinguished Flying Cross. Lieutenant Ries served in the elite Torpedo Squadron No. 8. This photograph was taken January 1, 1943. (Courtesy Decatur Public Library.)

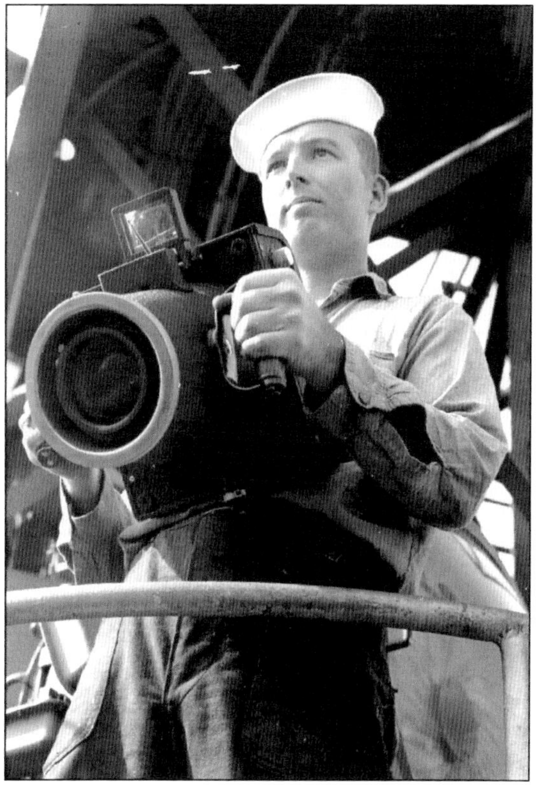

THE PHOTOGRAPHER PHOTOGRAPHED. This October 1945 photograph dates to the Occupation Period in Japan. The image shows Photographer's Mate Third Class Vernon Stogsdill, taking a picture from the bridge of the U.S.S. *Savo Island*, as the ship steams into Mutsu Bay, Northern Honshu, Japan. Before enlisting, Stogsdill was employed by the Eastman Kodak Company. (Courtesy Decatur Public Library.)

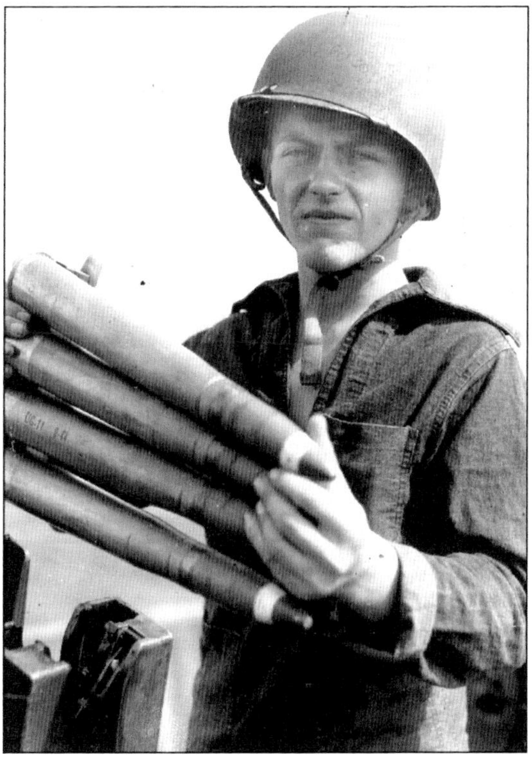

ANTIAIRCRAFT SHELLS. In this official U.S. Navy photograph taken in August 1945, during the last days of the war, Seaman First Class James E. Smallwood handles antiaircraft shells as he prepares to load a gun aboard an aircraft carrier somewhere in the Pacific. Manpower was an essential requirement to keep the fleet operating. (Courtesy Decatur Public Library.)

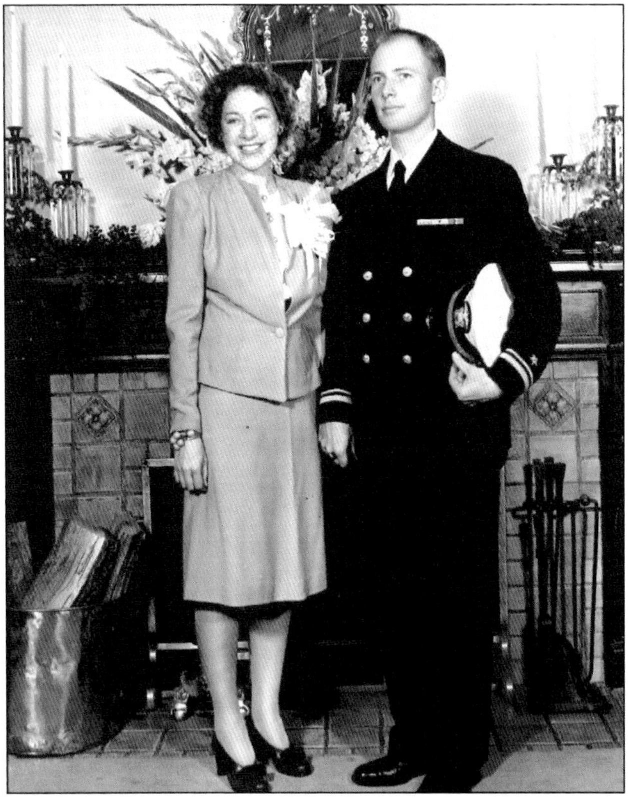

Married in Portland. Lt. J. G. Bartlett Field Cole married Janet Dillehunt in Portland, Oregon, in late June 1945, after a tour of duty in the Pacific that lasted for 17 months. The honeymoon was brief, since he was due to report at the Great Lakes Naval Station on July 1, 1945. (Courtesy Decatur Public Library.)

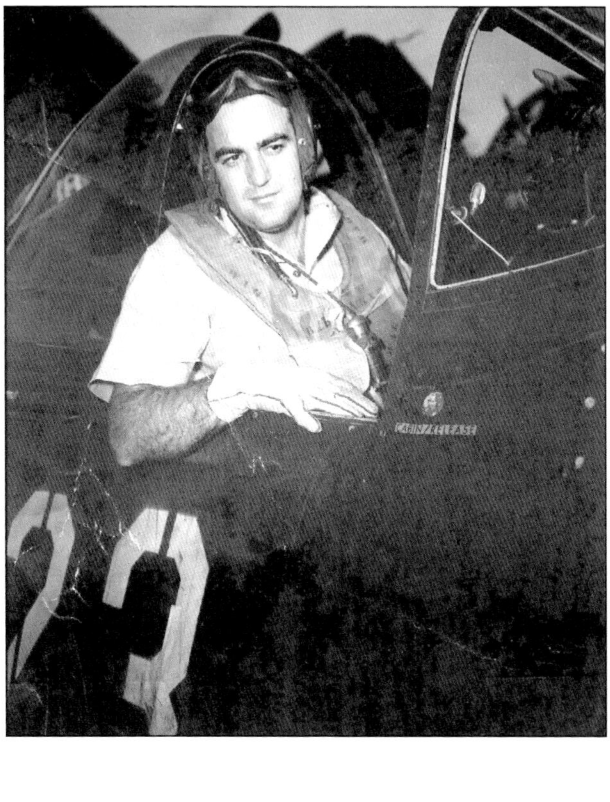

Naval Pilot in a Corsair Fighter. This photograph, taken during the occupation period in September 1945, shows Lt. Walter Clarke, a 1938 Millikin graduate, at the controls of the Corsair Fighter. The most effective fighter aircraft of World War II included the Mustang P-51, the British Spitfire, the Corsair, the Hellcat, and the Japanese Zero—in that order. (Courtesy Decatur Public Library.)

HELLDIVERS. John Joseph Molloy, aviation radioman third class, shown on the right in this June 1945 photograph, participated in the sinking of the battleship *Yamato* off Kyushu on April 7, 1945. Molloy was a 1943 graduate of Decatur High School and did his training in Chicago and DeLand, Florida. Molloy and the pilot are standing in front of their Helldiver naval aircraft. (Courtesy Decatur Public Library.)

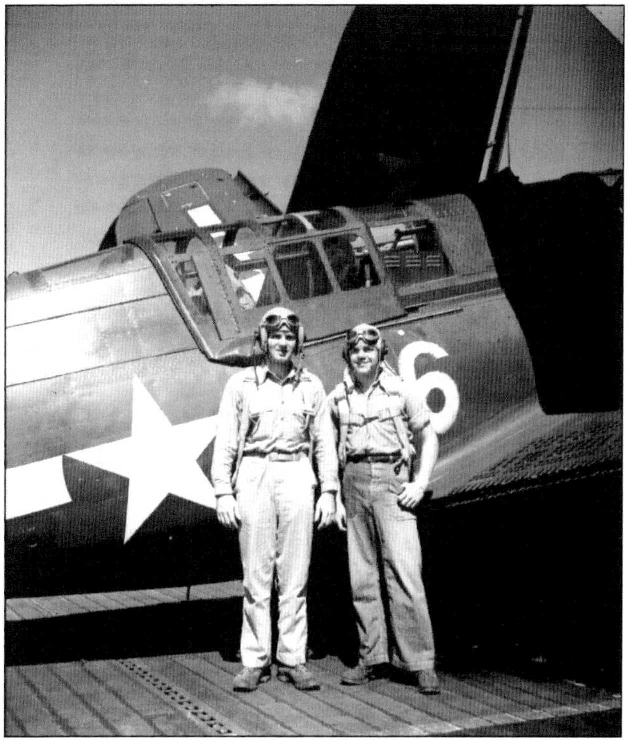

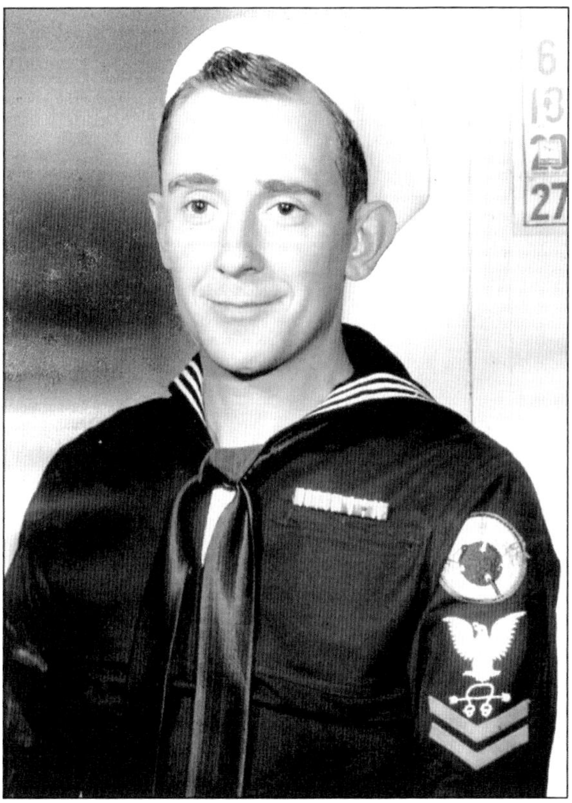

AT THE YALTA CONFERENCE. Sound Man Second Class Willard Stalker, who usually served on a minesweeper, was given the honor of standing guard at Yalta, where he had a chance to see Roosevelt, Churchill, and Stalin. Churchill puffed on a cigar, while Stalin was "short and quick of movement." In Sardinia he saw children eating out of garbage cans. The photograph was taken in May 1945. (Courtesy Decatur Public Library.)

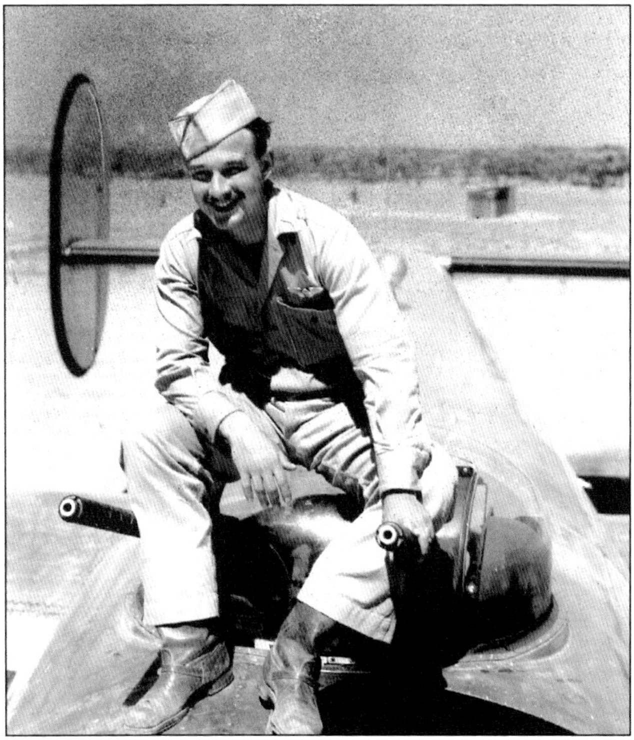

Top Turret Gunner. S.Sgt. Richard J. Lake, is seated atop his turret guns on a Liberator Bomber somewhere in Italy in this July 1945 snapshot. He is probably smiling because he had just completed 40 bombing missions, single-handedly shooting down two German fighter aircraft, and winning the Air Medal and one Oak Leaf cluster. He was serving with the 15th Army Air Force. (Courtesy Decatur Public Library.)

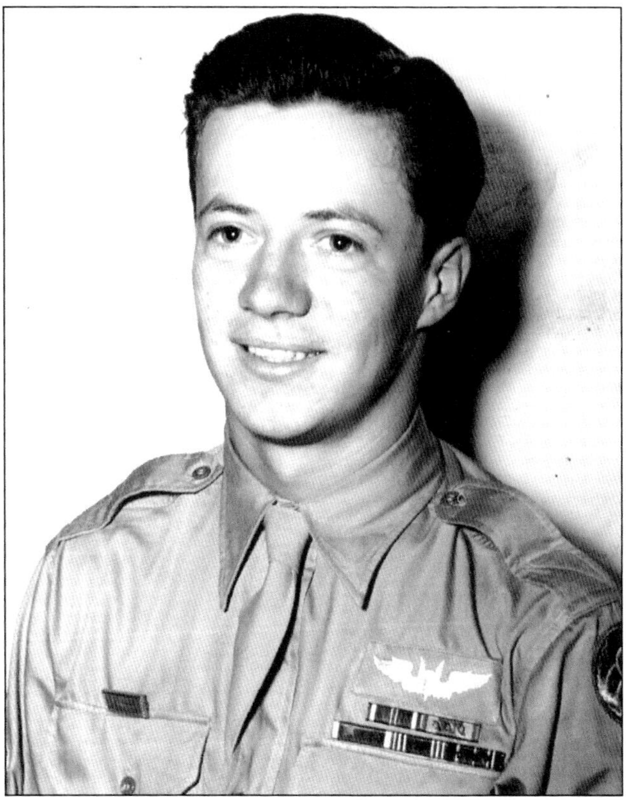

Togglier on a B-24 Bomber. S.Sgt. J. Francis Watkins served as a "togglier" on a B-24 bomber—he was the man who actually dropped the bombs once the bomb bay doors opened over the target. On March 18, 1945, during a bombing run over Berlin, his plane was shot down. Watkins landed safely in a playground and later joined up with American troops. (Courtesy Decatur Public Library.)

SHOT DOWN OVER ATHENS. Lt. Delbert Huffman, a former clerk at Millikin Bank, has served as the pilot of a B-17 bomber over Rome, Naples, and Athens. His plane was ultimately shot down over Athens, and in the process he took three bullets in his left arm and injured his back. Note the cast protruding from under his left sleeve. This photograph was taken December 21, 1943. (Courtesy Decatur Public Library.)

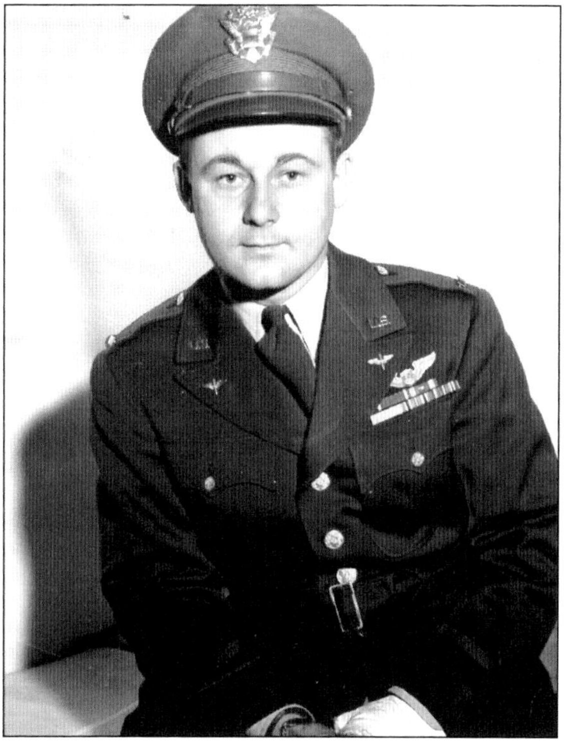

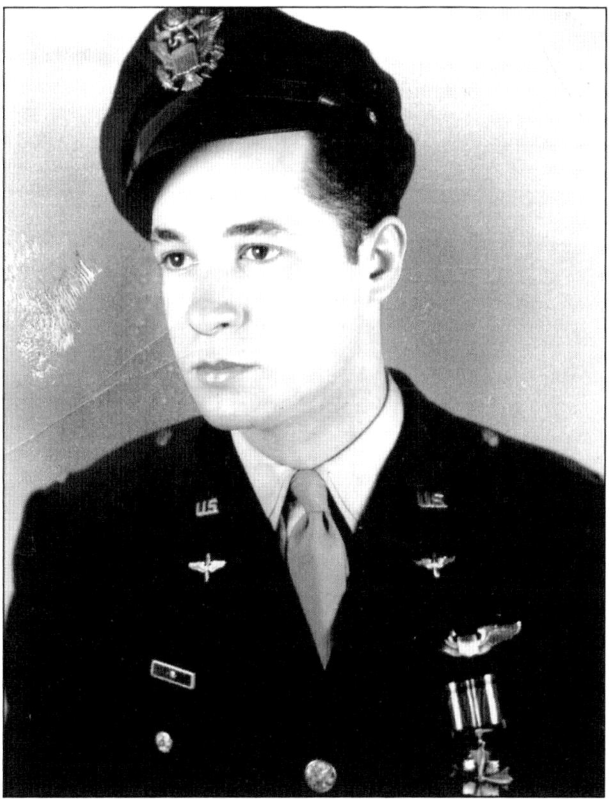

FLYING FORTRESS PILOT. A student at Illinois State Normal University before the war, 1st Lt. Dale J. Metzinger completed 30 missions over high-value military targets in Germany. He has been awarded the Distinguished Flying Cross and the Air Medal with three Oak Leaf clusters. The photograph is dated January 29, 1945. (Courtesy Decatur Public Library.)

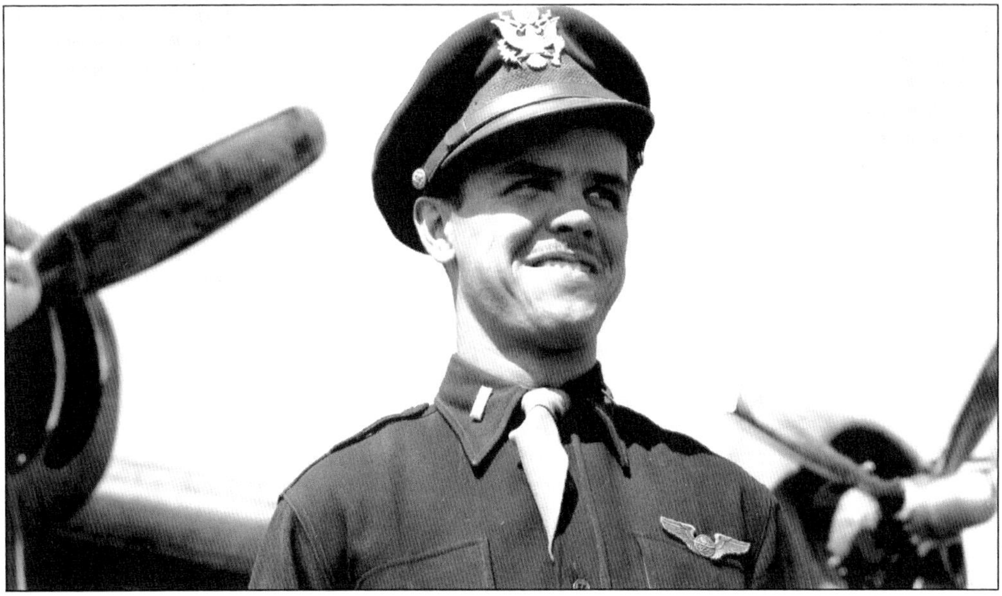

NAVIGATOR IN ITALY. In late March of 1945, 1st Lt. Robert D. Rutledge stands smiling in front of a Liberator Bomber somewhere in Italy. Lt. Rutledge had completed a total of 35 missions, serving as navigator for the crew. A winner of the Air Medal with over two years of service in the Air Force, Lieutenant Rutledge was previously employed at the Sangamon Ordnance Plant. (Courtesy Decatur Public Library.)

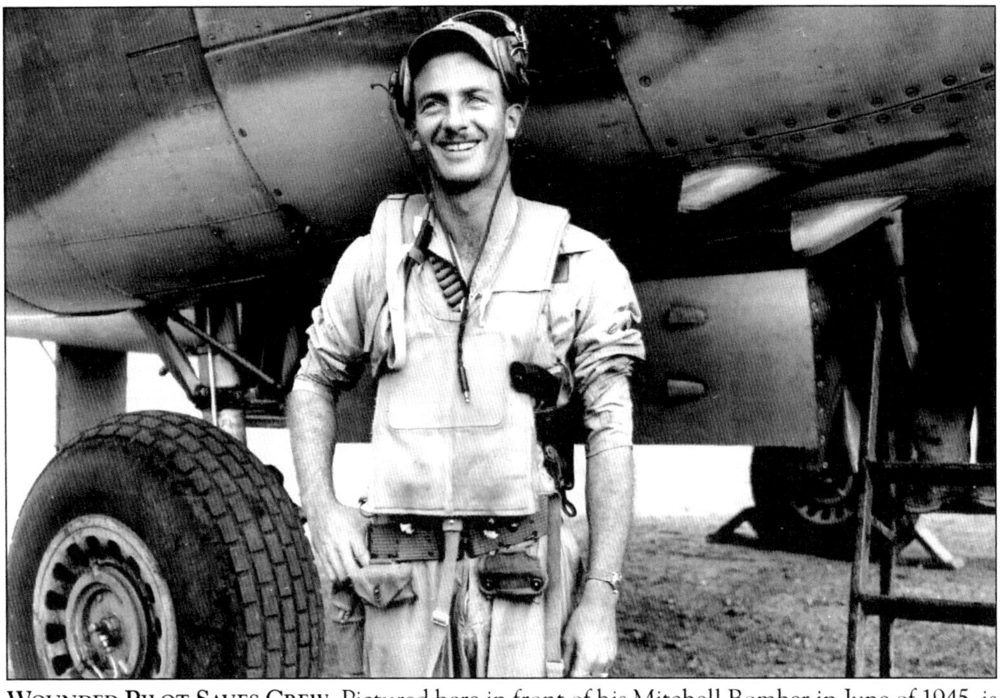

WOUNDED PILOT SAVES CREW. Pictured here in front of his Mitchell Bomber in June of 1945, is 1st Lt. Stewart R. Lauer who was hit by a barrage of Japanese flak over Mindanao in the Pacific. Even though he was badly wounded, and his eyesight was affected, he brought the bomber back to base and saved the lives of the entire crew. (Courtesy Decatur Public Library.)

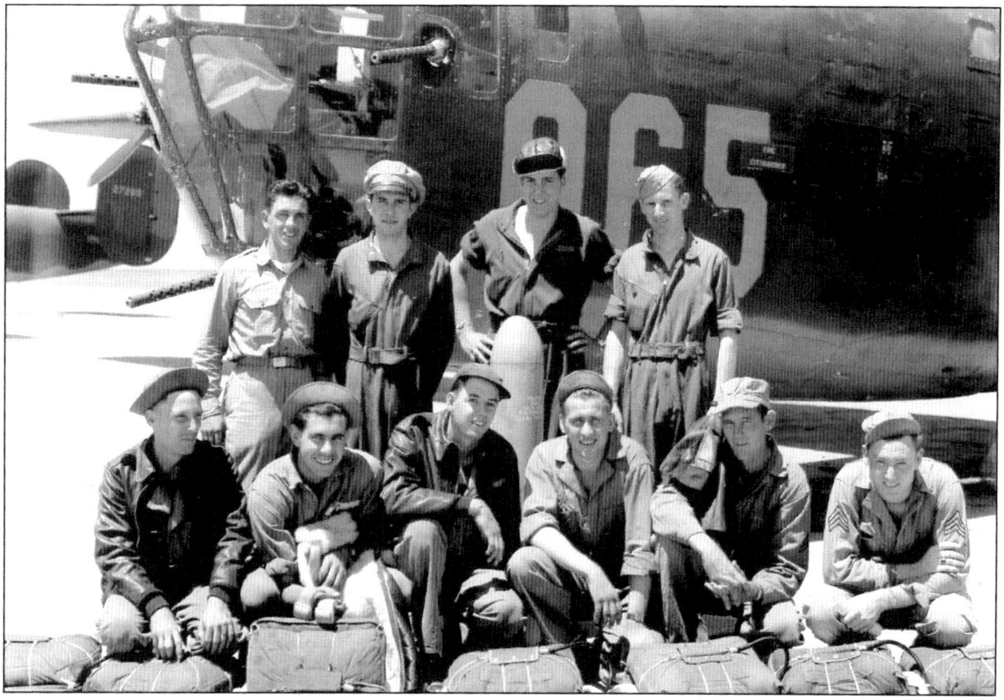

BOMBER CREW WITH PARACHUTES. In this 1945 photograph, taken somewhere in the pacific, Sgt. Samuel E. Conroy of Decatur (kneeling, third from the right), poses with his crewmates in front of their bomber. The leather bomber jackets were considered high-status possessions, and the men have also placed their indispensable parachutes proudly on display. (Courtesy Decatur Public Library.)

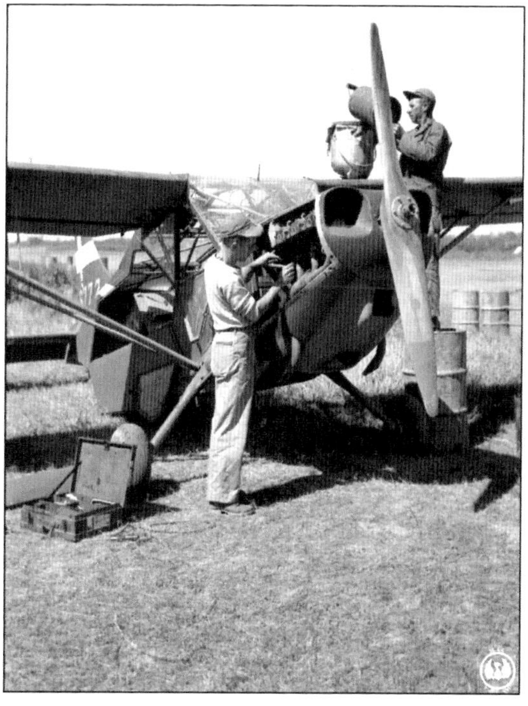

GASSING UP IN BURMA. Pfc. Bruce Gillespie of Decatur (left) is tuning the engine as Sgt. K. E. Piece of Oregon fills the tank. Both were serving as U.S. liaison pilots on Akyab Island off the coast of Burma. This is an official photograph of the South East Air Command taken January 27, 1945, by Sgt. Peter R. Voutsas. (Courtesy Decatur Public Library.)

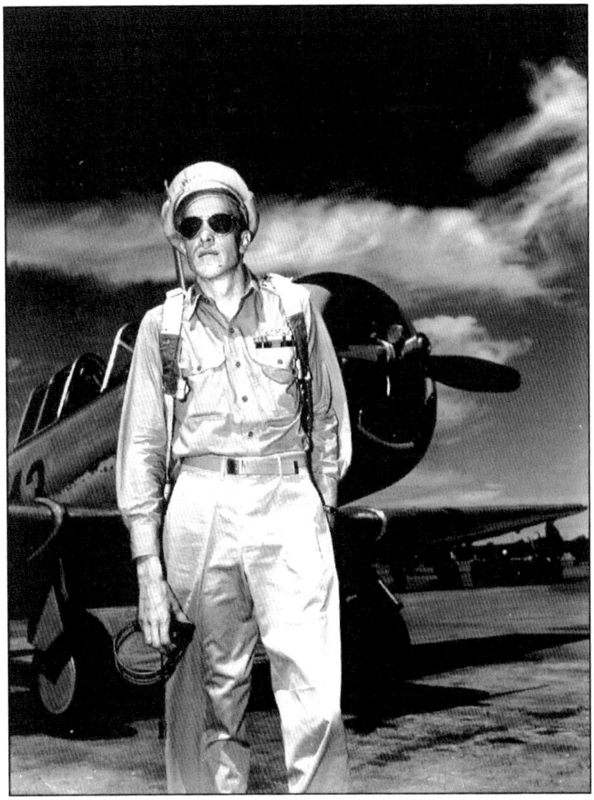

WINNER OF SIX MEDALS. Capt. Forrest Cox, former Millikin University student, was awarded six separate air medals while fighting German, Italian, and Japanese pilots. Captain Cox served in England, North Africa, India, China, and Assam, all in the space of 18 months. Before serving as a captain in the Army Air Force, Cox volunteered for the Eagle Squadron of the Royal Air Force (RAF). (Courtesy Decatur Public Library.)

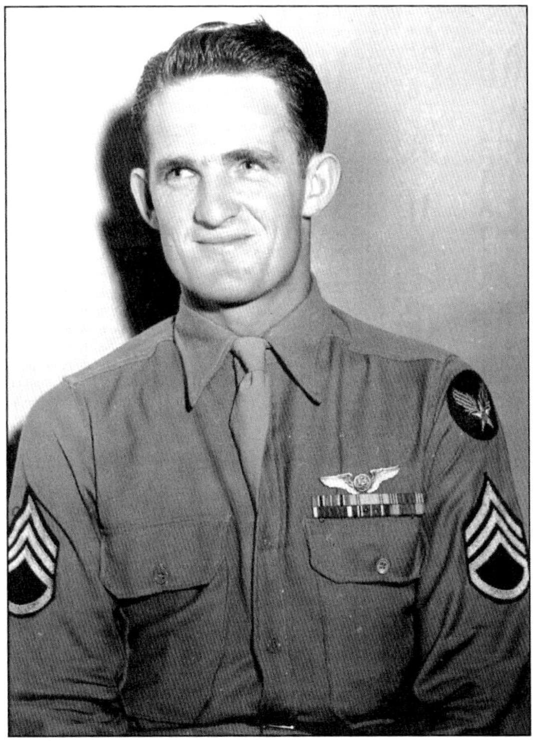

BOMBING PANZER TANKS. S.Sgt. Thomas O. Laughlin, an aerial gunner, flew in planes that dropped their bombs on German tanks from an altitude of only 35 feet. One of the planes crash-landed at a speed of 250 miles per hour. Sergeant Laughlin fought at the Kasserine Pass in North Africa, where Gen. George Patton dealt Field Marshal Rommel a decisive blow. (Courtesy Decatur Public Library.)

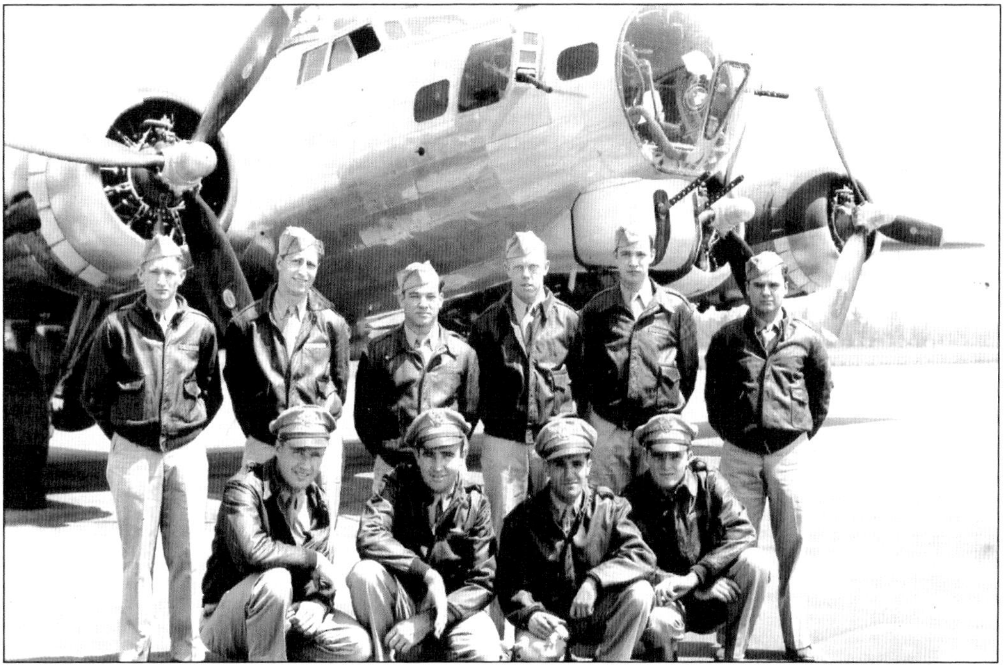

FLYING FORTRESS CREW IN LOUISIANA. Lt. La Verne Cummins of Decatur (kneeling, second from the left) is shown in this June 1944 photograph taken at Alexandria (Louisiana) Army Air Field, where the crew was completing their training. Lieutenant Cummins is the son of Mr. and Mrs. Gussie O. Cummins, 553 South Webster Street. (Courtesy Decatur Public Library.)

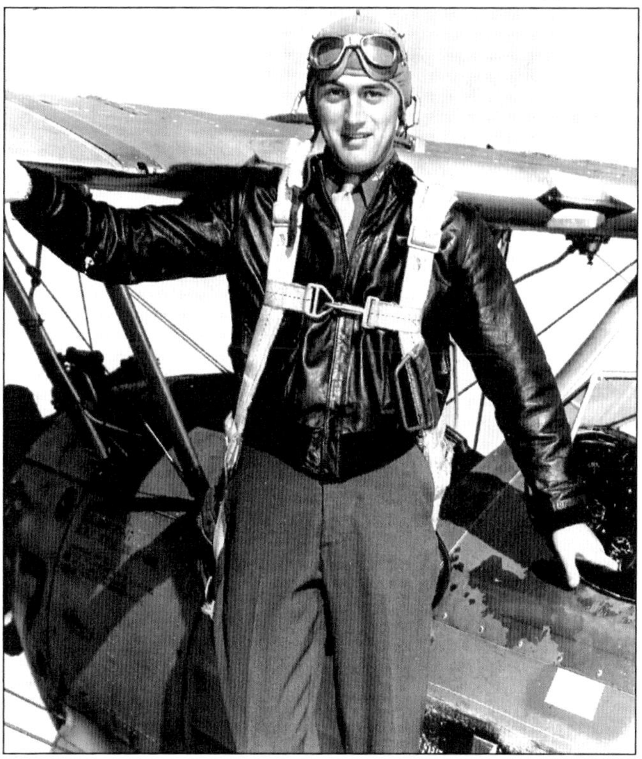

TRAINING ON A BIPLANE IN FLORIDA. When this photograph was taken, Sgt. Lynn C. Drew, formerly of the 46th Bomb Group, was training at Lodwick School of Aeronautics, part of the 216th Army Air Force Base at Lakeland, Florida. The Florida base, in turn, was under the direction of the Eastern Flying Command, Maxwell Field, Alabama. The photograph was taken in December 1944. (Courtesy Decatur Public Library.)

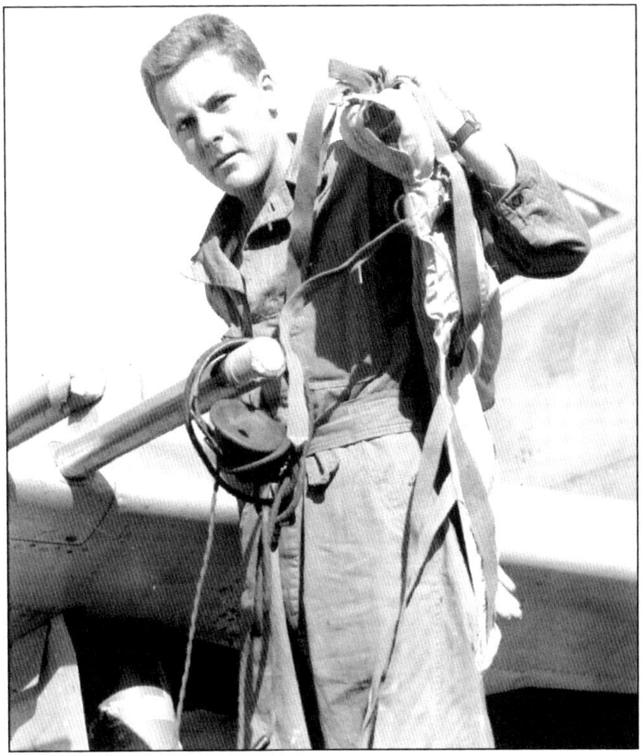

Lt. Robert Leslie Hawkins. Lt. Hawkins was only 18 years old when he received his commission as a second lieutenant and his pilot's wings. He is shown here, lugging his gear in a photograph taken February 16, 1944, shortly before he was killed somewhere over the skies of Germany. His twin brother, William, was serving in the Navy as a petty officer. (Courtesy Decatur Public Library.)

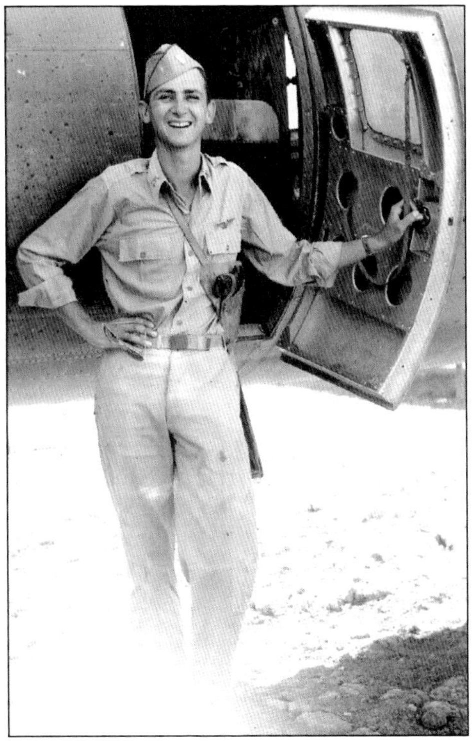

Raid on Rome. As a 50-mission pilot of a Flying Fortress, Lt. Carl D. Mitchell participated in a giant raid on the ancient city of Rome. "Rome wasn't any different from any of the other targets," Mitchell explained. "In fact, it wasn't as exciting . . . the flak wasn't as heavy and there weren't as many German fighters." This photograph was taken in October of 1943. (Courtesy Decatur Public Library.)

FLYING AMBULANCE DRIVER. Lt. Robert McEuen was one of the first pilots to go across the English Channel on D-Day, June 6, 1944. He regularly flew to France with a cargo of war materiel, returned to England with American wounded who needed hospitalization, and made his plane a "flying ambulance." (Courtesy Decatur Public Library.)

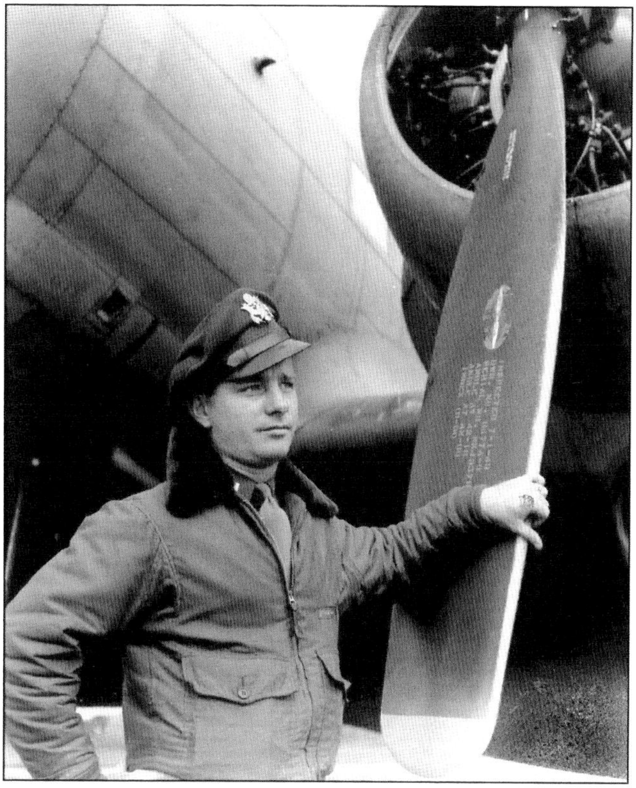

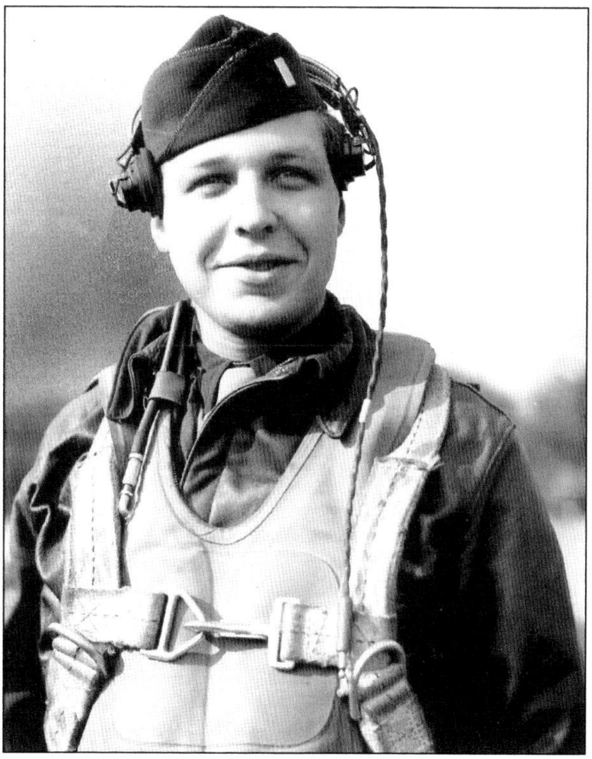

NAVIGATOR ON A FLYING FORTRESS. Previously a student at the University of Illinois, 2nd Lt. Robert C. Culp participated in some of the final air raids over communications facilities in the city of Berlin and other targets in eastern Germany. Based in England, Lieutenant Culp held the Air Medal and one Oak Leaf cluster. The photograph was taken in April 1945. (Courtesy Decatur Public Library.)

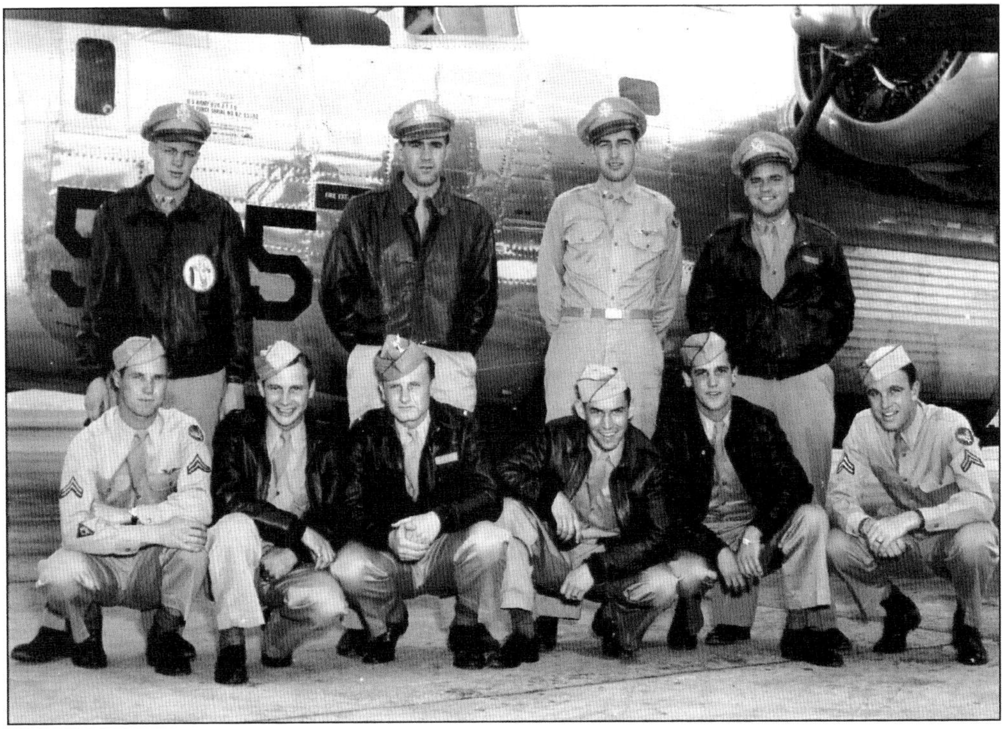

ENGINEER ON A B-24 BOMBER. This photograph was taken on July 25, 1944, at the Second Air Force Base, Gowen Field, Idaho. Sgt. Russell Ely (first from the left, kneeling) served as the engineer, and the entire crew was awaiting orders either to Europe or the Pacific. Before the war, Ely worked for the General Electric Company. (Courtesy Decatur Public Library.)

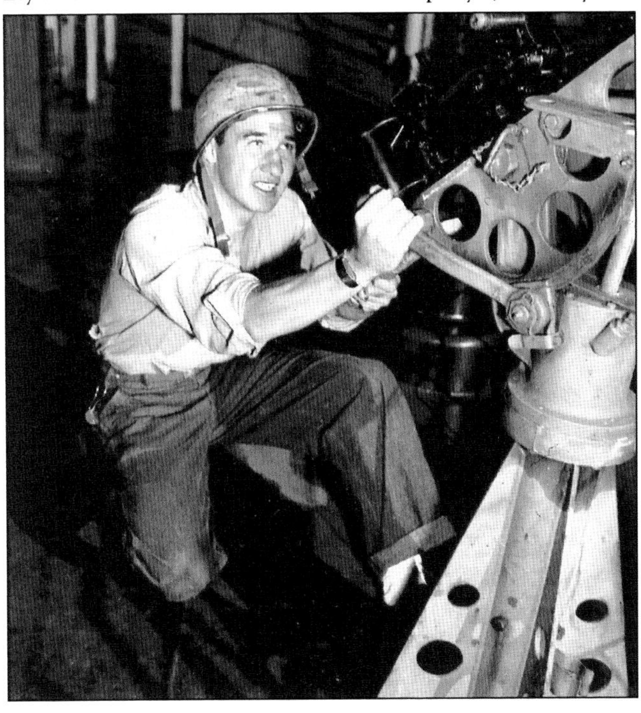

COAST GUARDSMAN ON RESCUE MISSION IN THE PHILIPPINES. Seaman First Class Llewellyn S. Knight, who served aboard a Coast Guard frigate, participated in a rescue mission that saved the lives of seven American Army scouts trapped behind the Japanese lines in the Philippines. The coast guardsmen were under constant enemy fire. Before the war, Knight was employed at the Western Electric Company. (Courtesy Decatur Public Library.)

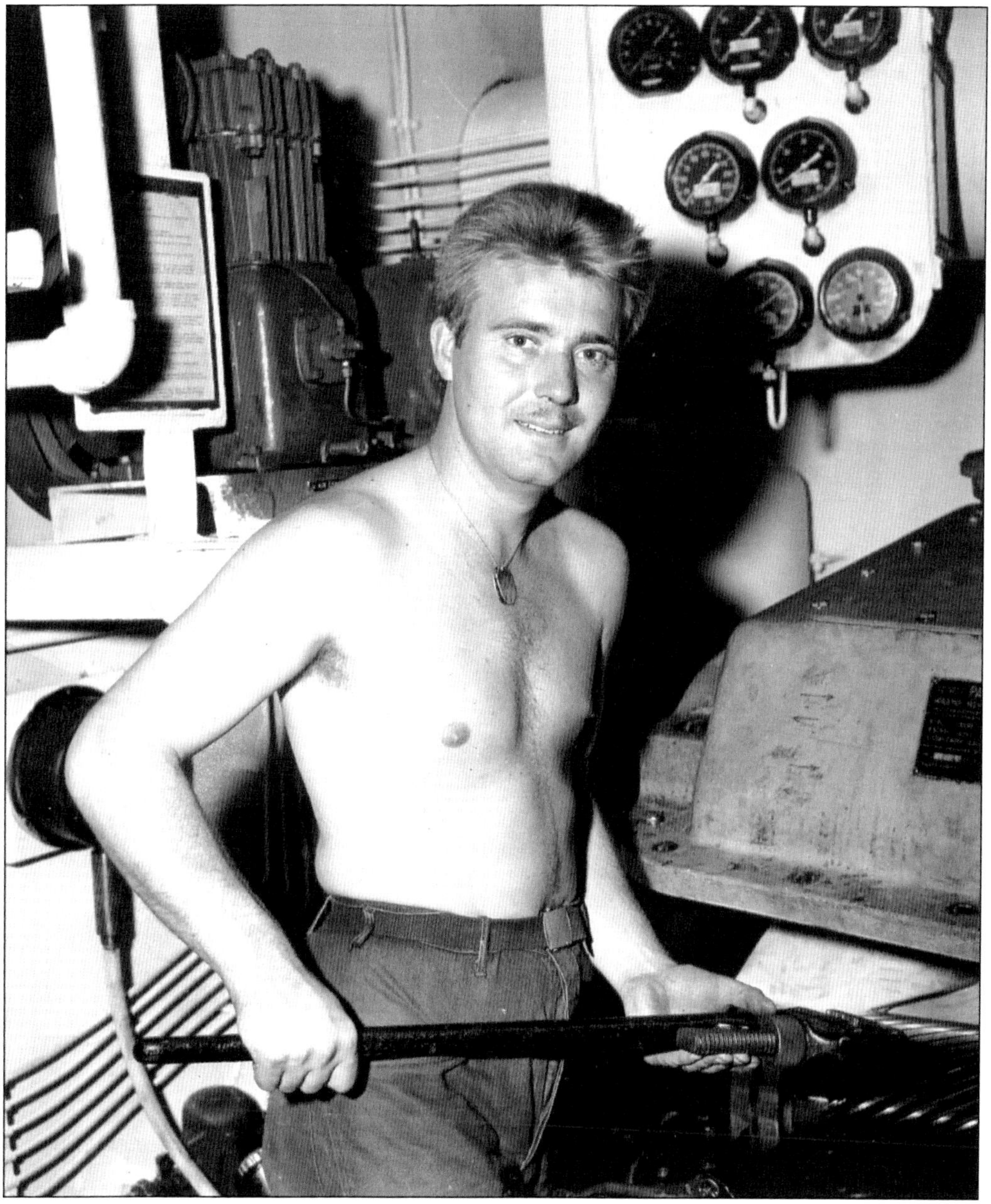

MOTOR MACHINIST'S MATE, SECOND CLASS. American servicemen and servicewomen served all over the world in places like Assam, Burma, India, China, Tunisia, Italy, France, England, Germany, the Philippines, and the Japanese home islands. They served in occupations as varied as clerks, gunners, medics, bombardiers, mechanics, pilots, radio operators, cooks, stenographers, carpenters, weather forecasters, truck drivers, surgeons, and riflemen. They wore khaki, navy blue, olive green, and white. They were adorned with various kinds of badges and insignias, from the globe and anchor of the Marines to the wings of the Air Force and the crossed cannons of the Artillery. They were all part of one massive organism. They all worked hard, sometimes stripping off their shirts, like Coast Guardsman Burrell F. "Bud" Reed, working in an overheated engine room on an LST ship in the Pacific, trying hard to fix the problem, and keep the momentum going. This photograph was taken in January of 1945. (Courtesy Decatur Public Library.)

For Further Reading

Banton, O. T., ed. *History of Macon County*. Decatur: Macon County Historical Society, 1976.
Guillory, Dan. *Decatur*. Chicago: Arcadia Publishing, 2004.
———. *Living With Lincoln: Life and Art in the Heartland*. Urbana: Stormline Press, 1989.
Irwin, Dayle Cochran. *Decatur Serving Others: A Pictorial History*. St. Louis: Bradley Publishing, 1999.
Johns, Jane M. *Personal Recollections of Early Decatur, Abraham Lincoln, Richard Oglesby, and the Civil War*. Decatur: Daughters of the American Revolution, 1912.
Richmond, Mabel, ed. *Centennial History of Decatur and Macon County*. Decatur: Decatur Review, 1930.
Sampson, Robert. "A Sense of Community: Italians in Decatur, Illinois: 1920-1940." Unpublished paper.
Smith, John W. *History of Macon County, Illinois, From Its Organization to 1876*. Springfield: Rokker's Printing House, 1876.